D1555537

The Law and
Occupational Injury,
Disease, and Death

Recent Titles from Quorum Books

The Law and Occupational Injury, Disease, and Death

WARREN FREEDMAN

QUORUM BOOKS

New York · Westport, Connecticut · London

Library of Congress Cataloging-in-Publication Data

Freedman, Warren.
  The law and occupational injury, disease, and death / Warren
Freedman.
    p. cm.
  ISBN 0-89930-410-9 (alk. paper)
  1. Industrial hygiene—Law and legislation—United States.
2. Industrial safety—Law and legislation—United States.
3. Workers' compensation—Law and legislation—United States.
I. Title.
KF3570.F74   1990
344.73'0465—dc20
[347.304465]   89-10746

British Library Cataloguing in Publication Data is available.

Library of Congress Catalog Card Number: 89-10746
ISBN: 0-89930-410-9

First published in 1990 by Quorum Books

Greenwood Press, Inc.
88 Post Road West, Westport, Connecticut 06881

Printed in the United States of America

(∞)

The paper used in this book complies with the
Permanent Paper Standard issued by the National
Information Standards Organization (Z39.48-1984).

10   9   8   7   6   5   4   3   2   1

Contents

The Law and Occupational Injury, Disease, and Death

1

Introduction to Injury, Disease, and Death in the Workplace

1.1 Definitions and Terminology

Each year more than 11,000 workers die and about 2 million workers are injured or fall victim to disease as a result of accidents or exposure to hazardous materials in the workplace.[1] Add to these numbers the millions of workers who sustain injury, death, or disease purely and simply from the myriads of other hazards, known and unknown, in the workplace, and the result is alarming. According to the National Safety Council, a Chicago-based research group, farms have become a deadly workplace, and farming has surpassed mining and construction in recent years as the deadliest occupation, claiming, in particular, the lives of thousands of children and leaving thousands more disabled.[2] In 1987 the farm death rate was 49 deaths per 100,000 workers compared with 38 deaths per 100,000 in mining and 35 deaths per 100,000 in construction. Indeed, "agriculture might be more hazardous than even these numbers indicate, some safety experts say," since many states "like Iowa, do not distinguish farm-related deaths from other accidental deaths and therefore are not included in these figures."[3]

Occupational disease, unlike occupational injury and death, which are relatively easily defined, may be delineated in terms of diseases, or even physical defects, that occur among people who perform a particular task and that do not occur among people who do not perform that particular task. The implication is clear that there is something about the task or work location that itself leads to development of the occupational disease. This conclusion is statistically true. In contrast is the environmental disease, which occurs in excess among people who live in a particular environment, perhaps near a factory, a hazardous waste site, or a common source of drinking water. Exposure to a pesticide, for example, is occupational for workers who manufacture pesticides or who apply the pesticide; however, exposure to pesticides can be environmental if the injury or disease occurs among people who live near the pesticide manufacturing plant or near the area of its application. The resulting disease or abnormality would depend on levels of exposure, and would vary among people in the occupational exposure and people in the environmental exposure. Accordingly, standards do differ between the workplace and the general environment; hence the need to differentiate. The potential hazards of the occupational area involve chemical agents, such as dusts, gases, vapors, and liquids; physical agents, such as noise, extreme temperatures, radiation, vibration, and electrical shock; and mechanical agents, such as defects in equipment and inadequate protective devices on machinery. Chemical agents make contact with workers by inhalation (entering the respiratory system), ingestion (entering the gastrointestinal tract), or dermal exposure (coming into contact with the skin). Inhalation is probably the problem of greatest importance in the occupational setting because breathing is a no-option, continuous process, although dermal exposure constitutes the greatest volume of diseases, to wit: occupational dermatitis. Chemical overexposure can produce respiratory distress, which effects include choking, coughing, difficulty in breathing, irritation of the respiratory mucosa, and even death. Chemical overexposure has also produced neurologic effects (from lead and mercury, for example), specific organ defects (from lead and cadmium, for example), liver angio-sarcoma (from vinyl chloride, for example), mutagenic action (from ultra-violet radiation and colchicine, for example), spermatotoxicism (from dibromochloropropane, for example), embryotoxicism (from chlorinated hydrocarbons, for example), and even death (from hydrogen cyanide, hydrogen sulfide, and nickel carbonyl, for example).

The incidence of chronic diseases, like lung cancer, liver disease, and heart disease, has increased in recent years, and it is believed that many of such chronic diseases are related to the man-made environment in both the workplace and the general environment. Chronic diseases usually have long latency periods, and the time lag makes determination of the causal relation difficult. In addition, chronic diseases may have multiple causes, and because they occur in the general population, too, the causal relation becomes even more complex.

The spread of occupational disease affects millions of workers in mines, factories, fields, research laboratories, and even office environments. Occupational disease can be termed an epidemic that only recently has been epidemiologically documented.[4]

Prevention of injuries, death, and disease in the workplace has occupied the attention of lawyers, labor unions, government officials, insurance companies, consultants, and scholars. One product-safety consultant advocates that workers be fully warned about hazards in the workplace and understand the warnings and the consequences of ignoring the warnings; that workers receive adequate information about how to work safely within the work environment; that workers use state-of-the art protective devices to minimize exposure to such hazards;[5] and that employers take action to make workers more safety-conscious in their work habits and attitudes.[6] Conversely, another writer takes the view that unsafe acts of workers are not the primary cause of workplace accidents,[7] pointing instead to the poorly designed equipment and the obsolete safety standards of the Occupational Safety and Health Administration (OSHA)[8] adopted from the American National Standards Institute's standards written before 1969. The same writer delineates such safety instrumentations as interlocked enclosures, presence sensors, pressure sensors, constant pressure devices, two-hand controls, fail-safe designs, integral instrumentation, zero-mechanical states, controlled failure devices, fail-evident devices, elevated workplaces, captive safety devices, and tamper-proof design devices.

It is prudent to distinguish between accidental injury and occupational disease: the adjective accidental describes injuries and deaths that have the "quality or condition of happening or coming by chance or without design, taking place unexpectedly or unintentionally."[9] In short, an accident is an unlooked for and untoward event that is not expected or designed by the person who suffered the injury or death.[10] Occupational disease, on the other hand, is defined in Section 42-11-10 of the South Carolina Code Annotated as

a disease arising out of and in the course of employment which is due to hazards in excess of those ordinarily incident to employment and is peculiar to the occupation in which the employee is engaged. A disease shall be deemed an occupational disease only if caused by a hazard recognized as peculiar to a particular trade, process, occupation or employment as a direct result of continuous exposure to the normal working conditions thereof. No disease shall be deemed an occupational disease when:

(1) It does not result directly and naturally from exposure in this State to the hazards peculiar to the particular employment;
(2) It results from exposure to outside climatic conditions;
(3) It is a contagious disease resulting from exposure to fellow employees or from a hazard to which the worker would have been equally exposed outside of his employment;
(4) It is one of the ordinary diseases of life to which the general public is equally exposed, unless such disease follows as a complication and a natural incident of an occupational disease or unless there is a constant exposure peculiar to the occupation itself which makes such disease a hazard inherent in such occupation;
(5) It is any disease of the cardiac, pulmonary, or circulatory system not resulting directly from abnormal external gaseous pressure exerted upon the body or the natural entrance into the body through the skin or natural orifices thereof of foreign organic or inorganic matter under circumstances peculiar to the employment and the processes utilized therein; or
(6) It is any chronic disease of the skeletal joints.

NOTES

1. See Mason, "OSHA's Hazard Communications Standard," Vital Speeches (December 1986) at 118.
2. See New York Times (September 26, 1988) at 1 and A21. In tough economic times, farmers rely increasingly on their children to work in the field, and children are

susceptible to injury and death from tractor rollovers, farm machine gears, and a host of other modern apparatuses in use today on farms.

3. Id. at A21.

4. See Baron, Handling Occupational Disease Cases (Lawpress, 1981) at ix.

5. See section 9.3 hereinafter.

6. See McGuire, "Hazards in the Workplace: What Is the Employer's Duty?" Trial Magazine (June 1988) at 24.

7. See Gallagher, "Exploding the Myths: How to Prevent Industrial Accidents," Trial Magazine (April 1988) at 53.

8. Note Section 6.4 hereinafter.

9. See Murch-Jargis Co. v. Townsend, 193 S.W.2d 310 (Ark., 1946), and Hiers v. Brunson Construction Co., 70 S.E.2d 211 (S.C., 1952).

10. See Hodge, "Accident v. Occupational Disease: Practical Considerations," Trial Magazine (June 1988) at 36.

1.2 Occupational Diseases and Diseases Caused by Accidents

Occupational illness and disease as well as disease caused by accident are today covered by nearly every state workers' compensation statute. Occupational disease is therein defined as any disability arising out of exposure to hazardous or harmful conditions in employment when such conditions are present in a peculiar or increased degree by comparison with other employments or the environment generally. Under the Colorado statute occupational disease is "a disease which results directly from the employment or the conditions under which work was performed, which can be seen to have followed as a natural incident of the work and as a result of the exposure occasioned by the nature of the employment, and which can be fairly traced to the employment as a proximate cause and which does not come from a hazard to which the work would have been equally exposed outside of the employment." [1]

It should be observed that occupational disease or illness cannot generally be "expected to be unexpected" or accidental, since by definition the occupational disease or illness is recognized and presumably accepted as an inherent risk of continued exposure to the conditions of the particular employment. Indeed, even an individual employee's inherent "weakness" or susceptibility to hazardous substances is immaterial if the particular condition of employment, in fact, did cause the disability. [2]

Unfortunately there have been many problems in compensating for occupational disease owing to restrictive statutory definitions of compensable disease and owing to time limitations on suit and rules of minimum exposure or recent exposure to particular disease-causing agents. [3] Litigation has also resulted in delayed payments or no payments; the chief judge of a Florida appellate court remarked that the number of workmen's compensation cases was "five times too many for the health of the court, for the health of the system, and for the health of the parties, including both claimants who are waiting months for benefits, carriers who are absorbing appellate costs, and employers who must pay premiums."[4]

Today the growing hazard of toxic chemicals in the workplace has prompted even an insurer's task force to recommend the adoption of a new standard definition of occupational disease, as well as a new system of evaluating worker injuries, and the creation of a reinsurance pool for occupational disease. Too many states still distinguish between hazardous and nonhazardous employment, and too many states still accept exclusions for agricultural workers, domestics, and small employers as well as limitations on the scope of compensable diseases. There are still hard questions of proof of causation with respect to occupational diseases, for simply calling a rose a rose does not make a weed a rose, or indeed an occupational disease an occupational disease.[5] In Matter of Amoroso v. Tubu[6] the New York Court of Appeals reversed a workmen's compensation board award for the death of an employee from carcinoma of the right lung allegedly caused by exposure for seventeen years to fumes in the plating and polishing department of his employer, a manufacturer of plumbing supplies. Proof of causal relation between death and the exposure was unconvincing, although the dissent carefully pointed out that

in this case three physicians testified unequivocally to causal relationship, and the respondent so concedes. It is argued, however, that their testimony should be rejected as a matter of law because it ignored pathological studies of autopsied tissues of the bronchi and lungs which did not reveal the presence of chromates. As a matter of fact two physicians who testified to causal relation were examined as to this very matter and dismissed the findings as not significant, chiefly on the ground that the spectographic tissue analysis was not made until some two or three years after the autopsy when the slides were prepared. This, of course, is a controversial issue, but one that is within the realm of fact which the board had power to resolve.[7]

In Grayson v. Gulf Oil Co.[8] the South Carolina court was faced with a workers' compensation claim from a worker in a gasoline company who experienced symptoms of what was later diagnosed as dysfunction of her immune system caused by her chemical sensitivity to gasoline products. Her employer contended that her disability was an occupational disease resulting from chronic exposure to petrochemicals and not the result of an accident, as required for recovery by South Carolina statute.[9] But the court bent over backward to provide coverage for her disability, citing with approval 82 Am. Jur. 2d, Section 303 (Workmen's Compensation): "Where a sudden illness or collapse is precipitated by the inhalation of harmful elements at a definite time, which brings to a climax the cumulative deleterious effects of the inhalation of such elements in the course of the employment over a period of time, it is generally considered that the disability is attributable to an accidental injury rather than to occupational disease."[10] In short, the court approved the employee's right to state workers' compensation benefits by circumstantial evidence, as did an earlier South Carolina case[11] in which the court found that the claimant had been exposed to a greater risk than the general public and that the resulting disease was unexpected, unusual, and, therefore, accidental; the court thereupon opined that "the settled rule is that where the work and its own environment of circumstance expose the employee to the happening of an event causing an accident, the accident arises out of the employment."

It should be noted that 75 percent to 80 percent of all cancers are caused by environmental or workplace exposures, according to the World Health Organization.[12] A recent OSHA report confirmed that more than 20 percent of all cancer deaths in the United States can be attributed to occupational exposure.[13] The National Institute for Occupational Safety and Health has classified more than 2,000 substances as playing some role in causing cancer.[14] In the state of Connecticut, for example, the most commonly diagnosed occupational disease is asbestos-related; almost 300,000 residents have been exposed to this carcinogenic substance linked with lung disease and with several types of cancer.[15]

Two interesting facets of occupational disease recognition relate to (1) recovery of damages owing to current increased risk of contracting the disease in the future and (2) the dilemmas facing occupational disease surveillance. The latter is intertwined with the problem of how to collect personal health data without infringing on individual rights of privacy, confidentiality, and even due process of law plus fear of fundamental discrimination in employment.[16] The role of insurance companies that cover workers is complicated by their need for overall research and trend analysis, which mandates some form of surveillance. Employers are generally reluctant to conduct surveillance of workers; there are indeed dis-incentives for the employer to collect individual case histories and chart trends of occupational disease. The former facet has perhaps an easier acceptability, as many courts have consistently held that damages for future complications of current injury are recoverable because of the likelihood that these effects will occur and, therefore, may be stated with reasonable medical certainty.[17] The New Jersey Supreme Court in Coll v. Sherry[18] opined that "while allowing recovery for future damages, the courts have adopted various formulae to restrict the elements of speculation and conjecture which may enter into a jury's assessment of them. Although the accepted verbal rituals are widely diversified . . . reasonable probability or its equivalent is sufficient." But, as illustrated in Laswell v. Brown,[19] courts have rejected claims for recovery of damages based solely on increased risk of future disease: "The complaint is conspicuously void of any allegation that the children have sustained any damage other than exposure to higher risk of disease and cellular damage. . . . A lawsuit for personal injuries cannot be based only upon the mere possibility of future harm."

The American Medical Association (AMA) guidelines to the evaluation of permanent impairment were before the Florida Supreme Court in Dayron Corp. v. Morehead.[20] The corporate employer claimed that a provision of the Florida workers' compensation law dealing with permanent impairment required the evaluation of the employee's claim under the AMA guidelines. But the court ruled that the AMA guidelines are not applicable when "they preclude a finding of permanent impairment where the claimant suffered a disability due to an occupational disease which permanently impairs his ability to work and results in economic loss but does not affect his activities of daily living." Interestingly, workers' compensation laws were once bitterly opposed by employers, but have become a shield against expanded liability and adequate awards. What was viewed as a way to establish a security of compensation with fixed damages instead of the uncertainty of litigative roulette became, over the years, a straitjacket on traumatic injury and occupational disease recovery as well as an obstruction to the corporate liability for latent occupational diseases.[21]

NOTES

1. Section 8-41-108 of Colo. Rev. Stat.
2. See Herrera v. Fluor Utah, Inc., 550 P.2d 144 (N.M., 1976).
3. Note generally Crum & Forster's Occupational Disease Task Force, "Role of the State Workers' Compensation System in Compensating Occupational Disease Victims," (1983) at 26–29.
4. See Fla. Bar News (August 15, 1982), No. 15 at 1.
5. See McAllister v. Workmen's Compensation Board, 445 P.2d 313 (Cal., 1968).
6. 194 N.E.2d 694 (N.Y., 1963).
7. Id.
8. 357 S.E.2d 479 (S.C., 1987).
9. Section 42-1-160 of S.C. Code Ann.
10. See Hodge, "Accident v. Occupational Disease: Practical Considerations," Trial Magazine (June 1988) at 37.
11. Sturkie v. Ballenger Corp., 235 S.E.2d 120 (S.C., 1977).
12. See "Cancer and the Worker," N.Y. Academy of Sciences (1977) at 2.
13. See Zubrensky, "Establishing Causal Relationship in a Claim for Occupational Cancer," 53 Wis. Bar Bull. (March 1980) at 8. See also Section 3.11 hereinafter.
14. Id.
15. See Hartford Courant (November 14, 1987) at D4.
16. See generally Freedman, The Employment Contract: Employer v. Employee (Quorum Books, 1989).
17. Note Remon v. Sooter, 274 N.E.2d 200 (Ill. App., 1971).
18. 148 A.2d 481 (N.J., 1959).
19. 683 F.2d 261 (8th Cir., 1982).
20. —— So.2d —— (Fla., 1987).
21. See Baron, Handling Occupational Disease Cases (Lawpress, 1981) at x.

1.3 Workers' Compensation Coverage and Employer Liability

It is said that workers' compensation insurance in the United States is a composite of tort principles and both British and German models of the right of injured employees to receive benefits designed to cushion the economic strain and prevent destitution during recovery for work-related injuries.[1] But the U.S. workers' compensation insurance program is predicated on unilateral employer liability without any direct contribution from the state or from the injured employee. Also, the injured employee in the United States may receive additional benefits under the Dual Capacity Theory[2] (i.e., when an employer acts in a capacity other than as an employer, the employer may incur responsibilities distinct from those imposed for his status as an employer[3]), the Dual Injury Theory[4] (i.e., when the injury is clearly compensable but the employer inflicts with respect to the first injury [which is covered under workers' compensation] a second and separate injury outside the scope of worker's compensation[5]), and the Intentional Acts Theory[6] (i.e., the employer severed the employment relationship by committing the intentional acts against the employee[7]).

Workers' compensation was first established in 1910 in the state of New York,[8] but the next year the New York Court of Appeals determined that the new law was unconstitutional because the state had exceeded its police powers in imposing strict liability without fault on certain designated occupations.[9] But the U.S. Supreme Court, in its 1917 decision in New York Central Railroad Co. v. White,[10] validated compulsory, elective, and optional compensation systems, so that within three years thereafter forty states had enacted workers' compensation programs.[11] The state programs today typically describe automatic entitlement to benefits for personal injuries by an accident arising out of and in the course of employment; no-fault liability against employers;[12] sliding scale benefits and expenses; elimination of employee rights to sue the employer at common law for negligence;[13] overall supervision by state insurance departments; and mandatory insurance coverage by employers, either self-insured, state fund, or private. Probably the most litigated aspect of these programs concerns "whether claimant's injuries arose out of or in the course of her employment," as illustrated by the recent New York Court of Appeals decision in Matter of Lemon v. New York City Transit Authority.[14] Here the female plaintiff was a train conductor who generally worked the "midnight shift." On her way home she fell "while climbing the (subway) stairs leading to the street, . . . fractured her knee," and was unable to return to work for six months. When her employer denied her claim for workers' compensation benefits, she appealed to the Workers' Compensation Board, which awarded her benefits, "concluding that the accident occurred within the precincts of claimant's employment." The New York Appellate Division affirmed,[15] on the basis of the free passes that the transit authority gave its employees to use the subway to return home, meaning that the employer "implicitly assumed the responsibility of transporting claimant to and from work"; but the highest New York court reversed, pointing out that "only if an injury flows as a natural consequence of the employee's duties can it be said to arise out of the employment." The court expounded at length as follows:

The question here is whether claimant's journey to and from work should be characterized as part of the service performed by the employee. The well-established rule is that "employees are not deemed to be within the scope of their employment while commuting," since "the risks inherent in traveling to and from work relate to the employment only in the most marginal sense." . . .

We have recognized a number of exceptions to this general rule. As long as there existed some reasonable nexus between the risk to which a claimant was exposed and the employment, recovery has generally been upheld, even though the injury was sustained while traveling to or from work. . . .

We agree, however, with the Transit Authority that none of the exceptions to the general rule are applicable here. According to her own testimony at the hearing, claimant's duties ended when she signed out of work at approximately 4:00 A.M. at the Woodlawn terminal in the Bronx. She was injured one hour and twenty minutes later while climbing the stairs on her way home at the Utica Avenue station in Brooklyn. Given the remoteness in terms of time and space from the Woodlawn terminal, we can see no reasonable connection between claimant's injury and her employment.

The dissenting opinion pointed out that:

The Workers' Compensation Law was enacted by the Legislature for economic and humanitarian reasons to protect employees and their families by providing "no fault" recovery for injuries arising out of and in the course of employment (*Matter of Richardson v. Fiedler*, 67 N.Y.2d 246, 250–251; *Surace v. Danna*, 248 N.Y. 18, 20–21). To carry out this purpose and to implement the underlying legislative policy, the Legislature created the Workers' Compensation Board and entrusted it with the authority of determining whether particular claims are compensable (see, Workers' Compensation Law §§ 10, 20). Respecting this broad delegation of authority, we have consistently held that the Board's factual findings and the inferences it draws therefrom are conclusive on the courts if supported by substantial evidence (see, *Matter of Richardson v. Fiedler*, supra, at 249–250; *Matter of Malacarne v. Parking Auth.*, 41 N.Y.2d 189, 193). Even where the facts are undisputed, the Board's determination of whether a particular injury is compensable is a mixed question of law and fact which is beyond our review unless it lacks a rational basis or is based on erroneous legal principles (see, *Matter of Fisher*, 36 N.Y.2d 146, 150; *Matter of Van Teslaar*, 35 N.Y.2d 311, 317–318; *see also, Matter of Richardson v. Fiedler*, supra). Here, I believe that the Board's determination that claimant is entitled to compensation is rational, consistent with established case law, and supported by substantial evidence. I, therefore, respectfully dissent.[16]

Certain workplaces are more prone to injuries that give rise to workers' compensation claims, and one of the more fascinating workplaces or fields is the professional football field. Statistics from the National Football League Players' Association indicate that every player (whose average professional career is only 3.7 years) will at some point sustain serious compensable injury.[17] As outlined by the California appellate court in Hurwitz v. Workers' Compensation Appeals Board,[18] "the employer has a duty to notify the employee of the potential right to benefits, and if the employer fails to do so, and if as a consequence the employee fails to file an application for workers' compensation benefits until after the applicable period of limitation has expired, the employer is estopped to assert the statute of limitations.'' One of the drawbacks to suit against third-party tortfeasors who may be responsible for injuries to professional football players is the ruling of the Tenth U.S. Court of Appeals in Hackbart v. Cincinnati Bengals, Inc.[19] to the effect that another professional player or professional team can be legally responsible for injuries caused to another player; here plaintiff was severely injured when he was illegally tackled by an opposing player after the play had ended. The federal district court dismissed the suit against the offending player and his professional football team on the ground that plaintiff had assumed the risk of injury.[20] But the federal appellate court reversed, holding that a professional football player can recover for injuries sustained that were recklessly and intentionally caused by another player. In short, the workers' compensation system may be the easier path to economic recovery for injuries sustained during the course of employment! However,

no one would contend that the awards and judgments (under workers' compensation) are full compensation for losses sustained. . . . The purpose of [workers' compensation] is to only partly reimburse for the impairment in earning capacity on the theory that such partial reimbursement without expense and delay and without the uncertainty of litigation is more desirable than the opportunity of full compensation for all loss and damages at the hands of courts and juries, with all the attendant delays, risks and expenses.[21]

Indeed, the workers' compensation payment is not a replacement of wages, but is limited to correcting interference with earning capacity in an amount sufficient to keep the injured employee from destitution or becoming a ward of the state.[22]

The definition of employee for purposes of workers' compensation is not always clear, as seen in Jack Hammer Associates, Inc. v. Delmy Productions, Inc.[23] Here plaintiff contracted with defendant to perform in a musical play, and he was injured when defendant permitted two of his "co-employees to drink alcoholic beverages backstage during the performance"; both "co-employees" allegedly "assaulted him and caused physical injuries for which he seeks $1 million in damages.'' The defense of the employer was that plaintiff was an "employee" relegated to workers' compensation and is not entitled to sue the employer. The New York appellate court agreed with the employer:

It is undisputed that Hammer entered into a written contract for a stipulated sum for a term certain, and that the time and place where he would work was determined by BBS. He was required to perform in a certain number of shows, which were presented at a specified time during certain days of the week. BBS determined the country and theater in which Hammer was to perform, and Hammer was obligated to follow the script and was subject to the supervision of the play's director. We conclude upon these facts that Hammer was an *employee,* as a matter of law, and not an independent contractor as he suggested (see, Matter of Morton, 284 N.Y. 167; Matter of Berman v. Barone, 275 App. Div. 867).

NOTES

1. See Larson, The Law of Workmen's Compensation (1984) at Sections 2.20, 3.10, and 3.20. Also see Harvey, "Insuring and Defending Employer Liability in a Blankenship/Jones Action: A Contemporary Analysis of Workplace Intentional Torts in Ohio," Def. Counsel J. (April 1987) at 226–251.

2. See Section 9.9. hereinafter.

3. See, for example, Guy v. Arthur H. Thomas Co., 378 N.E.2d 488 (Ohio, 1978).

4. See Section 9.9 hereinafter.

5. See, for example, Delamotte v. Unicast of Midland Ross Corp., 411 N.E.2d 814 (Ohio, 1978).

6. See Section 9.10 hereinafter.

7. Note Jones v. V.I.P. Development, 472 N.E.2d 1046 (Ohio, 1984).

8. See Section 674 of New York Workers' Compensation Law.

9. See Ives v. South Buffalo Railway Co., 94 N.E. 431 (N.Y., 1911); also, supra note 1 at 229.

10. 243 U.S. 188 (1917).

11. Note Mountain Timber Co. v. Washington, 243 U.S. 219 (1917) and Hawkins v. Bleakley, 243 U.S. 210 (1917).

12. See Section 2.6 hereinafter.

13. See Section 8.1 hereinafter.

14. 512 N.E.2d 744 (N.Y., July 7, 1988). See McLaughlin v. Stackpole Fibers Co. Inc., —— N.E.2d —— (Mass., November 9, 1988), holding that a widow was barred from suing her husband's employer once she received workers' compensation benefits.

15. 128 A.D.2d 943 (App. Div., 2nd Dept., 1987).

16. In a footnote the dissent observed: "It should be noted that the majority's position and the principles it relies on are opposed to the weight of American authority (see, 14 Am. Jur. 2d § 759; 82 Am. Jur. 2d § 256; Owens v. Southeast Arkansas Transp. Co., 216 Ark. 950, 228 S.W.2d 646; City and County of San Francisco v. Industrial Accident Commission 61 Cal. App. 2d 248, 142 P.2d 760; Radermacher v. St. Paul City Ry. Co., 214 Minn. 427, 8 N.W.2d 466; Micieli v. Erie R.R. Co., 131 N.J.L. 427, 37 A.2d 123; Brown v. Pittsburgh Ry. Co., 197 Pa. Super. 68, 177 A.2d 5 [equally divided court])."

17. See Trial Magazine (June 1988) at 87.

18. 158 Cal. Rptr. 914 (1979).

19. 601 F.2d 516 (10th Cir., 1979).

20. 435 F. Supp. 353 (Colo., 1977).

21. See Industrial Commission v. Drake, 134 N.E. 465 (Ohio, 1921).

22. Note Epstein, "The Historical Origins and Economic Structure of Workers' Compensation Law," 16 Ga. L. Rev. 775 (1982).

23. 499 N.Y.S.2d 418 (App. Div. 1, 1986).

1.4 The Inadequacy of Workers' Compensation

There appears to be universal recognition that benefits under workers' compensation are not only inadequate in amounts, but also unconscionably low and even unobtainable in many occupational disease cases.[1] Low payments and complicated recovery procedures hardly are commensurate with the avowed purpose of workers' compensation to preserve the dignity of the injured employee while concurrently expediting complete rehabilitation.[2] The counterargument is that benefits were purposefully set below full compensation to minimize fraudulent claims, to encourage job site safety, to keep operating expenses low, and to induce employers into hiring and maintaining additional workforce.[3]

A review of several recent cases points up some of the inadequacies in the evaluation of injuries, both from the viewpoint of the injured employee and from the viewpoint of the employer and insurer. In Breidenbach v. Mayfield[4] the legal representative of the estate of the injured employee, to wit, his wife, was denied the right to appeal the denial of the claim; the Ohio Supreme Court reasoned that the appeal abated by reason of the wife's death! And in Frank E. Brown & Sons, Inc. v. Commission[5] the same court on the very same day determined that an injured employee is not entitled to an additional workers' compensation award for violation of a specific safety requirement if his own negligence created that violation; and the highest Ohio court held that his unilateral negligence precluded a finding of violation of specific safety requirement liability on the part of the employer.

On the other hand, the employer was the loser in such claims as delineated in Harvey v. Raleigh Police Department,[6] Lujan v. Houston General Insurance Co.,[7] and Oelrich v. Schlagels, Inc.[8] In the Harvey case an employee's suicide was deemed to have been caused by an occupational disease compensable under the North Carolina Workers' Compensation Act; the employee's death was judged to have resulted from his depression, an occupational disease, brought on by a shift in his tour of duty as a policeman and not as a result of a "willful intent to kill or injure oneself." The "occupational disease" of suicide was characterized as preceded by anxiety, impotence, and violent bursts of anger. In short, his mental condition was supported by the disappointment in his shift of duty, and was the proximate cause of the compensable suicide! Workers' compensation death benefits were allowed in the Lujan case, in which the worker was saturated with gasoline on the job but flames igniting his clothing and person did not result until he got home; the Texas Supreme Court ruled that the injury was still sustained in the course of his employment. And a worker injured while performing services for the benefit of a trainer during an on-the-job training rehabilitation program after a prior work injury was awarded workers' compensation benefits by the Minnesota Supreme Court in the Oelrich case; this time the second injury was traceable to the trainer and not to his employer!

Part of the inadequacy in evaluating and compensating injuries in the workplace is based on the requirement under most workers' compensation acts that the origin of the occupational disease, for example, be traced to an identifiable toxic substance.[9] Because occupational diseases characteristically have long latency periods, it is frequently impossible to determine exactly where the disease came from or to prove that it came from a single exposure or a group of exposures to a given substance by that particular employee or employees. Furthermore, the injured employee may have worked for a number of employers in various industries before the onset of the occupational disease. The concept of "cumulative injury,"[10] as defined in the California case of Beveridge v. Industrial Accident Commission[11] and as expanded in Peoria County Belwood Nursing Home, Inc. v. Industrial Commission of Illinois[12] encompassing "repeated trauma," also points up other inadequacies in the workers' compensation system. A minority of jurisdictions do not follow this expansive concept that "when a worker's physical structures give way under the repetitive stresses of their usual work tasks, the law views it as an accident arising out of and in the course of employment."[13] Even the same Illinois court in Downs v. Industrial Commission[14] did not accept the concept of a compensable "cumulative injury" in dealing with a meat wrapper in a supermarket who claimed a spinal injury that developed over a period of time from his "back-breaking" job. The statute of limitations with respect to the "cumulative injury" may bar the claim.[15] In Miller v. Workers' Compensation Appeals Board[16] the California court "merged" separate, specific injuries within the cause of action for "cumulative injury" and held that there was no statute of limitations defense!

The inadequacy of workers' compensation programs is further characterized by the numerous options given to the injured employee to sue the third-party tortfeasor, including the employer, under such doctrines as Dual Capacity,[17] Dual Injury,[18] and Intentional Acts,[19] all delineated hereinafter in Chapter 9 on defenses to the claim for liability.

The time-consuming nature of workers' compensation is well illustrated by the California case of Billik v. Hughes Aircraft Co.,[20] which was litigated over an eight-year period before the California Workers' Compensation Appeals Board. Much of the long delay was allegedly due to federal security regulations that precluded the attorney-client relationship from enjoying the full benefits of that confidential privilege, and precluded doctors from receiving a full history so that a proper diagnosis could be made. The employee's physical injury emanated from symptoms of joint pain in almost all parts of his body, general malaise, headaches, and vision problems that gradually developed over a two-year period.[21] Subsequently he experienced blood coagulating in his arteries, all his bodily hair changing from white to black because of the presence of lead in his hair, and other inexplicable physical signs of occupational injury or occupational disease.

In Perez v. Tru-Fit Manufacturing Co.[22] the New York Supreme Court, New York County, ruled that tort recovery in New York was not barred by New

Jersey workmen's compensation benefits. Here a New York resident was injured in a fall in her employer's New Jersey parking lot, so she applied for and received workmen's compensation benefits under New Jersey law. Thereupon she sued her employer in New York for damages, and the defendant employer moved to dismiss the suit, contending that the New Jersey law limited plaintiff's remedy to the workers' compensation benefits. The court denied defendant's motion and explained:

Plaintiff argues that New York law on workers' compensation is controlling and that it will not bar recovery. Plaintiff contends that from the late 1970's through 1981, the parking lot where the injury occurred was in the possession of Tru-Fit, a distinct and separate corporate entity which was later merged into TFM. Plaintiff alleges that Tru-Fit negligently performed work in the parking lot during this time period which created the conditions which caused the accident. Plaintiff claims that since the basis of liability against Tru-Fit is totally independent from the employer-employee relationship between TFM and plaintiff, then under New York's Workers' Compensation Law there is no bar to her claim against TFM, regardless of the merger (citing Billy v. Consolidated Machine Tool Corp., 51 N.Y.2d 152).

Though the Workmen's Compensation Law does not define its territorial scope, it does create a presumption that in the absence of substantial evidence to the contrary, "the claim comes within the provision of this chapter" (Workmen's Compensation Law [21, subd. 1]). While our courts recognize this presumption, there has also been articulated a pragmatic test based on the sufficiency of significant contacts between the employment and this State, with each case being determined on its own particular facts (Rayford v. National Union of Hospital and Nursing Home Employees, 57 A.D.2d 975). In Hartham v. George A. Fuller Co. (89 A.D.2d 720), the court, citing numerous Court of Appeals and Appellate Division cases, held that "Whether the board has jurisdiction over a claim depends upon whether a claimant's employment is found to have sufficient contacts with New York reasonably to say that the employment is located there, and is determined in each instance by the facts of the particular case."

In addition, in Stacy v. Matthew Bender Co. (86 A.D.2d 913), the court stated that "the fact that another state has sufficient contact with the employment such that the other state would be able to take jurisdiction of a workers' compensation claim does not preclude a finding of jurisdiction in New York."

NOTES

1. See Baron, Handling Occupational Disease Cases (Lawpress, 1981) at 3.
2. See Section 2.5 hereinafter.
3. See Young, Workmen's Compensation Law of Ohio (2nd ed., 1984) at 5–6.
4. 524 N.E.2d 502 (Ohio, June 15, 1988).
5. 524 N.E.2d 482 (Ohio, June 15, 1988).
6. 355 S.E.2d 1417 (N.C. App., 1987).
7. 756 S.W.2d 295 (Texas, July 6, 1988).
8. —— N.W.2d —— (Minn., July 29, 1988).
9. Supra note 1.

10. See Parker, "Solving the Puzzle of Cumulative Injury," The Brief (Summer 1988) at 20–37.

11. 346 P.2d 545 (Cal., 1959): "We think the proposition irrefutable that while a succession of slight injuries in the course of employment may not in themselves be disabling, their cumulative effect in work effort may become a destructive force. The fact that a single but slight work strain may not be disabling does not destroy its causative effect, if in combination with other such strains, it produces a subsequent disability. The single strand, entwined with others, make up the rope of causation. The fragmentation of injury, the splintering of symptoms, into small pieces, the atomization of pain into minor twinges, the piecemeal contribution of work-effort to final collapse, does not negate injury. The injury is still there, even if manifested in disintegrated rather than in total, single impact. In reality the only moment when such injury can be visualized as taking compensative form is the date of the last exposure, when the cumulative effect causes disability."

12. 487 N.E.2d 356 (Ill. App., 1985).

13. See General Electric Co. v. Industrial Commission, 433 N.E. 2d 671 (Ill., 1982).

14. 493 N.E.2d 595 (Ill. App., 1986).

15. Supra note 10 at 22.

16. 65 Cal. Rptr. 835 (1968).

17. Section 9.9 hereinafter.

18. Section 9.9 hereinafter.

19. Section 9.10 hereinafter.

20. —— P.2d —— (Cal., 1988).

21. See The Brief (Winter 1988) at 7 et seq.

22. ——N.Y.S.2d —— (New York County, November 30, 1988).

1.5 Constitutionality of Environmental Laws Generally

Although environmental laws appear to be beyond the ken of occupational injury, occupational disease, and occupational death, it should be noted that environmental laws, whether federal, state, or local, do have a close relation. Injury, disease, or death may result to an employee in his environment and not necessarily in his workplace. Therefore, a brief scan of the constitutionality of environmental laws is in order. In the first place, environmental laws control the use and development of privately owned land and even workplaces, and these laws are subject to such issues of federal constitutional law as the General Welfare Clause,[1] the Commerce Clause,[2] the Due Process Clause,[3] the Preemption of the Supremacy Clause,[4] and the Taking Without Eminent Domain procedure.[5]

The General Welfare Clause has been relied on as authority for a number of federal environmental land use controls.[6] In the course of providing for the common defense and for the "general welfare of the United States" the federal government has, for example, preempted all state and local controls over the development and use of atomic energy.[7] The General Welfare Clause has justified federal programs for flood control, reforestation, prevention of soil erosion, and establishment of game preserves.[8]

The Commerce Clause vests power in Congress to "regulate commerce with foreign nations and among the several states." The Clean Water Act, for example, encompasses the "waters of the United States,"[9] including navigable and nonnavigable waters; even a mountain trout stream[10] and a dry desert arroyo[11] fall within that expansive definition. The Commerce Clause sustains the land use controls of the Safe Water Drinking Act (1974).[12] The Clean Air Act[13] regulates motor vehicle use in urban centers that have not attained "primary air quality standards," a level of air quality that is safe for public health. The Commerce Clause also serves to prevent state or local government from enacting laws that burden interstate commerce without sufficient justification as a police power measure to protect local environmental interests. In H. P. Hood & Sons Inc. v. DuMond[14] the U.S. Supreme Court explained:

The Commerce Clause is one of the most prolific sources of national power and an equally prolific source of conflict with legislation of the state. While the constitution vests in Congress the power to regulate commerce among the states, it does not say what the states may or may not do in the absence of congressional action, nor how to draw the line between what is and what is not commerce among the states. Perhaps even more than by interpretation of its written word, this court has advanced the solidarity and prosperity of this nation by the meaning it has given to these great silences of the constitution.[15]

In Soap and Detergent Association v. City of Chicago[16] the federal district court invalidated the municipal ban on the sale of phosphate detergents because the city had failed to make findings adequate to support its exercise of the police power and because the city sought to curb such pollution of waters outside the city. On the other hand, Vermont's 1953 law barring the sale of beverages in non-returnable containers was upheld.[17] In Huron Portland Cement Co. v. City of Detroit[18] the U.S. Supreme Court upheld the city of Detroit's Smoke Abatement Code as a legitimate exercise of local police power not violative of interstate commerce under the Commerce Clause.

The Due Process Clause enforces procedural rights and procedural regularity with respect to notice, nonambiguities in statute, and opportunity to be heard. Fair procedures entail assurance that the federal government has not violated the Fifth Amendment (i.e., deprivation "of life, liberty or property, without due process of law) or the Fourteenth Amendment (i.e., no state "deprive(s) any person of life, liberty or property, without due process of law"). Generally, a hearing or opportunity to be heard must be provided within a reasonable period of time before or after imposition of an environmental regulation or standard.[19] Failure to establish standards and regulations by an agency may be held to be a denial of fair hearing.[20] Due Process requires that before government may constrain a person's life, liberty, or property, the person must be fairly apprised of the government's requirements. Reasonable notice also depends on a statute that is not constitutionally deficient for vagueness; statutory precision is mandatory so as to give notice of proscribed behavior, guidance for enforcement, and protection of First Amendment rights.[21] The U.S. Supreme Court in 1960 declared that a legitimate, substantial purpose of a state "cannot be pursued by means that broadly stifle fundamental personal liberties when the end can be more narrowly achieved."[22]

The preemption of the Supremacy Clause also finds a basis in the Tenth Amendment to the U.S. Constitution, which reserved to the states, or the people, all "powers not delegated to the United States by the Constitution, not prohibited by it to the States." When both state and federal laws cover the same environmental subject matter, Supremacy Clause evaluation must be made to ascertain whether Congress had legislated so as to exclude the states from concurrent legislation, to wit: (a) when compliance with both statutes is physically impossible, the "federal exclusion of State law is inescapable"[23]; (b) when Congress has manifested its intent to preempt the field, federal law must prevail[24]; and (c) when no express preemption intent has been shown by Congress, the fact of preemption will nevertheless be implied.[25] However, in Askew v. American Waterways Operators[26] the U.S. Supreme Court held that federal and state oil pollution abatement laws were compatible, and that preemption was not necessary. Yet five years later the highest court in Ray v. Atlantic Richfield[27] invalidated the state of Washington's statute regulating the size, design, and movement of oil tankers in Puget Sound, although the state was allowed to exercise indirect authority with respect to design of the oil tankers.

The Taking Without Eminent Domain procedure has generally been upheld even when the property in question is restricted in its use and development based on aesthetics[28] or the desirability of maintaining open spaces and green acreage.[29] The deprivation of the right to maximize development profits from a parcel of land by prohibiting its "highest and best use" is not per se a taking of land without eminent domain.[30] However, the opposite is true when there is a clear trespass or invasion of private property by government.[31]

The Federal Employees' Compensation Act (FECA) of 1916[32] provides the exclusive remedy for civilian employees of the federal government. According to the President's Private Sector Survey on Cost Control (January 1984), approximately $880 million in compensation benefits, excluding medical expenses, were paid in 1982 to claimants under FECA. But the system was found to be "open to fraud and abuse because of an excessively permissive claims payment policy and because the current Automated Data Processing systems are not effective." The survey also found the following discrepancies:

The system does not correlate specific disabilities with recovery periods in order to identify those instances where absence exceeds established medical guidelines. The Government does not make use of comprehensive experience data to aid in identifying possible abuse.

The current system does not require that the medical credentials of physicians certifying disability be verified as a prerequisite to claim payment.

Claims submitted to more than one Region cannot be detected.

There is no cross reference to other wage replacement systems (such as unemployment insurance, black lung compensation, etc.), and thus the possibilities for duplicate payment of benefits are great.

The system does not verify wage earnings (available in 38 states) to identify individuals who may be employed while collecting benefits.

Claims offices emphasize paying claims quickly with little emphasis on controlling potential abuse.

NOTES

1. U.S. Constitution, Art. I, Sec. 8 (1): "The Congress shall have power to lay and collect taxes, duties, imposts and excises, to pay the debts and provide for the common defense and general welfare of the United States; but all duties, imposts and excises shall be uniform throughout the United States."

2. Art. I, Sec. 8 (3) U.S. Constitution.

3. See Matthews v. Eldridge, 424 U.S. 319 (1976).

4. U.S. Constitution, Art. VI (2): "This Constitution, and the laws of the United States which shall be made in pursuance thereof; and all treaties made, or which shall be made, under the authority of the United States, shall be the supreme law of the land; and the judges in every State shall be bound thereby, anything in the constitution or laws of any State to the contrary notwithstanding."

5. U.S. Constitution, Fifth Amendment: "nor shall private property be taken for public use, without just compensation."

6. See, for example, Texas Landowners Rights Association v. Harris, 453 F. Supp. 1025 (D.C., 1978).

7. 42 U.S.C. 2012, Atomic Energy Act; see Freedman, Hazardous Waste Liability (Michie, 1987) at Section 3.5 therein.

8. See In Re United States, 28 F. Supp. 758 (SD N.Y., 1939).

9. 33 U.S.C. 1251; see Freedman, Hazardous Waste Liability (Michie, 1987) at Section 3.7 therein.

10. See United States v. Earth Sciences, Inc., 559 F.2d 368 (3rd Cir., 1979).

11. See United States v. Phelps Dodge Corp., 391 F. Supp. 1181 (Ariz., 1975).

12. See Freedman, Hazardous Waste Liability (Michie, 1987) at Section 3.22 therein.

13. Id. at Section 3.6 therein.

14. 336 U.S. 525 (1949).

15. Id. at 534–535.

16. 357 F. Supp. 4 (Ill., 1974).

17. See Anchor Hocking Glass Corp. v. Barber, 105 A.2d 271 (Vt., 1954).

18. 362 U.S. 440 (1960).

19. Supra note 3.

20. See White v. Roughton, 530 F.2d 750 (7th Cir., 1976).

21. See Grayned v. City of Rockford, 408 U.S. 104 (1972).

22. See Sheldon v. Tucker, 364 U.S. 479 (1960).

23. See Florida Lime & Avocado Growers, Inc. v. Paul, 373 U.S. 132 (1963) at 142–143.

24. See Campbell v. Hussey, 368 U.S. 297 (1961).

25. See Northern States Power Co. v. Minnesota, 447 F.2d 1143 (8th Cir., 1971).

26. 411 U.S. 325 (1973).

27. 435 U.S. 151 (1978).

28. See Penn Central Transportation Co. v. City of New York, 438 U.S. 104 (1978) at 129.

29. See Jenad v. Village of Scarsdale, 218 N.E.2d 673 (N.Y., 1966).

30. See Steel Hill Development, Inc. v. Town of Sanborton, 469 F.2d 956 (1st Cir., 1972).

31. See Kaiser Setan v. United States, 444 U.S. 164 (1979).

32. See Freedman, Federal Statutes on Environmental Protection (Quorum Books, 1987) at 49 (note 5 V.S.C. 8101–8193).

1.6 The Right to Know Laws

Employees' interests are somewhat bolstered by the prevalence in many states of right to know laws that, in simplest terms, require employers to keep their employees posted of hazards in the workplace.[1] Workplace hazard warnings must be clear and unambiguous, and the employee must be realistically apprised of the warnings (i.e., know or appreciate the danger or hazard, as well as the recommended means to avoid the danger or hazard). The right to know statutes in the various states recognize the employees' right to know about all hazards and dangers in the workplace. The scope of federal workers' right to know regulations was delineated by the Third U.S. Court of Appeals in United Steelworkers of America v. Pendergrass.[2] Here the plaintiff union contended that the Office of Management and Budget had illegally blocked portions of the so-called hazard communication standard requiring employers to inform workers about dangerous substances in the workplace.[3] The court agreed that the federal agency had indeed done so under the guise of the Paperwork Reduction Act of 1980. Earlier in 1988 in the U.S. Senate the Reagan Administration had rejected legislation that would have required warnings to workers that they risk cancer and other diseases from on-the-job exposure to toxic chemicals because such legislation would "cost businesses up to $7 billion if workers began filing and winning liability suits against employers. Up to 300,000 workers a year could have been affected by the measure."[4]

The right-to-know principle has, on the other hand, been enforced in civil litigation, as when a company physician negligently fails to disclose his knowledge of the state of an employee's health to the employee.[5] The duty of an employer to disclose its knowledge of an employee's health condition or status was established in Union Carbide & Carbon Corp. v. Stapleton.[6] Here the employer had made fourteen chest x-rays of the employee during an eight-year period of employment, and the x-rays disclosed that plaintiff had an arrested case of pulmonary tuberculosis; the plaintiff-employee was never apprised of the state of his physical health. He subsequently became ill, and his condition was aggravated when his personal physicians did not take chest x-rays because they were aware of the company x-rays, which they presumed to be normal because the employer had not communicated with the employee about any adverse reading of the x-rays. The Sixth U.S. Court of Appeals ruled that the employer's duty to disclose was breached: the employer had no obligation to give the employee a physical examination or take chest x-rays, "but, when it undertook to do so, Stapleton was entitled to and did rely on the expectation that he would be told of any dangerous conditions actually disclosed by that examination. The appellant-employer was therefore liable for the injury to Stapleton caused by its negligent omission to advise him of his tubercular condition." Once the employer insists on a physical examination of the employee, the employer conducting the physical examination has almost a duty to discover injuries and diseases![7] It would appear that this duty of the employer rests on Section 323 of Restatement (Second) of Torts that one who undertakes to act must not act negligently.[8]

In Dougherty v. Hooker Chemical Corp.[9] the Third U.S. Court of Appeals ruled that whether or not the manufacturer of trichloroethylene was relieved of its duty to warn employees of Boeing Aircraft Co. when the employer of the employees had previously been given warnings, was a question for the jury. In deciding for the plaintiff-employee, the court cited Comment n of Section 388 of Restatement (Second) of Torts to the effect that "it may be improper for the supplier to trust the conveyance of the necessary information of the actual character of a highly dangerous article to a third person of whose character he knows nothing. It may well be that he should take the risk that information may not be communicated." Note that the negligence of the intermediary-employer does not affect the product manufacturer's duty to warn; the negligence of the intermediary-employer only relates to the causation of the injury.[10]

However, in Thomas v. Arvon Products Co.[11] the product manufacturer prevailed, since it had fulfilled its duty to warn. An employee was injured from exposure to fumes from varnish that defendant had sold plaintiff's employer. The evidence revealed that the defendant had sent a representative to the employer several times to explain the safe use of the varnish product, that the representative had criticized the manner of use of the product by the employee, and that the representative had taken other steps to ensure against misuse of the product. A compound containing hydrochloric acid was misused by an employee in Uptain v. Huntington Laboratories, Inc.,[12] and the evidence showed that the injured plaintiff-employee had been instructed by her employer to wear gloves in handling the product and that plaintiff had refused to do so; the jury verdict in favor of the product manufacturer was upheld on appeal.

NOTES

1. See generally McGuire, "Hazards in the Workplace," Trial Magazine (June 1988) at 24 et seq.

2. 819 F.2d 1263 (3rd Cir., 1988); also see N.L.J. (September 26, 1988) at 3.

3. Note United Steel Workers of America v. Auchter, 783 F.2d 728 (3rd Cir., 1986), and United Steel Workers of America v. Pendergrass, 819 F.2d 1263 (3rd Cir., 1987).

4. See New York Times (March 30, 1988) at A23.
5. See Betesh v. United States, 400 F. Supp. 239 (D.C., 1974).
6. 237 F.2d 229 (6th Cir., 1956). See Baron, Handling Occupational Disease Cases (Lawpress, 1981) at 56–57.
7. See Jines v. General Electric Co., 303 F.2d 76 (9th Cir., 1962). See also Bedmarski v. General Motors Corp., 88 Mich. App. 482, 276 N.W.2d 624 (1979); Blue Bell Globe Mfg. Co. v. Lewis, 200 Miss. 685, 27 So.2d 900 (1946); Brown v. Scullin Steel Co., 364 Mo. 225, 260 S.W.2d 513 (1953); and Atchison, T. & S.F.R.R. v. Perryman, 200 Okla. 266, 192 P.2d 670 (1948).
8. Supra note 6 at 61.
9. 540 F.2d 174 (3rd Cir., 1976). Also note Buser, "Failure to Warn in Toxic-Tort Cases," Trial Magazine (October 1987) at 21 et seq.
10. See Neal v. Carey Canadian Mines, Ltd., 548 F. Supp. 357 (ED Pa., 1982).
11. 227 A.2d 897 (Pa., 1967).
12. 723 P.2d 1322 (Colo., 1986).

1.7 Criminal Responsibility of Employers

In the late 1980s, according to the *New York Times*,[1] state courts reversed a trend upholding criminal convictions of companies and their executives for workers' injuries and workers' deaths. The article cited Sabine Consolidated Co. v. Texas Peabody Southwest,[2] in which the Texas appellate court opined that the criminal prosecution of employers for workplace injuries conflicted with federal law (i.e., OSHA), and the court overturned the convictions of two construction companies that had been found guilty of criminally negligent homicide in the trench cave-in deaths of construction workers. In People v. Chicago Magnet Wire Co.[3] the Illinois court in 1987 dismissed an aggravated battery indictment of an employer charged with exposing its workers to toxic chemicals on the ground of conflict with OSHA. A Brooklyn, New York, jury found company executives in People v. Pymm Thermometer Co.[4] guilty of assault for exposing workers to unsafe levels of mercury fumes in their factory, but the New York court set aside the verdict as contrary to OSHA. It should be noted that OSHA has relied almost exclusively on civil fines to punish violations of the federal law; hence the zest of state prosecutors to seek criminal responsibility for employers found guilty of workplace injuries, diseases, and deaths. The federal preemption here is particularly aggravating to state prosecutors who contend that Congress, in enacting OSHA, did not intend to create a shield behind which careless or reckless employers could hide.[5]

It should be apparent that OSHA has not been effective in curbing workplace injuries, diseases, and deaths, and the Reagan Administration in the 1980s was seemingly loathe to take decisive action. One such example is the multimillion-dollar property loss and the deaths of twenty-eight workers at the L'Ambiance Plaza building collapse in 1987 in Bridgeport, Connecticut, in which OSHA was unwilling to become involved: OSHA initially proposed "a $360 penalty against the general contractor on the site."[6] OSHA finally waived all fines, running into millions of dollars, and settled for reimbursement of its expenses in investigating the building collapse. One labor union leader commented, "I can only wonder how many construction workers could have been spared injury and death if OSHA had met the extent of the legislation that created it."[7]

NOTES

1. See Glaberson, "States Are Toppling Workplace-Injury Convictions," New York Times (September 19, 1988) at 1 and D5.
2. 756 S.W.2d 865 (Tex., 1988).
3. 510 N.E.2d 1173 (Ill. App., 1987).
4. 515 N.Y.S.2d 949 (1988).
5. Supra note 1 at D5.
6. See Hartford Courant (November 8, 1987) at B1.
7. See Hartford Courant (November 11, 1987) at A1 and A11.

2

Recognition of Occupational Injury, Disease, or Death

2.1 Facts and Figures

The U.S. Bureau of Labor Statistics released figures in 1988 illustrating the "riskiest" industries as of 1986, based on reported injuries and illnesses per 100 full-time workers.[1] The meat-packing industry achieved 33.4, followed by mobile-home manufacturing, vending-machine manufacturing, structural-wood manufacturing, raw cane sugar processing, prefabricated-wood building, rubber recycling, sawmills making wood shingles and other special products, boat building and repairing, and vitreous plumbing manufacturing, in that order.

The National Institute for Occupational Safety and Health similarly produced facts and figures for 1980–1984 occupational deaths, revealing that farming had the highest death rate, followed by mining, construction, forestry and fishing, transportation, communications, and public utilities.[2]

There can be little doubt that occupational injury, disease, and death are major economic problems as well, costing billions of dollars in lost time to industry and countless time in grief among workers and their families.

A prime concern is recognition, particularly of occupational disease, which has physical, biological, and chemical aspects.[3] A physical agent refers to an entity without substance that is capable of adversely affecting the biological mechanisms of the exposed worker (i.e., air pressure, vibrations, noise, and even radiation). Biological hazards encompass infections caused by bacteria as well as allergic responses or reactions to plant and animal agents.[4] Brucellosis in meat packers is particularly cited as an example of biological disease caused by occupational exposure.[5] Chemical aspects are probably the most common cause of occupational disease, since both the raw materials and the finished product in the manufacturing plant are frequently indicted as the causes, whether such occupational disease is achieved by inhalation, skin contact, or ingestion.

Exposure to toxins in the air and water and on land can also occur outside the employment relationship and present the employee with disease, injury, or death. Frequently victims are not aware of the fact of exposure until the injury, disease, or death manifests itself many years later. It is this "environmental exposure" that has also aroused political and economic concern because the price of injury, disease, and death is astronomically large.[6]

Employee safety involves recognition of the employer's liability in many fact situations such as those illustrated hereinafter: (a) Iandiorio v. Kriss & Senko Enterprises, Inc.,[7] in which an eighteen-year-old employee, as a gas station attendant, spilled some gasoline on his clothing and walked into the building where another employee lit a cigarette, and plaintiff-employee's clothing ignited, causing severe burns about his body; the Pennsylvania court found the employer responsible for failing to prohibit smoking on the premises; (b) Roberdo v. M. P. Industries, Inc.,[8] in which an employee crane operator was crushed to death when the crane toppled as he was endeavoring to lift an excessive weight without changing the boom angle of the crane; the Maryland court found that the employer had failed to train and supervise the deceased employee; (c) Jordan v. International Paper Co.,[9] in which the plaintiff iron worker fell sixty-five feet to the ground while climbing a steel column, losing the use of his pituitary gland and severely injuring his right foot and shoulder; the Alabama court upheld a finding that the employer had failed to provide him with a safe workplace, despite the employer's safety rule that prohibited unprotected climbs of more than thirty feet; and (d) Olivito v. GBS Associates, Ltd.,[10] in which the platform on which the plaintiff-employee was working in an elevator shaft in a hotel collapsed, causing the employee to fall five stories and sustain severe fractures of the pelvis, ribs, and spine; the New York court ruled that the platform was indeed a "scaffold" within the definition of Section 240 of the New York Labor Law, and that the fall of the unloaded scaffold was prima facie evidence of negligence on the part of the employer.

NOTES

1. See *New York Times* (January 10, 1988) at E5.
2. Id.
3. See Baron, Handling Occupational Disease Cases (Lawpress, 1981) at 7 et seq.
4. See Freedman, Allergy and Products Liability (Central Book, 1961).
5. See Supra note 3 at 8.
6. See Freedman, Hazardous Waste Liability (Michie, 1987) at 14.
7. 517 A.2d 530 (Pa. Common Pleas, Allegheny County, 1987); note that the Pennsylvania Supreme Court in 1986 (517 A.2d 530) had reversed an 1982 trial that had awarded the employer a compulsory nonsuit on the basis that the coemployee had engaged in a personal act outside the course of his employment. Note 31 ATLA Rep. 123–124 (April 1988).

8. —— A.2d —— (Md., Baltimore City, 1987).
9. —— So.2d —— (Ala., Montgomery County, 1987).
10. —— N.Y.S.2d —— (Kings County, 1988).

2.2 Recognition of Disability and Payment of Benefits

The recent New York decision in Surano v. Equitable Life Assurance Society[1] ruled that laryngectomy, total removal of the voice box, presumed a total loss for purposes of disability benefits. The defendant-insurer had refused to make payment, claiming that plaintiff-employee was not totally disabled, since he could still communicate by writing and esophageal speech. But the court refused to accept this heartless and cruel defense, and held that the insurance policy provisions are "clear in enumerating the loss of speech as presumptive total disability, not loss of communication."

Plaintiff-employee was injured in an automobile accident while driving his employer's vehicle and acting within the scope of his employment. The employer had purchased both workers' compensation insurance and no-fault insurance, and the defendant-insurer had derived a formula that paid the injured employee about $214 weekly or about $12 less than his weekly earnings. The federal district court in Georgia was asked to award him this "shortfall" for fifty-eight weeks. The court construed the Georgia statutes as forbidding double recovery of benefits but at the same time mandating full recovery of lost wages up to the combined limits of the two policies of insurance. The proper computation, according to the court, was a payment of about $150 under the workers' compensation policy and about $76 under the no-fault insurance policy. To do otherwise would allow the insurer to reap a windfall and deprive the plaintiff-employee of the benefits of both policies.[2]

In Fox v. Atlantic Mutual Insurance Co.[3] the New York Appellate Division, 2nd Department, ruled that in New York, workers' compensation benefits paid to employees injured in job-related vehicular accidents involving uninsured motorists are intended only as compensation for loss of economic benefits and cannot be used to relieve no-fault insurers of liability for noneconomic losses such as pain and suffering. Consequently, even if the compensation payments exceeded the uninsured provisions' maximum of $10,000 per person, these compensation payments could not be applied to noneconomic losses, nor could these compensation payments provide the unintended result of absolving insurers of much of their financial exposure.[4] According to the court, "any holding to the contrary would effectively subvert the intent of the Legislature and would deprive an injured employee of the right to obtain compensation for losses other than basic economic loss, in direct contravention of the no-fault scheme."

NOTES

1. —— N.Y.S.2d —— (Bronx County, August 23, 1988).
2. See Shipes v. Hanover Insurance Co., 670 F. Supp. 354 (MD Ga., 1987).

3. 521 N.Y.S.2d 442 (App. Div., 2nd Dept., 1987).
    4. Note Fox, "Compensation Payments Held to Cover Only Economic Loss," N.Y.L.J. (November 30, 1987) at 1.

2.3 The Rehabilitation Experience

The Rehabilitation Act of 1973[1] is a comprehensive statute designed to promote the interest of handicapped people by enabling them to share in the opportunities for education, transportation, housing, health care, and, most important, employment. The Act provides, inter alia, for increased federal programs for the handicapped in vocational training and in education generally. A handicapped person is defined as "any person who . . . has a physical or mental impairment which substantially limits one or more of such person's major life activities, . . . has record of such an impairment, . . . or is regarded as having such an impairment."[2] Regulations promulgated by the U.S. Department of Health and Human Services delineate physical impairment as "any physiological disorder or condition, cosmetic disfigurement or anatomical loss affecting one or more of the following body systems: neurological, musculoskeletal, special sense organs, respiratory, including speech organs, cardiovascular, reproductive, digestive, gastrourinary, hemic and lymphatic, skin and endocrine."[3] Major life activities are defined as "functions such as caring for one's self, performing tasks, walking, seeing, hearing, speaking, breathing, learning, and working."[4] The U.S. Supreme Court in School Board of Nassau County v. Arline[5] described the rights of a tuberculosis victim under the Act who, as a schoolteacher, had been discharged because of "the continued reoccurrence of tuberculosis." The federal district court found that the schoolteacher was not a handicapped person under the Act because Congress had not intended to include contagious diseases within the scope of the Act. The Eleventh U.S. Court of Appeals reversed, holding that a person with a contagious disease could be handicapped as defined in the Act, and the U.S. Supreme Court affirmed: the schoolteacher was "physically impaired" by her tuberculosis, since it existed in an active form and significantly affected her respiratory system and also substantially limited one of her major life activities. The highest court concluded that plaintiff-employee was dismissed because of her handicap, which also exhibited physical symptoms.

The Rehabilitation Act of 1973 is applicable only to activities or programs that receive federal financial assistance. In United States v. Baylor University Medical Center[6] the Fifth U.S. Court of Appeals declared that the acceptance of Medicare and Medicaid funds by the university hospital was sufficient to require that the hospital's emergency and inpatient activities and programs comply with the Act.

It would appear that there are at least five elements essential to state a cause of action under the Act, to wit: (1) plaintiff is handicapped as defined under the Act; (2) plaintiff is otherwise qualified for the treatment or the benefit sought;

(3) plaintiff has been excluded from participation in or denied a benefit of, or is the subject of discrimination in regard to the activity or program; (4) the program or activity is federally funded or assisted with federal funds; and (5) such discrimination is the sole reason of the handicap.[7]

In addition to the Rehabilitation Act of 1973, the Education of the Handicapped Act[8] prohibits discrimination against the handicapped in schools that receive federal funding. But it is the Rehabilitation Act that fully recognizes the rights of the handicapped: in Kohl v. Woodhaven Learning Center[9] the Eighth U.S. Court of Appeals in 1989 ordered all staff members of the defendant−learning center who came into contact with a blind, mentally retarded person with hepatitis B to be inoculated. The federal appellate court also enjoined the defendants from denying admission to the handicapped worker.

NOTES

1. 29 U.S.C. 700 et seq.
2. See Section 504 of the Act at 29 U.S.C. 706(7).
3. 45 C.F.R. 84.3(5) ii (1985).
4. 45 C.F.R. 84.3(v)2 ii (1985).
5. 107 S. Ct. 1123 (1987); for lower court opinion, see 772 F.2d 759 (11th Cir., 1985).
6. 736 F.2d 1039 (5th Cir., 1984), cert. den., 105 S. Ct. 958 (1984).
7. See Prewitt v. United States, 662 F.2d 292 (5th Cir., 1981).
8. 20 U.S.C. 1400 et seq.
9. —— F.2d —— (8th Cir., January 10, 1989), aff'g 672 F Supp 1221.

3

Identification of Specific Exposures in the Workplace

3.1 Introduction

Occupational disease is not easy to track down; identifying the specific exposures in the workplace is also a difficult task. Workers come into contact with myriads of chemicals, for example, some of which may have toxic potential and some of which involved the employee's exposure many years ago, perhaps even at another workplace.[1] Toxicologists[2] and epidemiologists[3] are but two experts that can help to identify the specific exposures in the workplace.

Hereinafter set forth are brief dissertations on the following specific exposures: (a) "Black Lung" and Other Lung Claims[4]; (b) Cancer Risk Assessments[5]; (c) Chemicals[6]; (d) Acquired Immunodeficiency Syndrome (AIDS)[7]; (e) Acid Rain and Other Pollutants[8]; (f) Cigarettes and Smoking[9]; (g) Radiation and Video Display Terminals[10]; (h) Heart Disease and Stress[11]; and (i) Repetitive Trauma and Aggravation of Preexisting Disease.[12]

NOTES

1. See Baron, Handling Occupational Disease Cases (Lawpress, 1981) at 25 et seq.
2. Note: Gardner, "Approach to Toxicological Evaluation," 31 Food, Drug & Cosm. L.J. 640 (1976); Gosselin, Robert E., Chemical Toxicology of Commercial Products (Williams & Wilkins, 4th ed. 1976); Hamilton, Alice, and Hardy, Harriet, Industrial Toxicology (Publishing Science, 3d ed. 1974; Kirschman, "Toxicology—The Exact Use of an Inexact Science," 31 Food, Drug & Cosm. L.J. 455 (1976); Loomis, Ted A., Essentials of Toxicology (Lea & Febiger, 2d ed. 1974); and Patty, F.A., Industrial Hygiene and Toxicology (Wiley, 2d ed. 1958).
3. Note: Fox, Hall, and Elveback, Epidemiology: Man and Disease (Macmillan, 1970);

Morris, J.N., Uses of Epidemiology (1975); Occupational Exposure to Asbestos, Criteria Document (NIOSH 1972); Revised Recommended Asbestos Standard (NIOSH Pub. No. 77–169); Stewart, Gordon T., M.D., Trends in Epidemiology: Application to Health Service Research and Training (1972); and Susser, Mervyn, Causal Thinking in the Health Sciences: Concepts and Strategies of Epidemiology (Oxford University Press, 1973). (Supra note 1 at 32–34).
4. See Section 3.2 hereinafter.
5. See Section 3.3 hereinafter.
6. See Section 3.4 hereinafter.
7. See Section 3.5 hereinafter.
8. See Section 3.6 hereinafter.
9. See Section 3.7 hereinafter.
10. See Section 3.8 hereinafter.
11. See Section 3.9 hereinafter.
12. See Section 3.10 hereinafter.

3.2 "Black Lung" and Other Lung Claims

For a hundred or more years, thousands of coal miners have developed the occupational disease of pneumoconiosis, a serious and irreversible pulmonary disease called "black lung." Pneumoconiosis literally means dust in the lungs, although not all dusts that can be deposited in the lungs cause recognizable disease, so that the disease must also delineate the tissue reaction to the presence of dust (defined as an aerosol composed of solid inanimate particles) in the lungs.[1] In 1972 Congress created a special program to benefit victims of black lung in the enactment of the Black Lung Benefits Act[2] based on congressional findings and declaration of purpose:

(a) Congress finds and declares that there are a significant number of coal miners living today who are totally disabled due to pneumoconiosis arising out of employment in one or more of the Nation's coal mines; that there are a number of survivors of coal miners whose deaths were due to this disease; and that few States provide benefits for death or disability due to this death to coal miners or their surviving dependents. It is, therefore, the purpose of this title to provide benefits, in cooperation with the States, to coal miners who are totally disabled due to pneumoconiosis and to the surviving dependents of miners whose death was due to such disease and to ensure that in the future adequate benefits are provided to coal miners and their dependents in the event of their death or total disability due to pneumoconiosis.

Earlier legislation had assured the constitutionality of the Act as not depriving mine operators of their property without due process of law or denying them equal protection of the law.[3] The purpose of the legislation was to fill the gap in traditional state workers' compensation coverage as it relates to coal miners.[4]

The applicable disease of pneumoconiosis means "a chronic dust disease of the lung and its sequelae, including respiratory and pulmonary impairments, arising out of coal mine employment."[5] Liability or entitlement can be based on five "particular rebuttable presumptions," to wit:

(1) If a miner who is suffering or suffered from pneumoconiosis was employed for ten years or more in one or more coal mines, there shall be a rebuttable presumption that his pneumoconiosis arose out of such employment.

(2) If a deceased miner was employed for ten years or more in one or more coal mines and died from respirable disease, there shall be a rebuttable presumption that his death was due to pneumoconiosis.

(3) If a miner is suffering from a chronic dust disease of the lung which (A) when diagnosed by chest roentgenogram, yields one or more large opacities (greater than one centimeter in diameter) and would be classified in category A, B, or C in the International Classification of Radiographs of the Pneumoconioses by the International Labor Organization, (B) when diagnosed by biopsy or autopsy, yields massive lesions in the lung, or (C) when diagnosis is made by other means, would be a condition which could reasonably be expected to yield results described in clause (A) or (B) if diagnosis had been made in the manner prescribed in clause (A) or (B), then there shall be an irrebuttable presumption that he is totally disabled due to pneumoconiosis or that his death was due to pneumoconiosis, or that at the time of his death he was totally disabled by pneumoconiosis, as the case may be.

(4) If a miner was employed for fifteen years or more in one or more underground coal mines, and if there is a chest roentgenogram submitted in connection with such miner's, his widow's, his child's, his parent's, his brother's, his sister's, or his dependent's claim under this title and it is interpreted as negative with respect to the requirements of paragraph (3) of this subsection, and if other evidence demonstrates the existence of totally disabling respiratory or pulmonary impairment, then there shall be a rebuttable presumption that such miner is totally disabled due to pneumoconiosis, that his death was caused by pneumoconiosis, or that at the time of his death he was totally disabled by pneumoconiosis. In the case of a living miner, a wife's affidavit may not be used by itself to establish the presumption. . . . The Secretary may rebut such presumption only by establishing that (A) such miner does not, or did not, have pneumoconiosis, or that (B) his respiratory or pulmonary impairment did not arise out of, or in connection with, employment in a coal mine. The provisions of this paragraph shall not apply with respect to claims filed on or after the effective date of the Black Lung Benefits Amendments of 1981 (see other provisions note to 30 USCS 901).

(5) In the case of a miner who dies on or before the date of the enactment of the Black Lung Benefits Reform Act of 1977 (enacted Mar. 1, 1978) who was employed for 25 years or more in one or more coal mines before June 30, 1971, the eligible survivors of such miner shall be entitled to the payment of benefits, at the rate applicable under Section 412(a) (2) (30 USCS 922 [a] [2]) unless it is established that at the time of his or her death such miner was not partially or totally disabled due to pneumoconiosis. Eligible survivors shall, upon request by the Secretary, furnish such evidence as is available with respect to the health of the miner at the time of his or her death. The provisions of this paragraph shall not apply with respect to claims filed on or after the day that is 180 days after the effective date of the Black Lung Benefits Amendments of 1981.[6]

Funding of benefits for black lung is provided by the Black Lung Disability Trust Fund[7]; both workers' compensation payments and social security disability awards, however, are offset against such black lung compensation payments.[8]

The U.S. Supreme Court in 1987, in Mullins Coal Co. v. Director, O.W.C.P.,[9] rendered an interpretation of Section 203(a) of regulations of the Secretary of Labor under the Black Lung Benefit Act. The section stated that a claimant who had worked in a mine for at least ten years is entitled to an *interim presumption* of eligibility for disability benefits under the act if he or she meets *one* of four prerequisites: (1) a chest x-ray confirming the presence of black lung; (2) ventilatory studies establishing the presence of any respiratory or pulmonary disease of a specified severity; (3) blood gas studies showing an impairment in the transfer of oxygen from the lungs to the blood; or (4) other medical evidence establishing a totally disabling respiratory impairment. This *interim presumption* in favor of the miner-victim is rebutted, however, if the evidence discloses that the claimant is then doing his usual work or comparable work or is capable of doing such work, and that the disability did not arise from coal mine employment, or that the claimant did not in fact have black lung. The victim here filed his claim in 1976 after having worked in a coal mine for sixteen years; he offered one x-ray interpretation, two ventilatory studies, and one supporting physician's diagnosis. But seven x-ray interpretations, four ventilatory studies, and five physician's diagnoses all supported a finding that he did not have black lung. Both the administrative law judge and the Benefits Review Board agreed with the negative findings, but the Fourth U.S. Court of Appeals reversed, holding that the victim only needed to submit *one* item of qualifying evidence.[10] But the U.S. Supreme Court again reversed and remanded, declaring that Section 203(a) of the regulations requires the claimant to establish one of the qualifying items of evidence by a preponderance of the evidence, which claimant here apparently did not do!

Earlier in Sebben v. Brock[11] the Eighth U.S. Court of Appeals had criticized the standards of the Secretary of Labor as being too restrictive, and ordered the Secretary of Labor to reconsider coal-induced pneumoconiosis claims filed by miners between December 30, 1969, and April 1, 1980, if the claimants submitted a positive x-ray as proof of black lung. Two years earlier, in Coughland v. Director, O.W.C.P.,[12] the same federal appellate court invalidated a rule of the Secretary of Labor that claimants must have worked in the coal industry for ten years to be eligible for benefits under the Act.[13] The U.S. Supreme Court on December 6, 1988, in an unanimous decision, ruled in Pittston Coal Group v. Sebben[14] that the Eighth U.S. Court of Appeals had erred in ordering the U.S. Department of Labor to reopen the old cases; but the highest court in a 5–4 vote found that the U.S. Department of Labor had improperly denied benefits to tens of thousands of coal miners who developed symptoms of black lung in the 1970s.[15] In ordering the U.S. Department of

Labor not to reopen the 93,000 claims because those miners had waived their right to benefits by failing to file proper appeals years ago, the Court shielded coal mine operators from paying as much as $13.6 billion.[16] Payments to the winning 7,000 miners opened up the enormous backlog of pending cases, particularly for short-term workers (i.e., those with less than ten years of work in the mines). The Court ruled that the presumption of black lung also pertained to these short-term miners: "We do not sit to determine what Congress ought to have done, given the evidence before it, but to apply what Congress enacted—and the exclusion of short-term miners from the benefits . . . finds no support" in the law aimed at making it easier for miners to seek benefits.

Inhalation of formaldehyde in particle board and plywood can cause symptoms ranging from sore throat to headache and nausea; chlorinated hydrocarbons in paint removers and contact cements, when inhaled, can cause cardiac arrest, and dust from pressure-treated lumber can expose an employee to arsenic.[17] The point is that there is little under the sun that cannot evince some lung problem (or other medical problem) in a susceptible person or employee. In Anderson v. Stauffer Chemical Co.[18] the plaintiff-employee sued his former employer, alleging that he was a victim of thirty years of exposure to asbestos, silica dust, phosphorus pentoxide, and other toxic substances, and therefore contracted interstitial lung fibrosis. This diagnosis was confirmed by medical testimony and chest x-rays. But the employer denied any causal connection, and furthermore pointed out that the statute of limitations in Florida barred the action for workers' compensation. The Florida Department of Labor and Employment Security[19] ruled that there was substantial evidence that his lung fibrosis was linked to the workplace exposure, that the two-year statute of limitations did not run because the claim of the plaintiff-employee had been filed within two years of the date of actual disability, and that the mandatory physical examination program of the employer had placed the employer on notice of the employee's lung condition.

NOTES

1. See Baron, Handling Occupational Disease Cases (Lawpress, 1981) at 323. Note also Occupational Diseases, A Guide to Their Recognition, U.S. Dept. of Health, Education and Welfare, NIOSH Pub. No. 77–181 (rev ed., June 1977).
2. 30 U.S.C. 901 et seq (1972).
3. See National Independent Coal Operators Association v. Brennan, 372 F. Supp. 16 (D.C., 1974), aff., 419 U.S. 955 (1975).
4. See Collins v. Weinberger, 401 F. Supp. 377 (Va., 1975).
5. Note Section 902(b) thereof.
6. Note Section 921(c) thereof.
7. See Section 9501 of the Internal Revenue Code at 26 U.S.C. 9501. Also, see generally Warren Freedman, Federal Statutes on Environmental Protection (Quorum Books, 1987) at 19–21.

8. Note Boyd v. Califano, 479 F. Supp. 846 (WD Va., 1978).

9. 108 S. Ct. 427 (1987). Note Bernstein, "Supreme Court Review," Trial Magazine (April 1988) at 14–15.

10. 785 F.2d 424 (4th Cir., 1986).

11. 815 F.2d 475 (8th Cir., 1987).

12. 757 F.2d 966 (8th Cir., 1985).

13. See A.B.A.J. (February 1, 1988) at 17.

14. 109 S. Ct. 414 (December 6, 1988).

15. See New York Times (December 7, 1988) at A26.

16. See Hartford Courant (December 7, 1988) at A9.

17. See Hartford Courant (November 8, 1987) at J11.

18. —— So.2d —— (Fla. Dept. of Labor and Employment Security, April 30, 1987).

19. Rule No. 428 30 1697.

3.3 Cancer Risk Assessments

The *New York Times* (March 20, 1984) published a major study of twenty substances, "all of which have been found or are now in the workplace," that are "known or suspected to have caused cancer in humans or animals."[1] These cancer risk assessments are but a small part of the total picture of dangers and hazards to which an employee is exposed in the workplace. The Environmental Protection Agency (EPA) in its "Risk Assessment Guidelines"[2] somewhat altered the usual proof of how cancer risk information is presented by insisting on explicit disclosure of scientific uncertainties. Thus the problem of proximate cause[3] was accentuated because causation ordinarily must be inferred by reference to an assessment of the probability that the exposure resulted in the cancer. Also, there is no scientific evidence that certain chemicals known to cause cancer at very high doses will also cause cancer at far lower levels. Yet workplace levels of exposure are presumably larger than environmental levels of exposure, although the differentiation cannot be scientifically proved. Thus scientists estimate the risk of cancer at very low doses from the effects observed at high doses.[4] But no one can predict which individuals will get cancer! And some chemicals, like fluoride, have beneficial uses in low concentrations, (i.e., fluoride in water because of its beneficial effects on teeth, but at high doses fluoride is deadly as used in rat poison!)[5] On the other hand, arsenic causes cancer at high doses but has recently been discovered to be an essential nutrient at very low levels, especially for animals.[6] Thus closing the door on arsenic and public exposure to it would actually be a loss to society.

As indicated above, the EPA "Risk Assessment Guidelines" of 1986 establish strict requirements for disclosure of the scientific uncertainties along with range-of-risk data. These guidelines also emphasize that cancer risk assessments must fully disclose the theoretical assumptions used in reaching the risk assessment conclusions.[7] Nevertheless, these cancer risk assessments hardly rise to the level of "reasonable probability" or "reasonable certainty," which are legal terminologies for measuring the duties and responsibilities for the potential tortfeasor. Courts have excluded cancer assessments based on animal data[8] as well as cancer assessments derivative of hypothetical suppositions.[9] Most courts have recognized the need to prove cause and effect in an individual plaintiff, even when epidemiological data disclose a connection between the chemical and a disease in humans.[10] In short, speculation and conjecture, even by scientific experts, is not admissible in evidence.[11] It should be apparent that science and case law do not support recovery for increased risk of current or future occupational disease.[12]

Today asbestos litigation is probably the fastest-growing area of tort law, as asbestos constitutes one of the clearest indications of cancer risk.[13] One asbestos manufacturer, after being sued by 20,000 persons, was forced into bankruptcy.[14] It is estimated that more than 700,000 public and commercial buildings are contaminated with asbestos.[15] In June 1988, according to the *Wall Street Journal*,[16] a federal district court in Georgia consolidated 3,500 asbestos claims into a single class action suit! The New Jersey Supreme Court in 1985 held that an employer who knew that an employee had developed an asbestos-related disease and yet willingly concealed that knowledge from the employee until the disease had progressed significantly was held to be subject to the ''intent to injure'' exception to the exclusivity of workers' compensation remedies. A direct suit against the employer by the injured employee was sanctioned.[17]

NOTES

1. See *New York Times,* May 2, 1984, at C12 and C13.

2. 51 Fed. Reg. 33, 992 (1986). See generally Scroggin, ''Cancer Risk Assessments: New Guidelines May Limit Their Use,'' Trial Magazine (October 1987) 49–54.

3. See Section 9.6 hereinafter.

4. Supra note 2 at 49.

5. Id. at 50.

6. Note 50 Fed. Reg. 46, 936 and 46, 960 (1985).

7. Supra note 2 at 52.

8. See Ethyl Corp. v. EPA, 541 F.2d 1 (D.C. Cir., 1976), cert. den., 426 U.S. 941 (1976).

9. See United States v. Brown, 557 F.2d 541 (6th Cir., 1977).

10. Note Johnston v. United States, 592 F. Supp. 374 (Kan., 1984).

11. See Calhoun v. Honda Motor Co., 738 F.2d 126 (6th Cir., 1984).

12. Note the following on the issue of claims of increased risk of contracting diseases: Ames, Magaw, and Gold, ''Ranking Carcinogenic Hazards,'' Science Magazine (April 1987) at 236; Claus and Bolander, Ecological Sanity (David McKay, 1977); Gleeson, ''A Primer on the Causation Issue in the Chemical Exposure Case,'' Defending Chemical Exposure Litigation (Defense Research Institute Monograph, March 1985); Gleeson, ''Chemically Induced Immune Disregulation: Closing Pandora's Box,'' Defending Chemical Exposure Litigation (Defense Research Institute Monograph, March 1985); Gleeson and Shelton, Reasonable Scientific Certainty: A Proposed Evidentiary Standard for the Disqualification of Experts in Toxic Tort Litigation. (Defense Research

Institute Monograph, August 1986); Gleeson, Challenging Medical Diagnosis in Toxic Tort Litigation (Defense Research Institute Monograph, August 1986); Gleeson, "Exclusion of Animal Data as Evidence of Chemically Induced Disease," 29 For the Defense 25 (October 1987); Gots, "Medical/Scientific Decision Making in Occupational Disease Compensation: Analytical System, Operational Approach," in Role of State Workers' Compensation System in Compensating Occupational Disease Victims, Crum and Forster's Occupational Disease Task Force (June 1983); Wilson and Crouch, "Risk Assessment and Comparisons: An Introduction," Science Magazine, 236:267–295 (April 17, 1987).

13. See A.B.A.J. (November 1987) at 74.
14. Note 20/20 Technology Review 20 (July 1987).
15. Id.
16. (June 13, 1988) at 17.
17. See Millison v. du Pont, 501 A.2d 505 (N.J., 1985).

3.4 Chemicals

Admittedly, there are 60,000 or more chemicals in the workplace and in the environment, constituting the most likely source of danger and hazard to working people and their environment. Only in recent years has the chemical industry, for example, begun to recognize its duty to assess toxic risks.[1] Among these many chemicals might be listed aniline,[2] which is not only irritating to the eyes, but may also cause corneal damage; systemically, exposure may cause cyanosis; arsenic,[3] which may cause skin cancer and other fatal toxic results; benzene,[4] which causes central nervous system depression as well as hemorrhage in the brain, and the urinary tract; beryllium,[5] which is highly toxic by inhalation and causes severe chemical pneumonitis with pulmonary edema; carbon monoxide,[6] which can cause death; carbon tetrachloride,[7] which can result in central nervous system depression, gastrointestinal symptoms, and acute renal failure; chromium,[8] which can cause lung cancer, inter alia; formaldehyde,[9] which can cause lung disease, chronic bronchitis, permanent asthma, and emotional distress; graphite,[10] which can produce a progressive and disabling pneumoconiosis; nitrogen oxides,[11] which may result in severe pulmonary irritation and methemoglobinemia, inter alia; sulfur dioxide,[12] which can cause chronic respiratory disease, inter alia; and trichloroethylene,[13] which can cause cancer.

There are also *unknown* chemicals that can cause workplace injury, as evidenced by the fact that chemicals called composites (used in airplane hangars) have caused workers to become too ill to work! The culprit appears to be phenolic resin and the chemical brew used to bond, cool, and clean it.[14] Reported ailments include rash, cramps, bloody urine, memory loss, and even cancer. Continued exposure to such hazardous substances may be deadly, according to Rogers v. Lockheed Corp.,[15] a multiplaintiff action filed in California court in 1988.

NOTES

1. See Warren Freedman, Hazardous Waste Liability (Michie, 1987) at 21.

2. Note Wetherhold, Linch, and Charsha, "Chemical Cyanosis: Causes, Effects and Prevention," Archives of Environmental Health (1960) 1:75.

3. Note Dinman, "Arsenic: Chronic Human Intoxication," Journal of Occupational Medicine (1960) 2:137.

4. Note Sherwood and Carter, "The Measurement of Occupational Exposure to Benzene Vapor," Annals of Occupational Hygiene (1970) 13:125.

5. Note Tepper, Hardy, and Chamberlin, Toxicity of Beryllium Compounds (Elsevier, 1961).

6. See Hartford Courant (February 10, 1988) at D5, reporting that in State of Connecticut v. PGP Industries the Connecticut court had ruled on February 8, 1988, that the employer, a reclaimer of precious metals, was not criminally negligent in the death of a security guard exposed to carbon monoxide. There were no state or local laws requiring the employer to install equipment that might have prevented the death, such as alarms designed to sound when levels of carbon monoxide exceeded acceptable levels.

7. See Nielson and Larsen, "Acute Renal Failure Due to Carbon Tetrachloride Poisoning," Acta Medica Scandinavica (1965) at 178.

8. See Barborik, "The Problem of Harmful Exposure to Chromium Compounds," Ind Med Surg (1970) 39:45.

9. See Crandall v. Eureka Fluid Works, Inc.,____F. Supp.____(Ariz., 1984), in which plaintiff developed lung disease from inhaling formaldehyde fumes while attempting to mop up spilled embalming fluid, and the jury awarded him $495,000; Tiderman v. Fleetwood Homes of Washington, 684 P.2d 1302 (Wash., 1984), in which plaintiff-teacher blamed her severe and permanent asthma on inhaling formaldehyde fumes in her newly purchased mobile home, and the jury awarded her $566,500; and Troensegaard v. Silvercrest Industries, Inc.,____Cal. Rptr.____(1984), in which the 84-year-old woman suffered emotional distress because of the strong odor of formaldehyde in her new mobile home, and the jury award exceeded $100,000.

10. See Harding and Oliver, "Changes in the Lungs Produced by Natural Graphite," British Journal of Industrial Medicine (1949) 6:91, and Penergrass, Vorwald, Mishkin, Whildin, and Werley, "Observations on Workers in the Graphite Industry," Medical Radiography and Photography (1967/1968) 43:71 and 44:2.

11. See Morley and Silk, "The Industrial Hazard from Nitrous Fumes," Annals of Occupational Hygiene (1970) 13:101.

12. See Ferris, Burgess, and Worcester, "Prevalence of Chronic Respiratory Disease in a Pulp Mill and a Paper Mill in the United States," British Journal of Industrial Medicine (1967) 24:26.

13. See Stites v. Sundstrand Heat Transfer, Inc., 660 F. Supp. 1516 (WD Mich., 1987), in which the court granted partial summary judgment for defendants on plaintiff's risk of cancer claim. Plaintiff failed to demonstrate with reasonable certainty that the future consequences will occur. Plaintiff's experts were unable to quantify the enhanced risk after defendants' experts showed that the likelihood that plaintiff would get cancer was significantly less than a reasonable certainty.

14. See Cox, "Stealth's Other Secrets," N.L.J. (March 6, 1989) at 1 and 46.
15. Id. (N.C.C. 31148).

3.5 Acquired Immunodeficiency Syndrome, or AIDS

AIDS is undoubtedly, in the 1980s, the nation's leading public health concern, for this disease is no longer impacting on only a small segment of our society, specifically homosexuals and intravenous drug users, but on workers and the society as a whole.[1] AIDS has also become an "employers' dilemma,"[2] as AIDS victims frequently bring lawsuits alleging unlawful discrimination under the Rehabilitation Act of 1973.[3] In the landmark case, Shuttleworth v. Broward County,[4] the employee was fired when he disclosed that he was an AIDS patient, although his employer explained the dismissal on the basis of the health risk to fellow workers. He filed a complaint before the Florida Commission on Human Relations and the Commission found for him in that the county employer had violated state and federal laws prohibiting employment discrimination against the handicapped. The commission specifically held that AIDS was a handicap under Florida law. Thereupon the employee filed a claim in federal district court alleging violation of Section 504 of the Rehabilitation Act as well as a violation of 42 U.S.C. 1983 claim based on violation of his equal protection and due process rights. The court found that the employee had stated a cause of action for discrimination, and that he did not have to exhaust Florida remedies before resorting to the federal claim.[5]

A word about the nature of the disease: AIDS is apparently a viral infection, and once it produces illness, death is certain, usually within eighteen months. Among the early symptoms are general weakness, nausea, headaches, weight loss, fever, diarrhea, and malaise; the virus inexorably eliminates the body's ability to combat infection. AIDS is not transmitted through casual contact but through intimate contact, through blood and semen, although the AIDS virus has been detected in human saliva, tears, breast milk, urine, and other body fluids. Recently in the New York case of New York State Society of Surgeons v. Axelrod[6] the plaintiff–medical association sought to compel the Commissioner of Health to designate human immunodeficiency virus (HIV) infection as a communicable disease under the New York Public Health Law. Plaintiff argued that the law's testing, reporting, and contact-tracing mechanisms were essential to control the spread of AIDS and to protect hospital staff and patients.[7] The court, however, distinguished AIDS from HIV seropositivity, and upheld defendant's refusal to list HIV infection as a sexually transmitted or communicable disease. Defendant's case was built on the fact that the designation "would require all local health officers, physicians, hospital administrators, laboratories, or people in charge of state institutions to report all cases or suspected cases of AIDS." Also, the designation would permit local boards of health and health officers "to isolate persons with communicable diseases"; mandatory contact-tracing "would not further the State's efforts in identifying

HIV seropositive persons. . . . [There are] many negative incentives which exist for intravenous drug users, homosexuals and other HIV positive persons which would inhibit their cooperation. . . . The State policy has been to encourage voluntary testing and counseling while ensuring the confidentiality of test results.'' The court cited the new Article 27F of the New York Public Health Law, effective February 1989,[8] as rejecting coercive measures because ''mandatory testing of broad population groups is neither effective nor desirable. Experience in other States has also shown that without effective assurances of confidentiality, voluntary testing efforts fail. The fight against AIDS can be won only with the voluntary cooperation of all our citizens, especially those most at risk.'' But the New York Court of Appeals, late in 1988, ruled that random drug testing of an elite police unit did not unreasonably invade the police officers' privacy interests. The highest New York court concluded that the officers' privacy claims were not protected by the rationale of Patchogue-Medford Congress of Teachers v. Board of Education,[9] in which the court in 1987 held that reasonable suspicion was required before schoolteachers could be tested for drug use.[10] In that 1987 case, according to the court, ''the school district's asserted interest in a drug-free teaching staff was limited to ensuring that its teachers are fit and that drug abuse does not impair their ability to deal with the students.'' But in the instant case[11] ''these officers are effectively on duty 24 hours a day,'' and therefore, the police department has a ''justifiable interest'' in keeping its ''mainline offense and defense in the war against drug trafficking'' free of drug use.[12]

In Massachusetts the case of Life Insurance Association v. Commissioner of Insurance[13] arose when the defendant attempted to prevent insurance companies in Massachusetts from testing applicants for HIV before issuing them health insurance policies. The court here opined that ''insurers have the right to classify risks and to elect not to insure risks if the discrimination is fair.'' The HIV antibody test to identify risks was deemed ''reasonable,'' and therefore, the defendant had overstepped his authority in telling insurers that they were not free to use the tests: ''If we were to accept the Commissioner's argument that he had implied authority to issue these regulations, it is hard to see what restrictions there would be on the Commissioner's right to control any and all activities of the insurers by regulation.''[14]

The death of the insured as a result of his contracting AIDS after receiving a blood transfusion to treat his hemophilia was held by the Maryland appellate court in Cheney v. Bell National Life Insurance Co.[15] not to fall within the coverage of an accidental death insurance policy, which excluded from coverage for any sickness or medical treatment. In rejecting the plaintiff's argument that the insured's death was ''accidental'' (i.e., the accident being the drawing of blood from a donor who had AIDS and injecting it into the insured), the court viewed the receiving of blood as ''no accident,'' since it was purposefully drawn from the AIDS donor.[16]

The use of tests to detect the AIDS virus in the employment context is prohibited by many states, for example, California,[17] Wisconsin,[18] and Florida.[19] The risk or even likelihood that an employee, because of AIDS, will be unable to perform the job in the future is generally insufficient to justify denial of employment or firing of the employee. In Chrysler Outboard Corp. v. Dilhr[20] the denial of employment of a person who had acute lymphocytic leukemia violated Wisconsin law prohibiting handicap discrimination; the prospective employee would have subjected the employer to higher insurance costs, higher absenteeism, and problems associated with prolonged recuperation and other complications, but he was currently able to do the job. In SDHR v. Xerox Corporation[21] the New York Court of Appeals ruled that the risk of future incapacity associated with obesity cannot justify a refusal to hire if the applicant is currently able to do the work.[22] On the other hand, the likelihood of harm to other employees might be a ground for denial of employment to an AIDS victim, although the Ninth U.S. Court of Appeals, in Mantolete v. Bolger,[23] held the employer to a very strict standard of proving a reasonable probability of substantial injury to other employees before sanctioning a denial of employment, particularly when the prospective employee was currently qualified and able to perform the essential requisites of the job. The federal district court for the Southern District of New York, in New York State Association for Retarded Children v. Carey,[24] had earlier ruled that restrictions placed on certain handicapped children with hepatitis B (analogous to AIDS) violated the Rehabilitation Act as discrimination against the handicapped. In Chalk v. U.S. District Court[25] the Ninth U.S. Court of Appeals in 1988 firmly stated that AIDS fell within the definition of handicap under the Rehabilitation Act.

It would appear that only one state, Delaware, and Puerto Rico and the Virgin Islands do not prohibit discrimination on the basis of handicap in employment.[26] Generally, such state laws are more encompassing than the federal Rehabilitation Act, since the latter finds attention principally from government contractors and recipients of federal funding. In the Massachusetts case of Cronan v. New England Telephone Co.[27] the court ruled that an "AIDS victim may also qualify as a protected handicapped person based solely on an employer's erroneous perception of him as someone contagious to co-workers." On the federal level, the employer cannot directly ask an applicant for employment whether or not the applicant has AIDS.[28] Similarly, laws that mandate blood tests and disclosure of the results would impact on the privacy rights of the employee or prospective employee.[29]

A review of recent court decisions on AIDS sheds light on the myriad of situations that can arise. In People v. Ward[30] the defendant had pleaded guilty to selling "crack" and was sentenced to prison. He moved to dismiss the criminal charge in the interest of justice because he had tested positive for AIDS and also had Hodgkin's disease. But the New York court found that the Hodgkin's disease was in remission, and that he was only "at risk" of contracting AIDS. In denying the motion the court held that there was no compelling factor dictating dismissal because defendant was simply not terminally ill! And the court delineated the issues:

The criteria that must be considered by this Court in deciding this motion is set forth in CPL section 210.40(1) as follows:

    (a) the seriousness and circumstances of the offense;
    (b) the extent of harm caused by the offense;
    (c) the evidence of guilt, whether admissible or inadmissible at trial;
    (d) the history, character and condition of the defendant;
    (e) any exceptionally serious misconduct of law enforcement personnel in the investigation, arrest and prosecution of the defendant;
    (f) the purpose and effect of imposing upon the defendant a sentence authorized for the offense;
    (g) the impact of a dismissal upon the confidence of the public in the criminal justice system;
    (h) the impact of a dismissal on the safety or welfare of the community;
    (i) where the court deems it appropriate, the attitude of the complainant or victim with respect to the motion;
    (j) any other relevant fact indicating that a judgment of conviction would serve no useful purpose.

Recently, there have been several so-called "AIDS cases" in which an application for dismissal in the furtherance of justice was granted by a trial court (see People v. Jose Osorigonlalez, Sup Ct Queens Co, NYLJ, 3–28–88, p54 col 4; People v. Richard Williams, Sup Ct NY Co, NYLJ, 9–18–87, p12 col 4; People v. Mike Camargo, 135 Misc 2d 987, Sup Ct Bronx Co (December 1986); People v. Jose Vasquez, Sup Ct Bx Co, NYLJ, 6–20–88, p30 col 2 and People v. Quinn, Sup Ct Queens Co, NYLJ, 10–20–88, p29 col 5). In each of these cases, the defendant was suffering from the AIDS disease and his prognosis for survival was poor. Each defendant was terminally ill and close to death and the courts therein found this to be a "compelling factor." . . . In the case at bar, defendant is not terminally ill. Defendant is not on his death bed, nor is defendant in his "last days." In fact, his physical condition is good and his appearance in court robust. The Hodgkin's disease is in remission, and he does not have the AIDS disease.

A dismissal of this charge would impact upon the confidence of the public in the criminal justice system. In this case, defendant was accused of selling crack, criminal sale of a controlled substance in the third degree, a class B felony, to an undercover police officer on three occasions at the Coachman Hotel, a shelter for the homeless in the City of White Plains. The two most pressing social and governmental problems in this County today are the explosion of crack use and a desperate need for safe and adequate housing for the homeless. A decision to release without prosecution an admitted drug seller in these circumstances would certainly cause the public to question the credibility of the criminal justice system in this County.

Defendant pleaded guilty to a reduced charge of attempted criminal sale of a controlled substance, a class D felony. As a predicate felon, the plea bargained sentence of 2–4 years is the mandatory minimum sentence. Mr. Ward was convicted of attempted robbery in the second degree in 1985.

I do not find the existence of some "compelling factor" to dismiss the instant (see People v. Viszoki, 99 AD2d 519). A denial of defendant's motion would not constitute or result in an injustice. Accordingly, in balancing the interest of the defendant and the State (see People v. Clayton, 41 AD2d 204, 208), and all the factors set forth above, defendant's request to dismiss the charge of attempted criminal sale of a controlled substance in the fourth degree in the furtherance of justice is denied.

In Matter of Hurwitz[31] a New York City dentist failed in his attempt to obtain a court order to stop the New York City Commission on Human Rights from conducting a hearing on a discrimination complaint that he had refused to treat a patient infected with AIDS. The dentist's defense was to the effect that a private dental practice was not covered by the Human Relations Law definition of "public accommodation." The court expounded:

The Education Law is intended to assure the professional medical competence of dentists. The Human Rights Law is intended to provide remedies for unlawful discrimination in . . . any public accommodation. . . . [T]he inclusion of dispensaries, clinics and hospitals in the definition of "place(s) of public accommodation" in both the state Human Rights Law and the city's Human Rights Law demonstrates that the legislators who enacted the statutes did not intend to exempt the medical field from scrutiny by the commission where discrimination is alleged. . . .

[However,] (i)n cases where access to treatment is based on an individual's disability, the inquiry is whether a good attempt was made at reasonable accommodation. The determination as to what constitutes reasonable accommodation is made with due deference to the judgments of responsible health officials, a procedure well within the purview of the commission.

And the court concluded:

Petitioner has presented no cases where a court held that a state or local anti-discrimination statute was pre-empted by a state regulatory statute. The pre-emption cases cited by petitioner are inapposite. The main thrust of petitioner's pre-emption argument is, in substance, that the Commission is not an agency qualified to deal with public policy questions of delivery of dental care where the spread of AIDS has raised serious issues of contagion and infection control measures, has caused mounting costs occasioned by responses to these issues, and raised further questions of where and how treatment is best delivered to individuals infected with AIDS. Petitioner argues that the Commission lacks the expertise to distinguish between a dentist's professional judgment and an unlawful discriminatory act.

It is clear to this court that the Commission "does not intend to obstruct the legitimate exercise of professional judgment" (Decision, Hearing Officer on pre-hearing motion, February 22, 1988, p.16) and that the Commission does not "require that every dentist must treat every patient" (Id.). On such issues the Commission can and does afford due deference to medical judgments. In cases where access to treatment is based on an individual's disability, the inquiry is whether a good attempt was made at reasonable accommodation. The determination as to what constitutes reasonable accommodation is made with due deference to the judgments of responsible health officials, a procedure well within the purview of the Commission. Petitioner has not shown that he is entitled to relief in the nature of prohibition on the issue of pre-emption.

On the broad subject of tort liability for the sexual transmission of AIDS, see Baruch, "AIDS in the Courts: Tort Liability for the Sexual Transmission of Acquired Immune Deficiency Syndrome."[32]

In January 1989 the U.S. Department of Labor proposed regulations that would require employers of the nation's 5.3 million health care workers to protect them from blood-borne diseases such as AIDS.[33] The regulations called for employers to adopt safety programs using a strategy called "universal precautions" in which all blood and body fluids are presumed to be infectious and handled accordingly. Fluids are placed in leakproof containers or color-coded bags, or labeled with a clear warning. Furthermore, employers would be required to provide workers with protective clothing such as rubber gloves, masks, and fluidproof aprons.

NOTES

1. See generally Fontana, "Government Liability as It Relates to Title VII Actions," 33 Tort & Ins. L. J. 642 (1988).

2. See Zellner, "Employers' Dilemma: The A.I.D.S. Crisis," For the Defense (May 1988) at 2.

3. See Section 2.3 hereinbefore.

4. Florida Commission on Human Relations, Case No. 85-624, dated December 11, 1985.

5. See also Thomas v. Atascadero Unified School District, 662 F. Supp. 376 (CD Cal., 1986).

6. _____ N.Y.S.2d _____ (Albany County, November 17, 1988).

7. "Petition sets forth that at the present time, with extreme risk to themselves and all health workers, the Petitioners, and all other physicians, surgeons and gynecologists, treat medical and surgical patients without having the necessary knowledge and information regarding whether these patients are infected with AIDS, which is, at present, incurable and always fatal; that the lack of necessary knowledge and information as to whether their patients are infected with the AIDS virus exposes the Petitioners, and all others similarly situated, to undue harm, requires them to practice in an atmosphere of fear and apprehension, and inhibits their ability to properly care for patients who might be infected with the AIDS virus without knowledge thereof; that if AIDS were designated a communicable and/or sexually transmissible disease, the testing, reporting, and contact tracing mechanisms authorized under those designations would begin the process of containment of the disease.

"Petition sets forth further that Petitioners are professionally and ethically responsible to assist in the prevention of disease in the general public, and in particular, because Petitioners are exposed to disease directly, Petitioners must act to seek protection from contracting disease themselves; that Petitioners have a legitimate interest and real concern with controlling the spread of communicable and sexually transmissible diseases; that Petitioners have a professional and ethical duty to ensure that patients are receiving quality care; that Petitioners have a legitimate interest in promoting safe treatment procedures for all who perform medical care, while providing quality care to all who need it; that Petitioners are injured when the Respondents interpret public health statutes and regulations in a manner which interferes with their ability to perform their ethical responsibilities to improve the public health, interferes with their ability to provide quality treatment to their patients, and interferes with their ability to adequately protect themselves from disease; that such testing, reporting, and contact tracing mechanisms, which have been successfully utilized in the past to control epidemics in New York State, would eventually result in fewer incidences of the disease and in fewer individuals being unaware that they were infected with the AIDS virus. . . .

"Petitioners who allege that they have an ethical mandate to provide adequate medical care, seek affirmative protection from AIDS by requesting the Commissioner and PHC to declare it to be a communicable disease and a sexually transmissible disease, so that routine epidemiological measures to control such epidemics may be implemented to contain the spread of AIDS; that in their work, they are exposed to AIDS in that they come into contact with a patient's blood; surgical gloves do not always provide an impervious barrier to such infection; that other members of the medical staff, unaware whether a patient they are treating is infected with AIDS, do not always take precautions to prevent transmission of the disease which they would if they had knowledge.

"Petitioners contend that taking such precautionary measures in all cases is an unworkable solution. Among other things, it would greatly increase costs and would extend the time required for surgery, thus increasing the patient's risk during surgery.

"Petitioners contend that because there are no public health measures under the communicable or sexually transmissible disease designations now being implemented to contain the spread of AIDS, an unknown number of individuals are becoming infected and are unaware thereof; that as a result, physicians, surgeons, gynecologists and obstetricians risk contracting the disease themselves during their performance of medical procedures and risk transmitting the virus to other patients in their care.

"The Petitioners contend also that surgeons, gynecologists, and health care workers now suffer irreparable harm due to potential exposure to AIDS from patients when they are ethically bound to treat.

"Petitioners contend further that without knowing whether or not a patient has contracted AIDS, a physician may engage in a course of treatment or prescribe medications that are not compatible with the AIDS infection; that not only may the AIDS patient not be receiving the most effective treatment, but he may be injured by the theory or medication prescribed."

8. "Section 1. Legislative Intent. The legislature recognizes that maximum confidentiality protection for information related to human immunodeficiency virus (HIV) infection and acquired immune deficiency syndrome (AIDS) is an essential public health measure. In order to retain the full trust and confidence of persons at risk, the state has an interest both in assuring that HIV related information is not improperly disclosed and in having clear and certain rules for the disclosure of such information. By providing additional protection of the confidentiality of HIV related information, the legislature intends to encourage the expansion of voluntary confidential testing for the human immunodeficiency virus (HIV) so that individuals may come forward, learn their health status, make decisions regarding the appropriate treatment, and change the behavior that puts them and others at risk of infection.

"The legislature also recognizes that strong confidentiality protections can limit the risk of discrimination and the harm to an individual's interest in privacy that unauthorized disclosure of HIV related information can cause. It is the intent of the legislature that exceptions to the general rule of confidentiality of HIV related information be strictly construed.''

9. 70 N.Y.2d 57 (1987).

10. See A.B.A.J. (February 1989) at 96.

11. Caruso v. Ward, 520 N.Y.2d 551 (October 25, 1988), aff'g 506 N.Y.S.2d 789.

12. Supra note 10.

13. _____ N.E.2d _____ (Mass., November 16, 1988).

14. Supra note 10.

15. 520 A2d 402 (Md App., 1987). Also see Prego v. New York, ____ N.Y.S.2d ____ (1988), holding that blood contaminated by the AIDS virus is a ''toxic substance'' within the meaning of New York's toxic tort revival statute. The suit here was brought by a doctor who contracted the disease when she was accidentally stuck by a needle hidden in gauze and other refuse in the patient's bed.

In another New York case, Hare v. State of New York, ____ N.Y.S.2d ____ (Ct. of Claims, April 4, 1989), an employee of a State hospital lost a claim against the State for damages for what he claimed was an ''AIDS phobia'' allegedly suffered after being bitten on the arm while helping to subdue a mentally disturbed prisoner. The court called the claim for psychological injuries ''too speculative'' and therefore non-compensable. (But the court did award $35,000 for the bite!) The court pointed out that ''clearly, there is no doubt that the defendant and its employees knew that the inmate . . . had attempted to commit suicide and had previously attempted to end his life by cutting his throat. . . . The officers at the hospital were charged with knowledge of the inmate's mental disturbance . . . and could reasonably have anticipated that he would try to do harm to himself again.'' Thus, the court found negligence on the part of the defendant State of New York: ''Although the court is aware that claimant may have lingering fears from the ordeal, it cannot, based on the evidence before it, award damages for AIDS phobia since every test has proven the claimant's fear to be unfounded. It is also important to note that the court had no evidence before it to indicate that the assailant suffered from AIDS.''

16. See New York Times (August 12, 1988) at A8, for a report on a major employer that had suspended a plan to cut off medical coverage of employees who became sick or injured as a result of AIDS.

17. See Cal. Health and Safety Code, Ch. 1.11 and 1.12, Sections 199.20 et seq., enacted by Ch. 22, Laws 1985, and Ch. 1519, Laws 1985.

18. See Wis. Stats, Sections 103.15 et seq., enacted by Act 73, Laws 1985.

19. See Fla. Stats, Sections 381.606 et seq., enacted by Ch. 85-82, Laws 1985.

20. 14 F.E.P. Cases 344 (Wis., 1976).

21. 65 N.Y.2d 213 (1985).

22. Cf. E.E. Black, Ltd. v. Marshall, 497 F. Supp. 1088 (Hawaii, 1980).

23. 767 F.2d 1416 (9th Cir., 1985).

24. 466 F. Supp. 479 (SD N.Y., 1978).

25. 840 F.2d 701 (9th Cir., 1988).

26. Supra note 2 at 5.

27. 41 F.E.P. Cases 1273 (Mass., 1986).

28. Note 29 C.F.R. Section 32.15; 34 C.F.R. Section 104.14; and 28 C.F.R. Section 41.55.

29. Supra note 1 at 648.

30. _____ N.Y.S.2d _____ (Westchester County, December 20, 1988).

31. 534 N.Y.S.2d 95 (New York County, December 21, 1988).
32. See 22 Tort & Ins. L.J. (Winter 1987) at 165–193.
33. See Hartford Courant (January 10, 1989) at 2.

3.6 Acid Rain and Other Pollutants

Acid rain is not only a pollutant that adversely affects the health of all persons, but also an occupational injury.[1] Outdoor workers, like construction workers, lumbermen, and even salespeople, must spend more time outdoors than the average person in the pursuit of their livelihood and are, therefore, more prone to the injury, disease, or death from acid rain and other pollutants. Acid rain, as delineated in the Acid Precipitation Act of 1980,[2] contributes to the corrosion of metals, wood, paint, and masonry used in construction and ornamentation of buildings and public monuments, as well as to human injury, disease, and death. A 1982 survey by the U.S. Congressional Office of Technology Assessment reported that half of the 9,400 lakes in twenty-three states had been adversely affected by acid rain; of the 117,000 miles of streams, 23,000 miles were reported as "acid-altered," and 37,000 miles were "seriously at risk."[3]

Unfortunately the District of Columbia Court of Appeals in Thomas v. New York[4] overturned a federal district court decision that upheld an action by plaintiffs seeking relief from acid rain damage. The plaintiffs were six states and four individuals who brought suit to compel the Environmental Protection Agency to abate the harm from acid deposition.[5] The state of Minnesota, on its own, however, has established stringent controls over acid rain pollution[6]; the Minnesota Acid Deposition Act of 1980[7] requires the State Pollution Control Agency to investigate the causes and effects of acid rain and to educate the people of the state about acid deposition. The Minnesota Acid Deposition Act of 1982[8] mandates the identification of areas in the state that are sensitive to acid rain and the establishment of standards and controls.

NOTES

1. See Freedman, Hazardous Waste Liability (Michie, 1987) at 26–27.
2. 42 U.S.C. 8901 et seq.
3. Supra note 1 at Section 1.8 (1988 update).
4. 802 F.2d 1443 (D.C. Cir., 1986).
5. In November 1988 nine states filed a new lawsuit against the Environmental Protection Agency (EPA) in their five-year legal effort to order new measures to curb acid rain. See New York Times (November 23, 1988) at D19. Suit was brought in U.S. Court of Appeals for the District of Columbia, and the petition spelled out the demand that the EPA immediately publish for public comment its determination that sulfur dioxide emissions from plants and factories were harming people.
6. See In Re Proposed Adoption of Minnesota Rules, pts. 7005.4010 to 7005.4050 (June 27, 1986). See generally Garland, "Dealing with Acid Rain: The Clean Air Act Is Not Enough," Trial Magazine (October 1987) at 58 et seq.

7. 1908 Minn. Laws Section 490.
8. Minn. Stats Sections 116B.42–.45 and 116C.69 (1982).

3.7 Cigarettes and Smoking

There are few artificial adjuncts of life that adversely affect so many workers as cigarettes and smoking. Not only is the smoker at peril for lung cancer, but his or her co-workers within the zone of smoking are also susceptible to the same cancerous possibilities. In 1986, in Perry v. Burlington Industries, Inc.,[1] the North Carolina appellate court reviewed an employee's workers' compensation claim for occupational lung disease allegedly caused by exposure to cotton dust in the textile mill where he worked; the defense of the employer was based on the employee's heavy cigarette smoking for more than thirty years. But the State Industrial Commission found that the employee's bronchial and pulmonary problems were caused by the working conditions at the textile mill; and the Commission concluded that he was totally incapacitated and entitled to workers' compensation. The court affirmed by holding that the employee's smoking did not invalidate the conclusion that the employee had a compensable occupational disease.[2] Later in 1986, in Dean v. Cone Mills Corp.,[3] the court affirmed the denial of compensation benefits because the claimant failed to clearly prove that exposure to cotton dust had caused his injury: "Those identified factors which likely contributed to that lung disease included his brief cigarette smoking, his cotton textile exposure, and unusual genetic susceptibility or other factors." And in Brisboy v. Fibreboard Paper Products Corp.[4] the Michigan appellate court opined that the employee's death was due to asbestos-related lung cancer, a result of the synergistic effect that occurs when asbestos fibers are inhaled by a cigarette smoker, rather than from purely cigarette-related lung cancer. Furthermore, the employee could not be said to have been negligent with regard to the specific hazard that he actually encountered in the workplace.[5] In Mack v. County of Rockland[6] the New York Court of Appeals reviewed a claim by a psychiatric social worker who suffered an aggravation of a preexisting eye disorder while in defendant's employment as a result of her exposure to cigarette smoking in a poorly ventilated room. The administrative law judge rendered a decision in her favor, but the Workers' Compensation Board reversed, holding that claimant's condition was not an occupational disease. The New York Appellate Division affirmed, as did New York's highest court:

It is settled that an "occupational disease," under the statute as it existed at the time of claimant's injury and claim, is restricted to medical conditions resulting from the ordinary and generally recognized risks incident to a particular occupation. An "occupational disease" derives from the very nature of the employment, not a specific condition peculiar to the employee's place of work (see, Matter of Paider v. Park East Movers, 19 NY2d 373, 377; Matter of Goldberg v. Marcy Corp., 276 NY 313, 318–319).

Because claimant's injury was caused solely by the environmental conditions of her work place, not by any distinctive feature of the occupation of a psychiatric social worker, the Board had a proper legal basis to deny her claim.

This claim arose prior to the enactment of an amendment to section 2(15) of the Workers' Compensation law which added a definition of "occupational disease" to the statute (L 1984, ch 659). We do not decide what, if any, change in the definition the amendment has effected.

Involuntary exposure to cigarette smoke is still a major issue in litigation, as illustrated by the Massachusetts case of Bernard v. Cameron & Colby Co.[7] Here the female plaintiff sued her employer when he transferred her to a work area where she was subjected to tobacco smoke. She specifically claimed that she was allergic to tobacco smoke, that her employer had previously provided her with a smoke-free workplace, and that her employer was totally aware of her allergy. But the highest Massachusetts court opined that the allegations were not sufficient to show that she was entitled to a smoke-free workplace, nor did she show that she was physically injured by the transfer. The court pointed out that the employer's action was not conduct that was so outrageous in character or extreme in degree as to be regarded as utterly intolerable![8]

Still, cigarette smoking is the major cause of lung cancer,[9] the major cause of coronary disease,[10] the major cause of chronic obstructive pulmonary disease,[11] a prime cause of cancer of the oral cavity, pharynx, larynx, esophagus, urinary bladder, pancreas, and kidney,[12] and the cause of approximately 300,000 deaths each year in the United States.[13] Safety in the workplace requires some restraints on cigarettes and smoking.

NOTES

1. 343 S.E.2d 215 (N.C. App., 1986).

2. See generally Rose and Ream, "Tobacco Litigation," For the Defense (February 1987) at 9.

3. 350 S.E.2d 99 (N.C. App., 1986).

4. 384 N.W.2d 39 (Mich. App., 1985).

5. Supra note 2 at 11.

6. _____ N.E.2d _____ (N.Y., June 2, 1988).

7. 491 N.E.2d 604 (Mass., 1986).

8. Supra note 2 at 8.

9. *The Health Consequences of Smoking, a report of the Surgeon General*, U.S. Dept. of Health, Education and Welfare (1979); *The Health Consequences of Smoking: Cancer, a report of the Surgeon General*, U.S. Dept. of Health and Education and Welfare (1982); *The Health Consequences of Smoking: Cancer and Chronic Lung Disease in the Workplace, a report of the Surgeon General*, U.S. Dept. of Health, Education and Welfare (1985).

10. *The Health Consequences of Smoking: Cardiovascular Disease, a report of the Surgeon General*, U.S. Dept. of Health, Education and Welfare (1983).

11. *The Health Consequences of Smoking: Chronic Obstructive Lung Disease, a report of the Surgeon General*, U.S. Dept. of Health, Education and Welfare (1984).
12. Supra note 9.
13. Supra note 10.

3.8 Radiation and Video Display Terminals

In recent years radiation hazards in the workplace have focused on the video display terminal, particularly with respect to the evils of miscarriages and birth defects in pregnant women. Other injuries associated with video display terminals include severe eyestrain, cataracts, fatigue, headaches, and muscle strain. A statistical correlation between miscarriages in working women and long hours of video display terminal use was found by the Northern California Kaiser Permanente Medical Care Program.[1] However, in 1984 the American College of Obstetricians and Gynecologists concluded that radiation emitted by video display terminals was "insufficient to cause spontaneous abortions and birth defects."[2] And in December 1986 the American Medical Association's Council on Scientific Affairs concluded that "no association has been found thus far between radiation emissions from VDT's and reported spontaneous abortions, birth defects, cataracts or other injuries."[3] It should be noted that cathode ray tubes also emit nonionizing electromagnetic radiation that could pose a biological hazard in the workplace.

More than 15 million video display terminals are in use in the United States, and by 1990 the number is expected to swell to 70 million.[4]

In June 1988 Suffolk County, New York, passed a law that required employers to subsidize annual eye examinations for video display terminal users and to provide eyeglasses or contact lenses if needed because of working on video display terminals. The local law was not based on concerns about radiation emissions, but on studies that detected such ailments as eyestrain, stiff neck, and crippling hand and wrist pain among workers who put in long hours at the video display terminals. The local law required employers to provide adjustable chairs and desks, fifteen-minute breaks every three hours, regular vision examinations, corrective eyewear, and education in ergonomics (i.e., the science that seeks to adapt work and working conditions to workers), all for permanent employees who use video display terminals more than twenty-six hours per week.[5] But the Suffolk County Executive vetoed the local law, stating that it would economically isolate Suffolk County and would also cost thousands of jobs.[6] The eighteen-member Suffolk County Legislature thereupon overrode the veto[7] and encouraged more than twenty-five states to consider similar legislation.

It is interesting to observe that plaintiffs who did not suffer a *current* physical injury from exposure to radioactive material were not permitted in Westrom v. Kerr-McGee Chemical Corp.[8] to maintain an action for negligent infliction of emotional distress.

NOTES

1. See New York Times (June 16, 1988) at 1 and B10.
2. Id. at B10.
3. Id.
4. See New York Times (June 23, 1988) at B11.
5. See Letters to the Editor, New York Times (July 1, 1988) at A30.
6. See New York Times (June 11, 1988) at 1 and 34.
7. See New York Times (June 15, 1988) at 1 and B2.
8. ___ F. Supp. ___ (ED Ill., 1983).

3.9 Heart Disease and Stress

There are myriads of claims for workers' compensation benefits based on heart disease and stress, but one of the more interesting cases concerned a fatal heart attack suffered by an employee after he was told that he would be fired! In Re Sara Black[1] the deceased salesman had a heart attack when informed by his employer that he would be fired, and his widow was awarded by the workers' compensation board a funeral benefit of $1,500 plus $135 weekly. The employer immediately appealed on the ground that the heart attack was "not job-related." The employer claimed that the stress the employee endured after he was told he would be fired was not undue or excessive, as required under the emotional stress injury standard in New York law. Furthermore, the employer argued that the decision to terminate his employment was a reasonable personnel decision. But the New York Court of Appeals found that the employee "had a history of heart disease and hypertension and that, on the day before his death, he was severely distraught because he had been told by his employer that he was being dismissed." And, according to New York's highest court, the workplace injury was therefore "job-related," and the notification of dismissal was a "major stress factor resulting in ventricular instability, subsequent fibrilation, and ultimately death," entitling the employee to workers' compensation.[2]

NOTES

1. 504 N.E.2d 400 (N.Y., May 3, 1988).
2. See Trial Magazine (August 1988) at 10.

3.10 Repetitive Trauma and Aggravation of Preexisting Disease

The employee was a disabled sheet metal worker whose wrists had deteriorated owing to thirty-eight years of work with heavy tin snips. The Washington State Labor Department denied his claim for disability benefits on the ground that his disability was not related to his work or occupation. In Dennis v. Department of Labor[1] the Washington Supreme Court in 1987 ruled that the employee was entitled to disability benefits, since his disability was caused by repetitive trauma or aggravation of preexisting illness. The court overruled an earlier Washington decision[2] that had required a worker to show that the conditions that induced the disease were generally "peculiar to and inherent in" that industry. The new rule meant that a worker only had to show that an occupational disease resulted from the condition of his job.[3]

NOTES

1. 745 P.2d 1295 (Wash., 1987).
2. See Kenville v. Department of Labor, 664 P.2d 1311 (Wash., 1983).
3. See Trial Magazine (May 1988) at 89–90.

4

Alcoholism in the Workplace

4.1 Introduction

A purchasing agent for the National Maritime Fisheries Service, a federal agency in Florida, was fired by his employer for alcoholism. The evidence revealed that the purchasing agent drank a pint of gin every day over a three-year period of employment and missed fourteen months' work during that thirty-six-month employment. In Ferguson v. U.S. Department of Commerce[1] the federal district court in Tampa, Florida, ruled that he was indeed a victim of discrimination in that he had not received the requisite counseling mandatory for handicapped federal workers before being fired. The federal government, as employer, had argued that the federal agency could not have offered him counseling because he had never said that he was an alcoholic, he had never staggered in the workplace, he had never been seen surreptitiously drinking, and he had never smelled of alcohol. But the court found that the agency "was ignorant of the common symptoms of alcoholism including chronic absenteeism, and this ignorance prevented the recognition of Ferguson's problem."[2] Indeed, the alcoholic faces many problems in finding and keeping work, problems that vary with the severity of his or her alcohol abuse.[3] As indicated above, the recovered alcoholic may find that the job opportunities are denied him or her on the basis of past alcoholism, without regard to current ability to do the job; and the current alcoholic may be denied new positions or may be fired from his current position on the basis of his or her diminished productivity and heightened absenteeism. Even the employee who has become unable to work may find his or her entitlement to disability benefits to be in jeopardy if his or her employer or the insurer can prove that the employee's disability is the willful product of alcoholism.[4]

Alcoholism leads to many disabling injuries, diseases, and deaths. For example, cirrhosis of the liver, often induced by alcohol, caused the deaths in 1984 of 11.6 persons per 100,000.[5] Alcoholism is responsible for fetal alcohol syndrome, a condition that causes mental retardation and physical deformity in babies born to mothers who drank heavily during pregnancy.[6]

Overindulgence in alcohol has been recognized from remote antiquity, not only as an evil in and of itself, but also as a cause of cruelty, indolence, neglect, and poverty, and therefore as a fit subject of moral and legal condemnation.[7] But in recent years studies indicate that the roots of alcoholism may stem from genetics: about 40 percent of the 10.6 million alcoholics in the United States in 1989 have at least one parent who is or was a confirmed alcoholic.[8] Typically, becoming an alcoholic is a two-step process in which alcohol abuse, relatively common, leads to more chronic abuse and addiction: "In alcoholism, the contribution of nature and nurture is mixed, the interaction between the hardware of one's genes and the software of one's experience is complex."[9] Inherited physiological differences exist in people that may very well attest to genetic factors that indicate a predisposition to alcoholism.[10] Alcoholics Anonymous (A.A.), an organization of self-help, has more than 1.5 million members throughout the world, half of whom reside in the United States and the other half in 114 other countries. Membership in the A.A. today includes young people, blacks, Hispanics, and homosexuals, attesting to the growing widespread problem of alcoholism.[11] Fortunately there has also been a growing recognition that alcoholism is a disease, not an intentionally inflicted injury. In July 1949 I coauthored "Alcoholism: Self-inflicted Injury or Disease Under Disability Provisions of Insurance Policies."[12] It took the prestigious American Medical Association another seven years for its trustees and house of delegates to declare that alcoholism was a disease, "thereby validating a central belief of A.A. from its founders on, that it is a sickness, not a sin."[13] In 1986 the Second U.S. Court of Appeals in Traynor v. Turnage,[14] however, refused to review a Veterans' Administration decision that barred disability benefits for the plaintiff on the ground that alcoholism was "willful misconduct." Here the plaintiff had a history of drinking going back to the age of eight; he was hospitalized for drinking five times while in the military service. However, he stopped drinking and joined A.A. but was denied veterans' benefits on the ground that he had engaged in willful misconduct. He brought suit in the federal district court for the Southern District of New York, alleging that the Veterans' Administration had violated the Rehabilitation Act of 1973[15] forbidding discrimination on the basis of handicap. The trial court agreed with him, ruling that denial of benefits amounted to discrimination against alcoholics.[16] In reversing, the federal appellate court simply and curtly cited 38 U.S.C. 211(a), which bars judicial review of final decisions of the Veterans' Administration! A parallel case, McKelvey v. Turnage,[17] prompted the U.S. Court of Appeals for the District of Columbia to hold that the Veterans' Administration could reasonably distinguish, as they did, between those who were responsible for their handicap from alcoholism and those who were not responsible for their handicap from alcoholism. (The plaintiff here had drunk up to half a gallon of bourbon a day after his honorable discharge from military service, and was hospitalized thirty-three times until he became an alcoholism counselor and stopped drinking.) The U.S. Supreme Court affirmed in 1988.

Since 1978, when Congress amended the Rehabilitation Act,[18] the definition of "handicapped" expressly included "alcoholics," and therefore discrimination against alcoholics is an unlawful act. Empathy with the alcoholic is also evident in the recent New York decision in Cooper Wireless Cable of New York, Inc. v. Local Union No. 3, IBEW, AFL-CIO.[19] Here the employer moved to set aside an arbitration decision reinstating an employee who had violated the employer's policy of terminating any employee who used alcohol or drugs during working hours. The employee was found drinking beer at work. The court held that although public policy did not encourage alcohol or drug use, there was no compelling public ethos offended by the reinstatement of the beer-drinking employee. Furthermore, the court found that the employee did not have sufficient notice of the no-alcohol policy of the employer, the violation of which would not justify punishment as harsh as dismissal from employment.

Interestingly, the virtues of alcohol have been sung by a new magazine, *Prost!* launched in 1988 to fight the negative image of alcohol.[20] The magazine toasts the pleasures of responsible drinking: "There have been so many mixed signals in the media about drinking that a good many people have such a guilt complex that they are afraid to buy a drink or afraid to go into a liquor store. We want everybody to get the facts and get them straight and take care of themselves." The magazine stresses the health benefits of moderate drinking; overindulgence occurs after the third drink!

NOTES

1. 680 F. Supp. 1514 (Fla., March 1, 1988).
2. See N.L.J. (March 21, 1988) at 10, and New York Times (March 4, 1988) at B9.
3. Note "Alcohol Abuse and the Law," 94 Harv. L. Rev. 1660 (1981) at 1687.
4. Id. at 1688.
5. See New York Times (December 24, 1987) at B9.
6. Id.
7. See 18 Mass. L.Q. 80 (1890), observing that "the early lawgivers of Babylon, China, and Israel strove to encourage sobriety and stamp out drunkenness among their respective peoples. Later, the Christian Church made attempts to bring about a more moderate use of the wine cup. St. Gildas dealt out severe punishment to any churchman guilty of drunkenness. Dunstan is said to have labored in the cause of temperance in England to the end that King Edgar at his instance restricted the number of taverns and the quantity of intoxicants that might be sold." Also, note Crowley v. Christensen, 137 U.S. 86 (1890): "By the general concurrence of opinion of every civilized and Christian community, there are few sources of crime and misery to society equal to the dramshop,

where intoxicating liquors, in small quantities, to be drunk at the time, are sold indiscriminately to all parties applying. The statistics of every state show a greater amount of crime and misery attributable to the use of ardent spirits obtained at these retail liquor saloons than to any other source."

8. See Hartford Courant (December 31, 1987) at F1.

9. Id.

10. See New York Times (November 10, 1987) at C1 and C2.

11. See New York Times Sunday Magazine Section (February 21, 1988) 40 et seq., adapted from "Getting Better: Inside Alcoholics Anonymous" (April 1989).

12. See 23 Temple L.Q. 39–62 (July 1949).

13. Supra note 11 at 57.

14. 791 F.2d 226 (2nd Cir., 1986).

15. See Chapter 2 hereinbefore, to wit: 29 U.S.C. 701–796i (1979).

16. 606 F. Supp. 391 (S.D.N.Y., 1985). Also see Neal, "Is Alcoholism a Disease?" A.B.A.J. (February 1, 1988) at 58.

17. 792 F.2d 194 (D.C. Cir., 1986); for lower court opinion, see 596 F. Supp. 1317 (D.C., 1984).

18. Supra note 15.

19. Unreported ____ N.Y.S.2d —— (New York County, 1980).

20. See Insight Magazine (October 3, 1988) at 54.

4.2 "Driving While Intoxicated" and Dram Shop Laws

Alcohol abuse is the single largest factor leading to traffic fatalities and is involved in one-half of all highway deaths.[1] A person with a blood alcohol count of 0.08 percent poses four times the risk of causing a fatal accident as a person who has not been drinking; at 0.15 percent, the risk is twenty-five times as great. These facts have prompted courts to deal with the problem in almost a rash manner: for example, in Solberg v. Johnson,[2] the Oregon appellate court held that a person who buys a drink for another may be held liable if that person subsequently gets into an automobile accident. Liability was predicated on the generous patron of the bar on the theory that the generous patron knew or should have known that the drinker had a drinking problem, that the drinker had in fact previously been convicted of drunken driving, and that the drinker had been in several accidents while drinking. The court spelled out the generous patron's liability for damages under a common law negligence theory that someone who "substantially assists or encourages" negligent conduct of another can be held liable.[3] The Utah appellate court, in Biswell v. Duncan,[4] even authorized punitive damages to be recovered against a drunk driver whose misconduct manifested a reckless disregard of another's and the public's safety. And in MacLean v. Sperry[5] the federal district court in New Hampshire upheld a substantial award to a father for a devastating emotional trauma from holding his dying fifteen-year-old son in his arms after a harrowing highway collision caused by a corporate defendant's drunk driver.[6]

It should be observed that all states have raised the drinking age to twenty-one, and that most states have adopted 0.10 % as the per se level of intoxication.[7] The National Beer Wholesalers Association has advocated that states issue different licenses to drivers under twenty-one years of age so as to effectively preclude drinking by underage people.[8] In New Philadelphia, Ohio, anyone convicted of driving while intoxicated must go to jail,[9] and in San Jose, California, the person charged with this offense must also pay for police-time and manpower-time associated with the arrest, even if the person is not found guilty![10] Interestingly, under Section 523 of the Bankruptcy Code, debts incurred for willful and malicious injuries to person or property are not dischargeable, especially a judgment or consent decree in which liability was predicated on the debtor's driving while legally intoxicated.[11] In Re Thomas[12] the debtor filed a bankruptcy petition just three weeks before the date set for trial of a personal injury claim against him based on his driving while intoxicated. The plaintiff-victim sought to have excepted from discharge her claim against the tortfeasor-defendant based on the drunk-driving exception under Section 523 (a)(9) of the Bankruptcy Code. The tortfeasor-debtor argued that the "debt" did not fit within the exception because a judgment or consent decree against him had not yet been obtained. But the court rejected his argument because otherwise, "quick-thinking drunks or their attorneys" would seek to avoid the exception to discharge merely by more quickly filing the bankruptcy petition! If the plaintiff-victim-creditor never obtains a drunk-driving judgment against the defendant-tortfeasor-debtor, the exception still stands, according to In Re Dougherty,[13] in which the bankruptcy court reasoned that the debtor's voluntary plea in the criminal action, coupled with his agreement to pay restitution and his voluntary execution of a promissory note, was "tantamount to a consent decree."

Dram shop laws, or third-party liability laws, impose strict liability on tavern owners and other commercial sellers who serve alcohol to intoxicated customers, and the damages awarded to the third-party victims are often spectacular, as seen in Hargraves v. Brown,[14] in which the Ohio court observed that the tavern and its owner were sued for $24 million by the widows of two men killed in a head-on automobile collision, and in Cansler v. Pineknob Investment Co.,[15] in which the Michigan court approved a settlement by the tavernkeeper's insurance company of the wrongful death claim for $10.8 million. Beyond the strict liability imposed on the tavern or bar is the application of the same set of rules on liability for social hosts, churches, hospitals, and even universities, as illustrated by Bearman v. University of Notre Dame,[16] in which the Indiana jury found the defendant university liable for $53,000 for its failure to exercise crowd control at a football game after a drunken fan assaulted another fan in the stadium parking lot! The New York Court of Appeals in D'Amico v. Christie[17] and Henry v. Vann[18] decided the "common issue whether employer or an employee's association should be liable for injuries caused by the off-premises drunk driving of adult, off-duty employees who have consumed intox-icants. We conclude that neither the Dram Shop Act nor the common law encompasses such liability." At the outset the court opined:

At common law, one who provided intoxicating liquor was not liable for injuries caused by the drinker, who was held solely responsible. Excessive alcohol consumption was deemed to be the proximate cause of injuries produced by the inebriate; selling or fur-nishing alcohol to an adult who elected to become intoxicated was not viewed as the root of the resulting harm (see, e.g., Reid v. Terwilliger, 116 NY 530, 533; Meade v. Stratton, 87 NY 493, 496; Bertholf v. O'Reilly, 74 NY 509, 524; Allen v. County of Westchester, 109 AD2d 475, app dismissed 66 NY2d 915; Edgar v. Kajet, 84 Misc 2d 100, affd 55 AD2d 597, lv dismissed 41 NY2d 802; Note, Special Project: Social Host Liability for the Negligent Acts of Intoxicated Guests, 70 Cornell L Rev 1058, 1063 [1985]).

By the Dram Shop Act, the Legislature created an exception to the common law rule (see Note, Liability Under the New York Dram Shop Act, 8 Syracuse L Rev 252 [1956–1957]). The statute provides:

"Any person who shall be injured in person, property, means of support, or otherwise by any intoxicated person, or by reason of the intoxication of any person, whether resulting in his death or not, shall have a right to action against any person who shall, by unlawfully selling to or unlawfully assisting in procuring liquor for such intoxicated person, have caused or contributed to such intoxication; and in any such action such person shall have a right to recover actual and exemplary damages."

The court concluded that it found

no basis for departing from the consistent interpretation of lower courts that the Dram Shop Act requires a commercial sale of alcohol. That the statute is properly limited to sellers of intoxicating liquors is made plain even by its title: "Compensation for injury caused by the illegal sale of intoxicating liquor." The body of the statute also speaks of "unlawfully selling" alcohol. When the Legislature intended to reach the broader category of alcohol providers—as it did in 1983 in adding General Obligations Law §11–100, applicable to minors—it said exactly that. General Obligations Law §11-100, in contrast to the Dram Shop Act, imposes liability for injuries caused by intoxicated individuals who have not reached the legal drinking age upon persons "unlawfully fur-nishing" alcoholic beverages to them. Nor does anything in the long history of the Dram Shop Act support the broader reading plaintiff now urges upon us. The Act ap-pears to have uniformly required an alcohol sale as the predicate for liability (see Laws of 1963, ch 516 §11-101).

In the end, plaintiff's plea is that the statute should include all alcohol providers because of the indisputable threat to society posed by drunk drivers. We are, however, constrained in applying a statute by the unequivocal intent expressed by the Legislature in enacting it; if there is to be a change in what the Legislature has clearly written it should come from the Legislature.

Based on the affirmed findings supported by the record, we agree with the conclusion reached by both courts below that the Association was not engaged in commercial sale of alcohol as contemplated by the Dram Shop Act. The Association made no direct sales of alcohol, and had no recognizable expectation of pecuniary gain from its social affairs. The availability of beer to co-employees who had chipped in to buy their own food and beverages for the picnic cannot be considered a commercial sale of alcohol within the Dram Shop Act.

There having been no commercial sale of alcohol, no claim is stated against the Association under the Dram Shop Act, and this claim against Schlegel obviously fails as well.

On the common law negligence claims, the highest New York court similarly found no basis for liability because neither the employer nor the employee's association owed any legal duty to the third-party victim.[19] The court stated:

Thus, plaintiffs have failed to demonstrate any legal duty in the existing law of this state that defendant can be said to have breached.

Nor, on these facts, should the common law be enlarged to permit plaintiff's recovery. It is plain that to do so would have broad ramifications, a factor we appropriately take into account in fixing the orbit of duty that will necessarily control other cases as well as this one (*see, Waters v. New York City Hous. Auth.,* 69 NY2d 229, 230, *supra; see also,* Morrison and Woods, *An Examination of the Duty Concept: Has It Evolved in Otis Engineering v. Clark?* 36 Baylor L Rev 375, 419–425, *supra*). Where is the line to be drawn on the legal responsibility of an employer terminating an employee in these circumstances? What is the responsibility to third persons; what is the responsibility to such an employee who then goes out onto crime-ridden streets? What action would be required of employers to satisfy this legal duty; what action do they have a legal right to take? Such vexing questions, for which no reasonable solutions are suggested or indeed discernible, persuade us that it would be unwise, on the facts presented here, to enlarge an employer's existing common law duties as plaintiff suggests.

Other New York decisions have recently held that the dram shop law does not apply to an employer who provided free drinks at a company outing where the intoxicated employee subsequently injured the third-party plaintiff; in Wasserman v. Godoy[20] the court dismissed the claim, holding that the dram shop law applied only to "commercial vendors" and not to "private hosts or employers." Although it dismissed the causes of action based on the statutory provisions, the court nevertheless found that causes of action based on the employment would not be dismissed:

It is the general rule that an employee is not acting in the scope of his employment when he drives to and from work. The exception to that rule is that an employee who uses his motor vehicle in furtherance of his employment is acting within the scope of his employment while driving home from his last business appointment inasmuch as such person is working and is under his employer's control from the time he leaves his house in the morning until he returns at night (Lundberg v. State of New York, 25 NY2d 467, 471).

Mr. Godoy's attendance at the outing was work related. He was required to attend that function or another function or appear for work at movant's offices in New York

City. Therefore, it could be found that Mr. Godoy was acting in the scope of his employment when he left the outing to drive to his home or to visit a relative.

Since movant provided the alcoholic beverages to be consumed by its employees at the outing, there is an issue presented as to whether movant knew of and contributed to Mr. Godoy's intoxication at the work related outing located at some distance from Mr. Godoy's usual place of business.

In Cowin v. Huntington Hospital,[21] in which plaintiff was injured in a car accident caused by defendant's employee who had reported to work drunk and was sent home by his employer, only to find himself in the accident while intoxicated, the court pointed out that the employer did not owe a separate common law duty to protect the general public from the dangerous behavior of its intoxicated employee. In dismissing the suit against the employer the court opined: "An employer will be liable for the negligence of an employee only while the employee is acting within the scope of his employment, . . . (Here the employee was not) as a matter of law, [acting within the scope of his employment] since his actions in becoming intoxicated prior to reporting to work can in no way be viewed as having been performed in furtherance of the employer's requirements and the employer did not participate in creating his condition."

Dram shop laws were probably a consequence of the temperance movement, although Wisconsin enacted a dram shop statute in 1849 that required all tavern owners to post a bond to "support all paupers, widows and orphans, and pay the expenses of all civil and criminal prosecutions growing out of or justly attributable to . . . traffic in alcoholic beverages."[22] Four years later, in 1853, the Indiana statute (although repealed two years later) presaged the Ohio and Pennsylvania statutes the next year, followed by the New York statute in 1857. Today more than thirty states have some form of liability for licensed alcohol sellers. In New York the "social host" was not liable under the Dram Shop Act in Quaranta v. Lessings, Inc.,[23] in which liability is based on the sale of intoxicating liquor, even though the defendant was a caterer of the office party that resulted in the damaging conduct of the intoxicated employee. The New Jersey Supreme Court had, in Keely v. Gwinnell,[24] held the "social host" liable for serving two or three drinks to a guest who soon thereafter had a head-on collision; the court reasoned that any loss in the conviviality of social gatherings was more than outweighed by the social interest in stopping people from driving while intoxicated.[25] In Maine the new Liquor Liability Act,[26] designed "to prevent intoxication-related injuries, deaths, and other damages," spells out liability for negligent or reckless service of liquor to minors or to those who are "visibly intoxicated" when served. There is a "cap" on damages of $250,000, and there are statutory and common law defenses, including proof of adherence to "responsible serving practices," such as the tavern keeper attending a server education training course! This Maine statute is evidently patterned after the Model Dram Shop Act,[27] which was drafted in 1985 by the

Prevention Research Group of the Medical Research Institute of San Francisco.[28] Today the Model Dram Shop Act is in force in Maine,[29] Rhode Island,[30] and New Hampshire,[31] and Section 10 of the Act (delineating the responsible business practices defense) has been enacted in Michigan[32] and Vermont.[33] In the state of Oregon[34] all license holders and all servers of alcoholic beverages are required to undergo training and receive state certification. In the state of Texas[35] an employer is exempt from civil liability under the dram shop law if the employer requires its employees to attend an officially approved seller training program, and if the employer has not directly or indirectly encouraged the employee to violate laws relating to the sale and service of alcoholic beverages.

It should be noted that an intoxicated patron of a tavern or bar who injures himself on a glass door when leaving the tavern or bar is not entitled to any protection under the dram shop laws. In Brower v. Robert Chappell & Associates[36] the North Carolina court held that Brower's act of becoming intoxicated constituted, as a matter of law, contributory negligence, thereby precluding recovery against the owner of the tavern or bar, even though the owner was negligent per se in continuing to sell him intoxicating liquor after he was noticeably intoxicated.[37] But in Cresswell v. Warden[38] the New York court did not protect the tavern owner; here plaintiff sued defendant to recover damages for assault, and defendant cross-sued the tavern for contribution, claiming that his intoxication caused the tort and that the tavern supplied the alcoholic drink. The tavern contended that there was no remedy of contribution under the Dram Shop Act in New York. But the court disagreed, and ruled that if plaintiff was injured as a result of intoxication from a violation of the Dram Shop Act, then the defendant may seek contribution from the tavern. As the court reasoned:

The simple rule of contribution is that if one tortfeasor is liable for any injury suffered, then he may seek contribution from any other tortfeasor who would also be liable for that injury (CPLR §1401). A tavern, in violation of the Dram Shop Act, would be a tortfeasor liable to an injured plaintiff. The intoxicated tortfeasor would also be liable to such an injured plaintiff. Accordingly, under CPLR §1401, either tortfeasor may seek contribution from the other tortfeasor. The third-party defendant Landmark's argument, that to allow the intoxicated tortfeasor to recover contribution from the tavern is in effect, construing a beneficial remedy on behalf of the intoxicated tortfeasor, is unpersuasive. In fact, the reverse would be true, in that to prevent the intoxicated tortfeasor to recover contribution from the violator of the Dram Shop Act would, in effect, construe a benefit on the other violating tortfeasor. Just as making a seller of intoxicating liquor liable to persons injured provides a remedy to such injured persons and futhers the Legislature's intent to discourage the unlawful sale of alcohol (see Mitchell v. The Shoals, Inc., 48 Misc. 2d 381, affd. 26 AD2d 78, affd. 19 NY2d 338), so, too, is the Legislature's purpose furthered by making said seller liable for contribution on a third-party claim.

Therefore, if it is found that Warden injured the plaintiff, Cresswell, as a result of Warden's intoxication and such intoxication was a result of the third-party defendant

Landmark's violation of the Dram Shop Act, then Warden may properly seek contribution from such third-party defendant Landmark.''

In Umlauf v. Gresen Manufacturing Co.[39] an employee discharged for reporting to work in an intoxicated condition may be denied unemployment benefits if his discharge is determined to have been for misconduct; but there is a ''chemical dependency'' exception to misconduct under the Minnesota Unemployment Compensation Statute that could change the determination. In short, if the employee's behavior or conduct was due to chemical dependency and he made reasonable efforts to retain his employment, he should receive unemployment compensation benefits. Reasonable efforts to retain employment did not require an employee in Minnesota totally to abstain from alcohol or achieve total success in treatment; rather, the employee must make consistent efforts to control his illness—the focus being on his efforts, not on the results. Here the Minnesota appellate court ruled that the employee should be denied benefits on the grounds that he had not made reasonable efforts to retain his employment, since he did not attend an aftercare treatment program, which he had previously agreed to do!

The use of a Breathalyzer in detecting ''driving while intoxicated'' is important in the law's enforcement, as illustrated in Bazza v. Banscher,[40] in which the New York court permitted the injured plaintiff to offer evidence of the tortfeasor's refusal to submit to a Breathalyzer test after the accident. Section 1194(4) of the New York Vehicle and Traffic Law does not preclude evidence of refusal to submit to a blood alcohol test in proceedings other than criminal prosecutions. According to the court, although evidence of refusal ''may be of limited probative force, the refusal may be regarded as conduct inconsistent with the defendant's position on trial that he was not intoxicated at the time of the accident.'' In People v. Close[41] the defendant was charged with driving while intoxicated and moved to suppress the results of the Breathalyzer test on the ground that the chemical solution in the ampules used in the machine was improperly prepared and that the test results could not be used because the integrity of the ampules could not be established. But the court rejected the argument, holding that the test's reliability was a matter for the jury in the criminal trial to determine.[42]

NOTES

1. See U.S. Department of Transportation, 1968 Alcohol and Highway Safety Report 11 (1986); also note 33 Q.J. Stud. Alcohol 160 (1972) and 94 Harv. L. Rev. 1660 (1981) at 1674 et seq.

2. 90 Or. App. 90 (March 9, 1988).

3. See N.L.J. (March 28, 1988) at 36.

4. 742 P.2d 80 (Utah App., 1987).

5. _____ F. Supp. _____ (N.H., April 8, 1988). Here the father's claim was for

"traumatic cancer" that was linked to the traumatic impact of the automobile accident. Note that the New Hampshire legislature in 1986 had prohibited punitive damages "in any action, unless otherwise provided by statute." N.H. Stats. Ann. Section 507:16.

6. Id.

7. See McAllister, "The Drunken Driving Crackdown: Is It Working?" A.B.A.J. (September 1, 1988) at 52 et seq.

8. See Hartford Courant (August 3, 1988) at A2.

9. See New York Times (May 22, 1988) at E6.

10. See New York Times (December 29, 1987) at A10.

11. See 11 U.S.C. 523(a)(9); see also N.Y.L.J. (December 19, 1985) at 1 and 28.

12. 51 B.R. 187 (ED Va., 1985).

13. 13 B.C.D. 443 (Colo., 1985).

14. _____ N.E.2d _____ (Ohio Ct. of Com. Pleas, Butler County, 1988); also see generally Goldberg, "One for the Road: Liquor Liability Broadens," A.B.A.J. (June 1, 1987) at 84 et seq.

15. _____ N.W.2d _____ (Mich., Oakland County, 1988).

16. 453 N.E.2d 1196 (Ind., 1983).

17. 71 N.Y.2d 76, 518 N.E.2d 896 (1987).

18. Id.

19. According to the court, "landowners in general have a duty to act in a reasonable manner to prevent harm to those on their property *(Basso v. Miller,* 40 N.Y.2d 233, 241). In particular, they have a duty to control the conduct of third persons on their premises when they have the opportunity to control such persons and are reasonably aware of the need for such control *(see, DeRyss v. New York Cent. R.R. Co.,* 275 NY 85). Applying this rationale, lower courts have recognized that a landowner may have responsibility for injuries caused by an intoxicated guest *(see, e.g., Joly v. Northway Motor Car Corp.,* _____ AD2d _____, 517 NYS2d 595; *Comeau v. Lucas,* 90 AD2d 674; *Huyler v. Rose,* 88 AD2d 755, *app dismissed* 57 NY2d 777). Significantly, however, these decisions have uniformly acknowledged that liability may be imposed only for injuries that occurred on defendant's property, or in an area under defendant's control, where defendant had the opportunity to supervise the intoxicated guest *(see, e.g., Delamater v. Kimmerle,* 104 AD2d 242, 244; *Comeau v. Lucas, supra; Wright v. Sunset Recreation,* 91 AD2d 701; *Huyler v. Rose, supra; Schimer v. Yost,* 60 AD2d 789; *Paul v. Hogan,* 56 AD2d 723; *Vale v. Yawarsk,* 78 Misc 2d 522 [Hancock J.]). That duty emanated not from the provision of alcohol but from the obligation of a landowner to keep its premises free of known dangerous conditions, which may include intoxicated guests.

"But that situation is materially different from the one at hand. First, unlike the cited examples, the Association was not engaged in serving alcoholic beverages: the picnic was a cooperative venture. Association members—all co-employees who gathered voluntarily for the social benefit of a summer picnic—in effect had purchased their own food and alcoholic beverages, and set up the party and served themselves; co-employees neither dispensed nor monitored the consumption of alcohol. The Association was not in the position of a bartender or even a host dispensing alcohol, who may deny the request of a patron or guest for another drink. Second, the injuries complained of did not take place on the picnic premises, or Association property; the accident occurred on a public highway several miles distant. The Association lacked the opportunity to supervise the control that defendants in the cited cases had. Thus, it is clear that the common law of this State relating to landowners who provide alcohol to their guests does not support recovery by plaintiff against the Association.''

20. 523 N.Y.S.2d 597 (N.Y. County, December 2, 1988).

21. 496 N.Y.S.2d 203 (Suffolk County, 1985).

22. Supra note 14 at 86.

23. Unreported ____ N.Y.S.2d ____ (Nassau County, 1987).

24. 476 S.2d 1219 (N.J., 1984).

25. See also Clark v. Mincks, 364 N.W.2d 226 (Iowa, 1985), and Ashlock v. Norris, 475 N.E.2d 1167 (Ind., 1985).

26. Supra note 2.

27. See Colman and Christy, ''Major Legislative Trends Emerge in Dramshop Liability Statutes,'' N.L.J. (February 1, 1988) at 18–19.

28. See ''The Model Alcoholic Beverage Retail License Liability Act of 1985,'' 12 Western St. U.L. Rev. 442–517 (Spring 1985).

29. Supra note 4; also Maine Rev. Stat. Ann., title 28, ch. 33, secs. 1401–1416 (1986).

30. Secs. 3-14-1 to 3-14-15 of R.I. Gen. Laws (1986).

31. Secs. 507-F:1 to 507-F:8 of N.H. Rev. Stat. Ann. (1986).

32. Mich. Comp. Laws Ann. Sec. 436.22 (1986).

33. Vt. Stat. Ann. Sec. 501, title 7 (1987).

34. Secs. 471.542 (1985) and 30.950 and 30.960 (1987) of Ore. Rev. Stat.

35. See Texas Alcohol Beverage Code, title 1, ch. 106.14 (1987).

36. 328 S.E.2d 45 (N.C., 1985).

37. See Freedman, Strict Liability (Hanrow Press, 1986) at 47–48. For recent decisions rejecting claims by plaintiffs, see Ling v. Jan's Liquors, 703 P.2d 731 (Kan., 1985); Cuevas v. Royal D'Iberville Hotel, 498 So.2d 346 (Miss., 1986); and Milligan v. County Line Liquor, 709 S.W.2d 409 (Ark., 1986).

38. ____ N.Y.S.2d ____ (Nassau County, January 3, 1989).

39. 393 N.W.2d 198 (Minn. App., 1987).

40. 533 N.Y.S.2d 285 (1988).

41. ____ N.Y.S.2d ____ (N.Y. County, January 26, 1989).

42. According to the court, ''the Breathalyzer [sic] has been in public use since 1954 and has been widely accepted and adopted by law enforcement agencies for use in testing blood-alcohol content. It operates on the firmly established principle that at normal body temperature the concentration of alcohol in the blood circulating through the lungs is 2,100 times greater than in the air discharged from the lungs (4 Gray, Attorneys' Textbook of Medicine, §133.73[1]). The apparatus is a semi-automatic analyzer designed to test a blood-alcohol percentage present in any breath sample. Scientifically, the Breathalyzer [sic] wastes all but the last portion of a long exhalation, trapping a measured volume which is then forced through a reagent and is ultimately photometrically measured resulting in a calculated reading of the subject's blood-alcohol percentage. Studies have shown that this device is considered to be ''fail safe'' and that as a general rule its readings are slightly lower than those obtained in a corresponding blood test; and any slight error caused either by mechanical defect or operator fault will usually produce lower rather than higher readings (45 N.C.L. Rev. 34, 56).

''The scientific reliability of the breathalyzer in general is no longer considered a litigable issue (People v. Mertz, 68 NY2d 136, 148 [1986]; People v. Donaldson, supra). The reliability of the particular administration of the breathalyzer test, however, is still viable (see Gerstenzang, Peter, Handling the DWI Case in New York [West Publishing Co., 1987] Chs. 8, 9, 29, and People v. Gower, 42 NY2d 117 [1977]).'' See also People v. Gatto, 536 N.Y.S.2d 851 (Bronx County, February 9, 1989).

4.3 "Willful Misconduct" Caused Alcoholism

The U.S. Supreme Court, in Traynor v. Turnage,[1] ruled that alcoholism is caused by "willful misconduct," thus upholding a Veterans Administration rule defining alcoholism as "willful misconduct." This ruling denies disability and other benefits to most veterans disabled by alcoholism.[2] Here the highest court, by a 4–3 vote, rejected the veterans' argument that the "willful misconduct" exception penalized them for their disability in violation of the Rehabilitation Act of 1973.[3] The majority of the court pointed out that the court had not decided if alcoholism is "a disease whose course its victims cannot control"; the court decided only that when Congress adopted the ten-year benefit period in 1977, it approved the policy that alcoholism is caused by "willful misconduct." The three-judge minority opinion stressed the fact that the four-judge majority view contradicted School Board of Nassau County v. Arline,[4] which earlier case of the court held that a teacher suffering from tuberculosis could not be removed from the classroom without an "individualized" determination that the teacher herself was contagious! The bare majority of the court here nevertheless concluded that "there is nothing in the Rehabilitation Act" that would require the Veterans Administration to give special treatment to veterans who have a disability that is partly of their own making![5] And furthermore, "veterans who bear some responsibility for their disabilities have no stronger claim to an extended eligibility period than do able-bodied veterans."

A New York court, in People v. Tocco,[6] in support of the proposition that alcoholism is not a disease, but a self-inflicted injury,[7] declared that taking a drink was recklessness per se! Here defendant, while severely intoxicated, set his apartment on fire after an argument with his wife in which he threatened her life and that of the couple's children. He was charged with reckless endangerment in the first degree, which charge requires proof that he had a general intent to commit the offense. He argued that his intoxication was involuntary and precluded him from having a general intent to endanger. But the court replied:

If an alcoholic knows that he is prone to commit criminal acts while drunk and the consumption of even one drink will destroy his ability to resist further drinking, to the point of intoxication, it must follow that his voluntary imbibing of the first drink is the very initiation of a reckless act. . . . Alcoholics should not be penalized for their conditions, but . . . should be held responsible for their conduct.

In Hon v. Stroh Brewery Co.[8] the Third U.S. Court of Appeals held that a beer manufacturer or brewery may be strictly liable for the wrongful death of a beer drinker from pancreatitis caused by the brewery's failure to warn of the health hazards from moderate, as distinguished from excessive, drinking.[9]

NOTES

1. 108 S. Ct. 1372 (1988); for lower court opinion, see 791 F.2d 226 (2nd Cir., 1986). Also note McKelvery v. Turnage, 792 F.2d 194 (D.C. Cir., 1986).

2. See A.B.A.J. (June 1, 1988) at 47.

3. See Section 2,3 hereinbefore.

4. 107 S. Ct. 1123 (1987).

5. See N.Y.L.J. (April 21, 1988) at 3.

6. 525 N.Y.S.2d 137 (Bronx County, February 5, 1988).

7. See Freedman and Lefcourt, "Alcoholism: Self-inflicted Injury or Disease Under Disability Provisions of Insurance Policies," 23 Temple L.Q., 39–62 (July 1949).

8. 835 F.2d 510 (3rd Cir., 1987).

9. See Section 4.6 hereinafter.

4.4 Public Policy on Drinking Alcoholic Beverages

According to the *New York Times* (December 21, 1987), state laws making twenty-one the legal drinking age, intended to combat driving while intoxicated among young people, have little effect on limiting drinking among college students.[1] Stiffer college regulations on drinking has led more students to drink off campus: according to a 1983 nationwide survey of about 4,200 students at public and private colleges and universities, "21% said they had six or more drinks at least once a week. The figure remained the same in 1985, and preliminary information from a 1987 survey shows similar figures."[2]

The state of New York has, since 1979, issued "guidelines" by its Division of Alcoholism and Alcohol Abuse to local government units governing the operation of local alcohol service plans and financing. In City of New York v. New York State Division of Alcoholism and Alcohol Abuse[3] the New York court refused to strike down these "guidelines" as "null and void" because of the state's alleged failure to comply with the Mental Hygiene Law, the State Administrative Procedure Act, the Executive Law, and the New York Constitution. Plaintiff contended that these "guidelines" were insensitive to the needs of an ethnically and economically diverse population residing in New York City. The court granted summary judgment to the state, pointing out that the city's "conclusory assertion that the guidelines were applied as rules is insufficient to require a trial of material questions of fact."

NOTES

1. At B1 and B15.

2. Id.

3. ____ N.Y.S.2d ____ (New York County, May 2, 1988).

4.5 Products Liability and Alcoholism

Alcoholism figures prominently in many products liability claims, and even breweries have become target defendants in injury suits brought by drinkers themselves. The Third U.S. Court of Appeals, in Hon v. Stroh Brewery Co.,[1] held the brewery strictly liable for the wrongful death of a beer drinker from pancreatitis because the brewery had failed to warn of the health hazards even from moderate beer drinking. In effect, the imposition of liability on the product manufacturer could "impose an impractical burden on manufacturers of alcoholic beverages to devise warnings suitable for the particular tolerance of each consumer."[2] Probably a more acceptable warning, like "Alcohol can have adverse effects on your health even when consumed in moderate amounts," would suffice. But the record here apparently allowed a jury to find that the moderate amount of beer consumed by the plaintiff-decedent was potentially lethal, a fact known neither to the decedent nor to the consuming public. Such a warning of its lethal quality on the label of the beer product would hardly be acceptable to the product manufacturer. And yet the applicable Pennsylvania law mandated that a product manufacturer need only warn of latent, hidden, or concealed defects.[3] In Fraust v. Swift & Co.[4] the federal court, applying Pennsylvania law, denied summary judgment for the product manufacturer whose peanut butter sandwich caused a sixteen-month-old baby to choke and suffer severe brain damage, concluding that the baby's mother, in the absence of a proper warning, might not have known of the choking risk of feeding defendant's product to her baby. What was defective about the labeling here in the instant case was its failure to warn of the fatal potentialities of disregarding any warning that might have been given in the very first place by the brewery![5] The brewery also had used television advertising to "cultivate a belief among the consuming public that moderate consumption of its (beer) product is safe."[6]

Indeed, in Penn v. Heublein, Inc.,[7] plaintiff boys sued two liquor companies for failure to have warned their mother about the possible harmful effects of alcohol on unborn infants. The suit filed in November 1987 in the federal district court in Seattle, Washington, accused the two defendants of having scientific evidence as early as 1968 that drinking during pregnancy could cause birth defects. Fetal alcohol syndrome is today recognized as one of the three major causes of birth defects associated with mental retardation in infants.[8] And, according to the Centers for Disease Control, about 2.2 babies per 10,000 are born with this syndrome! The mother of the boys drank Smirnoff vodka during her pregnancies in 1976 and 1979. Another pending law suit involving bourbon whiskey is Thorp v. James B. Beam Distilling Co.,[9] filed in the same federal district court in Seattle.[10] These and other lawsuits filed against the liquor industry have prompted market analysts to fear that product liability claims "similar to those faced by the cigarette industry" would soon arrest liquor sales growth.[11]

NOTES

1. 835 F.2d 510 (3rd Cir., 1987).
2. Id. at 514.
3. See 31 ATLA L. Rep. (May 1988) at 148 et seq.
4. 610 F.2d 711 (WD Pa., 1985).
5. Note Tampa Drug Co. v. Wait, 103 So.2d 603 (Fla., 1958), delineating the hazards of carbon tetrachloride.
6. According to the court, "if a jury finds that Stroh's marketing of its product has effectively taught the consuming public that consumption of beer on the order of eight to twelve cans of beer per week can be part of the 'good life' and is properly associated with healthy robust activities, this conclusion would be an important consideration for the jury in determining whether an express warning was necessary to make Old Milwaukee Beer safe for its intended purpose."
7. See Hartford Courant (March 5, 1988) at A1 and A9.
8. Id.
9. _____ F. Supp. _____ (Wash., 1988).
10. See N.L.J. (September 5, 1988) at 3 and 10.
11. See New York Times (July 26, 1988) at D10: "Cigarette stocks have already been discounted for the litigation problems. They stand at about a 30 percent discount to the market. Anheuser-Busch and other alcohol producers are not yet discounted for litigation worries and thus present a greater downside risk. . . . Alcohol producers dismiss the concern over the lack of a warning on their product. Some argue that women are warned by their doctors not to drink or smoke during pregnancy. Nevertheless, the demand for warnings is spreading along with the litigation.

"Starting next October, alcohol companies operating in California will be required to use signs at point of sale warning of birth defects during pregnancy. Such signs are already required in New York City, parts of California and elsewhere. Warning labels are also proposed in Federal legislation by Senator Strom Thurmond, Republican of South Carolina, and Representative John Conyers Jr., Democrat of Michigan."

4.6 Criminal Responsibility and Alcoholism

Alcohol abuse is involved in many serious crimes, particularly crimes of violence, and perhaps as many as one-half of homicide perpetrators are, to some extent, under the influence of alcohol.[1] It is said that alcohol reduces one's sensitivity to external cues to behavior and dulls self-control and self-criticism.[2] In general, intoxication does not relieve an offender of criminal responsibility, but intoxication does show that the offender may not have the specific intent to commit the particular crime.[3] Where proof of the commission of the crime only requires "general intent," such as for voluntary manslaughter, intoxication may not be a valid defense.

As to the crime of drunkenness and driving a vehicle while intoxicated (DWI), the rights of the defendant have generally been expanded, as illustrated by State of Oregon v. Spencer.[4] Here the Oregon court ruled that suspected drunken drivers have a state constitutional right to seek a lawyer's advice before deciding whether to consent to a Breathalyzer test. The court observed that under the Oregon Constitution[5] the accused "in all criminal prosecutions . . . shall have the right . . . to be heard by himself and counsel" when the suspect is "taken into formal custody."[6] In People v. Shaw[7] the New York Court of Appeals reviewed the argument of a defendant who was arrested for DWI and who consented to taking a Breathalyzer test, only to contend later that the test result should be suppressed because his Sixth Amendment rights were violated in that he was not advised of his right to counsel when requested to take the test. The highest New York court found that the defendant had

no constitutional right to refuse to consent to such a search. . . . The right is entirely statutory and, by its terms, may be waived without an attorney's assistance. . . . The Sixth Amendment does not require that the defendant be afforded counsel at this stage in the proceedings. Although the defendant was called upon to waive a statutory right, it was not a critical stage in the proceedings within the meaning of the Sixth Amendment because no judicial proceedings had been initiated against the defendant at that time.

In People v. Nigohosian a lower New York court, in 1988, ruled that the Breathalyzer test did not constitute testimonial evidence under the Fifth Amendment:

There is no absolute right to counsel, nor a constitutional right to refuse to take the Breathalyzer test. The fact that counsel did appear in the case does not, in the opinion of the court, prohibit the police from accepting a later consent to take the test and administering the test in the absense of counsel. However, the waiver of counsel would have been prohibited under People v. Arthur (supra), in a Fifth Amendment self-incrim-ination situation, unless counsel was present at the waiver. There is, at best, a qualified right to counsel and there is no requirement that any such waiver of that limited right be in the presence of counsel.

Since this is not a Fifth Amendment right to counsel situation, there exists only a limited right to counsel at best, which limited right was not denied. The cases which hold that the right to counsel once having been invoked cannot be waived in the absence of counsel, apply only in Fifth Amendment self-incrimination situations. Even in these situations, where counsel has appeared and the right to counsel has been invoked and interrogation stopped, a statement or admission occurring spontaneously and not the product of police interrogation, or prodding would be admitted. Accordingly, the court holds that the defendant's right to counsel has not been violated, and that the appearance of counsel is not a bar to the police administering the test to defendant's consent freely given. The Breathalyzer test results will not be suppressed, and may be introduced at the trial of this matter.

However, expert testimony is required to establish an adequate foundation for the admissibility of a police officer's testimony concerning results of a hor-izontal gaze nystagmus test performed on a suspected drunk driver, according to the Pennsylvania court in Commonwealth v. Miller.[8] The HGN test is based on the principle that alcohol consumption exaggerates and magnifies involuntary eye twitching. The defendant here was required to cover one eye and follow the path of an object with the other eye; by observing how well the defendant was able to follow the object, the police officer estimated that his blood alcohol content exceeded the legal limit for driving. The court excluded the results of the HGN test because the admissibility depends on presenting an adequate foundation and the general acceptance of the test by scientific experts active in the field.[9]

A defendant charged with vehicular manslaughter cannot suppress statements he made after being arrested for DWI; he was found to have waived his right to maintain silence because his statements were voluntary after he was read his *Miranda* rights and had indicated in a perfectly calm and rational manner that he understood them and was willing to talk to the police.[10]

In People v. Tocco[11] the defendant was found guilty of reckless endangerment[12] after having set fire to his apartment while excessively drunk.[13] The New York court, in a lengthy opinion, discussed the defense of intoxication and concluded:

Some commentators have speculated that courts will be required, some time in the future, to meet the argument that the intoxication of a chronic alcoholic is, on its face, involuntary (see The Criminal Responsibility of Chronic Alcoholics, supra, at 479). If such were the case, the chronic alcoholic could never be held liable for crimes that he committed while in a severely intoxicated state. As of yet, no court has extended the defense to preclude prosecution of an alcoholic for non-alcohol related crimes committed while in an intoxicated state. And, presently, alcoholism is not a defense even to alcohol related crimes that punish more than mere status.

In view of the Supreme Court holding in Powell, supra, it would appear that any change in the law would find basis only in conclusive medical evidence spurred by growing social concern, rather than constitutional pivots. Yet, if alcoholism is a disease characterized by an inability to control the consumption of alcoholic beverages, then the imposition of criminal liability for acts performed while drunk would at first blush defy logic.

Separating the physical act of drinking from the causative condition, alcoholism is the distinguishing factor to which we must pay heed. Alcoholics should be held responsible for their conduct; they should not be penalized for their condition. An enlightened society cannot otherwise justify itself.

If an alcoholic knows that he is prone to commit criminal acts when drunk and that the consumption of even one drink will destroy his ability to resist further drinking, to the point of intoxication, as in the instant case, it must follow that his voluntary imbibing of the first drink is the very initiation of a reckless act—and the concomitant disregard of the substantial and unjustifiable risk attendant thereto. If so, under our law the consumption of said drink by such alcoholic raises the act to the level of recklessness per se, subjecting him to strict accountability for crimes such as reckless arson and/or reckless endangerment now before the Court. No case has been uncovered imposing liability at this early threshold.

Arguendo, if we accept alcoholism as a disease, the hypothesis suggests that some (although probably not all) alcoholics lack the ability to control the taking of even the first drink. In paralleling the instant case, exculpatory legal argument on the proposition that the defendant's addictive conduct was involuntary—whether psychological, biochemical, genetic, cultural, and/or environmental—has not been shown. Nothing in the record was offered to explain or illuminate the defendant's condition. Under familiar rules, expert opinions are certainly admissible on subjects involving professional or scientific knowledge not within the range of ordinary training or intelligence (People v. Cronin, 60 N.Y.2d 430 [1983]; De Long v. County of Erie, 60 N.Y.2d [1983]; Dougherty v. Milliken, 163 N.Y. 527 [1900]).

Accepting the law as it now stands, then, it is clear that intoxication will negative the specific intent required in some crimes, but will not act as even a partial defense in general intent crimes. Moreover, though the law may evolve as new medical research on the nature of alcoholism becomes available, alcoholism is not, according to the prevailing view, accepted as a defense to any crime.

And the court concluded:

Accordingly upon the evidence adduced at the trial of this action, this Court finds the defendant not guilty of arson in the second degree, which is defined as "intentionally damag[ing] a building . . . by starting a fire" (Penal Law, Sec. 150.15), as he lacked the specific intent to damage a building. However, the Court finds the defendant guilty of the lesser included offense of arson in the fourth degree, which is defined as "recklessly damag[ing] a building . . . by intentionally starting a fire" (Penal Law, Sec. 150.05 [1]).

Further, and likewise, this Court finds the defendant guilty of reckless endangerment in the first degree. Here, the defendant voluntarily commenced a reckless course of action (i.e., the act of his taking an alcoholic beverage), a risk in itself, the natural consequences of which, the unjustifiable endangerment of the lives of others thus being intended. The Court opines that the chronic alcoholism of this defendant combines with the totality of circumstances extant to make his conduct of disregard that of recklessness per se. Even were this not the Court's finding, the defendant's having committed the arsonous act (i.e., lighting the fire[s]) would, nonetheless, make out the elements of the offense.

NOTES

1. See 94 Harv. L. Rev. 1660 (1981) at 1681 et seq.
2. See Bacon, "Alcohol, Alcoholism and Crime," 9 Crime & Delinq. 1 (1963).
3. See Note, 55 Columbia L. Rev. 1210 (1955) at 1211–1212.
4. 750 P.2d 147 (Or., March 5, 1988).
5. Art. I, Sec. 11 of the Oregon Constitution.
6. See N.L.J. (March 14, 1988) at 6.
7. 514 N.Y.S.2d 128 (Nassau County, March 7, 1988). See Miller, "Oklahoma's Constitutional Right Against Self-incrimination and the Introduction into Evidence of the Refusal to Take a Sobriety Test," 37 Okla. L. Rev. 245 (1984).
8. 532 A.2d 1186 (Pa., 1987).
9. See New York Times (January 3, 1988) at 20.
10. See People v. Paris, 525 N.Y.S.2d 913 (Kings County, March 30, 1988): "Be-

fore a statement may be submitted to a jury, the prosecution must carry the burden of proving voluntariness beyond a reasonable doubt. See People v. Valerius, 31 N.Y.2d 51, 55 (1972); People v. Huntley, 15 N.Y.2d 72, 78 (1965); People v. Brown, 33 A.D.2d 735, 735 (1st Dept. 1969). Similarly, the prosecution must prove—by the same standard, according to some courts—that a statement which was the product of a custodial interrogation was obtained after a knowing and intelligent waiver of the constitutional rights spelled out in the *Miranda* warnings. See People v. Winship, 78 A.D.2d 514 (1st Dept., 1980); People v. Camacho, 103 Misc.2d 791, 796–97 (Sup. Ct. N.Y. County 1980). See also Miranda v. Arizona, 384 U.S. 436, 475 (1966) ('a heavy burden rests on the government to demonstrate that the defendant knowingly and intelligently waived' his rights); People v. Jenkins, 85 A.D.2d 265, 276 (1st Dept., 1982) (same); People v. Tirado, 79 A.D.2d 907, 908 (1st Dept., 1981) (same).

"The prosecution in this case carried both burdens. Although the evidence indicates that the defendant was voluntarily intoxicated when the *Miranda* warnings were given, the defendant—as demonstrated by the videotape, as well as by the testimony—clearly understood what he was told, gave concise, intelligent, and responsive answers, and followed instructions appropriately.

"Nor did his intoxication rise to a level sufficient to affect voluntariness. It is true that a statement obtained from a voluntarily intoxicated person must be excluded if the defendant was unable to appreciate the nature and consequences of his remarks, or if the statement is unreliable (see People v. Adams, 26 N.Y.2d 129, 137 [1970]; People v. Schompert, 19 N.Y.2d 300, 305 [1967]). The record here, however, is virtually devoid of evidence of unreliability, suggesting the conclusion that perhaps the defendant shaded his admissions of alcohol intake to his own benefit."

11. 525 N.Y.S.2d 137 (Bronx County, February 18, 1988).

12. "At common law, intoxication was never a defense to criminal misconduct" (People v. Koerber, 244 N.Y. 147 [1926]). Instead, it was viewed as an aggravating circumstance that heightened moral culpability (People v. Koerber, supra, at 151–152). "The common law courts viewed the decision to drink to excess with its attendant risks to self and others, as an independent culpable act" (People v. Register, 60 N.Y.2d, 270, 280 [1980]). Later cases allowed evidence of intoxication to be introduced for limited purposes, such as to negative proof that the defendant possessed the physical capacity to commit the crime (People v. Register, supra, at 280).

Under the current state of the law voluntary intoxication is not a defense to a criminal charge; however, in crimes that have specific intent as an essential element voluntary intoxication has been found to negative such intent, thereby rendering the defendant not guilty of the crime charged (People v. Westergard, 113 A.D.2d 640 [2nd Dept., 1985]). The "intoxication defense" has been codified in New York as Penal Law, Section 25.25; it provides: "Intoxication is not, as such, a defense to a criminal charge; but in any prosecution for an offense, evidence of intoxication of the defendant may be offered by the defendant whenever it is relevant to negative an element of the crime charged."

The penal law does not define the term "element." "However, it does set forth what the 'elements' of an offense are and identifies them, as does the common law, as a culpable mental state (mens rea) and a voluntary act (actus reus) (Penal Law, Sec. 15.05)" (People v. Register, supra, at 276).

And although intoxication may negative the mens rea in a crime requiring specific intent, it may not negative the lower culpable mental state required in crimes of recklessness (Penal Law, Sec. 15.05[3]).

A "specific intent" crime is one that requires more than the mere intentional doing of an act. It requires, in addition, that the actor have the accompanying state of mind whereby he intends that certain further consequences flow from his act. A "general intent" crime, on the other hand, penalizes, in itself, the intentional doing of a proscribed act (Intoxication as a Criminal Defense, 55 Columbia L.R. 1210 [1955]).

Crimes in which the requisite mens rea is one of recklessness are classified as "general intent" crimes.

In New York recklessness is defined in Penal Law, Section 15.05 (3), which states, in pertinent part: "A person acts recklessly with respect to a circumstance described by statute defining an offense when he is aware of and consciously disregards a substantial and unjustifiable risk that such result will occur or that such circumstance exists."

Because recklessness requires awareness of the risk, it would seem reasonable that lack of awareness owing to voluntary intoxication would negative the mens rea required in any crime of recklessness. "[T]here is some authority for the proposition that, where awareness is required for criminal liability, lack of awareness because of intoxication negatives the crime; that so long as [the defendant] is actually unaware of the risk it makes no difference how he came to be unaware" (LaFave & Scott, Criminal Law, 2nd Ed. HB, Sec. 4.10 [c]). However, most cases in the United States create a special rule relating to intoxication, thereby not allowing an intoxicated person to avail himself of the defense in crimes of recklessness.

13. "Involuntary intoxication is a defense if it deprives the intoxicated person of understanding the nature and quality of his act or the knowingness that the act is wrong" (LaFave & Scott, Criminal Law, 2nd Ed. HB, supra, at 393, Sec. 4.10[f]; Intoxication as a Criminal Defense, 55 Columbia L. Rev., supra, at 1219).

This is so even when the crime requires only a general criminal intent. But although there are situations in which a defendant may avail himself of the defense, these are severely limited (cf. People v. Scott, 194 Cal. Rptr. 633 [1983], wherein the evidence established that the defendant unknowingly and therefore involuntarily ingested some kind of hallucinogen with his alcohol). "The paucity of successful pleas of involuntary intoxication has led one commentator to conclude that 'involuntary intoxication is simply and completely nonexistent' " (The Criminal Responsibility of Chronic Alcoholics, 52 Cornell L. Q. 470, at 473, citing Hall, Intoxication and Criminal Responsibility, 57 Harv. L. Rev. 1045, at 1054–56). In general, anything short of fraud, force, or coercion has been held to be voluntary (Intoxication as a Criminal Defense, supra, at 1219).

As we have seen, there is a recognition among physicians that alcoholism is a disease characterized by loss of control over the consumption of alcoholic beverages. Can, then, an alcoholic's inebriated state(s) ever be considered truly voluntary? This question and a related one dealing with narcotic addiction have been dealt with by some courts. One such case is Robinson v. California, 370 U.S. 660 [1961], wherein the Supreme Court held unconstitutional a statute making it a criminal offense to be "addicted to the use of narcotics." The Court based its opinion, in part, on the fact that addiction is an illness, and to hold a person criminally liable for an illness would be to inflict cruel and unusual punishment in violation of the Constitution (Robinson v. California, supra, at 667).

Relying in part on the opinion in Robinson, supra, some courts subsequently held that it would be cruel and unusual to punish a chronic alcoholic for the crime of public drunkenness, as such a person is powerless to stop drinking (Driver v. Hinnant, 356 F.2d 761 [4th Cir., 1966]; Easter v. District of Columbia, 361 F.2d 50 [D.C. Cir.,

1966]). These courts have said, in essence, that public drunkenness is an involuntary act when committed by a chronic alcoholic.

Subsequently, however, the Supreme Court, in Powell v. Texas, supra, upheld the conviction of a person for violation of article 477 of the Texas Penal Code, which provided that it was an offense to be "drunk or be found in a state of intoxication in any public place." The Supreme Court based its opinion, in part, on the lack of evidence in the trial court record relating to the nature of the defendant's drinking problem, the circumstances surrounding the drinking bout that resulted in his conviction, and, indeed, in the nature of alcoholism itself. The Court found that the medical profession lacked a true consensus as to the manifestations of alcoholism and even as to whether alcoholism is a separate disease in any meaningful biochemical, physiological, or psychological sense (Powell v. Texas, supra, at 522). The Court further held that Powell's conviction did not violate the Cruel and Unusual Punishment Clause of the Eighth Amendment (applicable to the states through the Fourteenth Amendment). It found the situation in Powell, supra, distinguishable from the one in Robinson v. California, supra, in that Powell was convicted not of being a chronic alcoholic, but for being drunk in a public place on a particular occasion. Thus he was being punished for the performance of an act, rather than for mere status (Powell v. Texas, supra, at 532).

The Supreme Court also emphasized the fact that when Powell was sober, the act of taking the first drink was a "voluntary exercise of his will," even though this exercise was undertaken under the "exceedingly strong influence" of a compulsion that was "not completely overpowering" (Powell v. Texas, supra, at 520).

Thus the Supreme Court, in Powell, supra, effectively short-circuited a developing line of cases (e.g., Driver and Easter) and threw aside the notion of an alcoholic's intoxication as being anything less than voluntary.

After the holding in Powell, supra, New York's Supreme Court, Appellate Division, upheld the conviction of a defendant for public intoxication (Penal Law, Sec. 240.40), finding that there is a direct relation between the conduct condemned by the statute and the legitimate interest that the community has in preserving the public order. The court emphasized that the statute does not exact punishment for merely a condition, but for a condition from which it might reasonably be expected that an annoyance or a danger might arise (People v. Myers, 39 A.D.2d 122 [2nd Dept., 1972]). Accordingly, the court upheld the constitutionality of the statute.

4.7 Rehabilitation and Treatment of Alcoholics

An estimated 6 to 10 million employees have drinking problems,[1] and this fact imposes substantial costs on employers, on the affected employee, and on society in general. More than $15 billion annually is lost through decreased productivity, excess absenteeism, increased welfare payments, and property damage. Not only are the costs of alcoholism in the workplace high, but the costs of possibly successful rehabilitation are equally high. These steps of rehabilitation and treatment of alcoholics in the workplace encompass both job protection and employer-sponsored programs, both of which are mutually interdependent for success. Congress promoted the establishment of occupational alcoholism programs in 1970 by creating the National Institute on Alcohol Abuse and Alcoholism (NIAAA).[2] To encourage private employers to establish alcoholism programs, NIAAA subsidizes experimental rehabilitation programs, funds consultants, and disseminates information on how to establish and operate such alcoholism programs.[3] As of 1975, more than 600 companies had established alcoholism programs for their employees, and the number of employers involved in the NIAAA programs has greatly increased over the succeeding years.

The Social Security Act[4] also addresses the needs of disabled workers by establishing a fund for the payment of money to people who are forced to terminate their employment because of a prolonged physical or mental permanent disability. In recent years courts have permitted recovery by alcoholics whose drinking had caused physical damage that in turn permanently disabled these alcoholic workers.[5] Other cases have focused on the alcoholic employee's long-term inability to perform any work.[6] The disabled alcoholic may also be eligible for payments under his employer's insurance or pension plan where the list of compensable disabilities includes alcoholism.[7] Many state laws require employers to provide insurance coverage for alcoholism.[8]

Alcoholism in the workplace is but a symptom of psychological causes. Psychological treatments exist now that relieve the emotional pain, fear, and rage that make alcohol so inviting.[9] In the state of Connecticut there are at least twenty-five large in-patient alcohol treatment facilities, ranging in size from 13 beds to 112 beds.

NOTES

1. See 94 Harv. L. Rev. 1660 (1981) at 1689 et seq.
2. 42 U.S.C. 4551 (1979).
3. Supra note 1 at 1692.
4. 42 U.S.C. 301 to 1397 (1979).
5. Note Lewis v. Celebreeze, 359 F.2d 398 (4th Cir., 1966).
6. Note Johnson v. Harris, 625 F.2d 311 (9th Cir., 1980).
7. See Weiss, Dealing with Alcoholism in the Workplace (1980) at 26.
8. Supra note 1 at 1699–1700.
9. See Letter to Editor by Director of the Bio Psychotherapy Institute of New York, in New York Times (December 19, 1987) at 26.

5

Drug-Testing in the Workplace

5.1 Mandatory Testing for Drugs

In March 1988 the President's Commission on Organized Crime recommended mandatory drug-testing for all federal employees as part of a comprehensive health and safety program aimed at identifying and treating drug abusers.[1] Although such blanket mandatory drug-testing appears to unnecessarily violate civil liberties, including the right of privacy,[2] the supporters of the federal employee drug-testing program contend that the procedure does not violate the unreasonable search-and-seizure restraints of the Fourth Amendment. In Allen v. City of Marietta[3] the defendant municipality fired several workers when their urine tested positive for marijuana, and the court deemed that the drug-testing procedure was not unreasonable in view of the fact that the workers were engaged in hazardous activities, and that the city had a legitimate need to know whether its workers were indeed using drugs.[4] On the other hand, even in occupations in which safety is a paramount issue, drug-testing without cause would appear to be impermissible, as shown in McDonnell v. Hunter,[5] in which the court opined that the Fourth Amendment allows a urine test ''only on the basis of a reasonable suspicion, based on specific objective facts and reasonable inferences drawn from those facts in light of experience, that the employee is then under the influence of alcoholic beverages or controlled substances.'' The U.S. Supreme Court, in Connick v. Myers,[6] had ruled that drug-testing of government employees is not a condition of employment, nor has the government a right to impose unlimited restrictions on its employees.

It should be observed that the Fourth Amendment applies only to searches and seizures by the government or by those employers acting under color of law. In the private sector, intrusions on privacy, such as mandatory drug-testing of employees, are not covered by the Fourth Amendment.[7] However, the First U.S. Court of Appeals, in Kelley v. Schlumberger,[8] in 1988, upheld an award of $125,000 for negligent infliction of emotional distress to an employee in the private sector, which employee was required to submit to a drug test on the job and who tested positive for marijuana. Here a private employer was held liable simply for requiring an employee to submit to a drug test![9] The action arose when plaintiff was fired from his job as barge engineer on an oil drilling rig in the Gulf of Mexico after two of his urinalysis tests showed positive for marijuana use. The drug-testing was part of the companywide program of "random" drug-testing of employees. The employer here required another employee to watch the plaintiff as he provided an urine sample to make sure that plaintiff did not cheat by switching samples or diluting his sample urine with water; and this direct observation of the employee urinating was the "hub" of plaintiff's complaint for invasion of his privacy. Applying Louisiana law, the federal trial court approved the jury award of $1 on the privacy claim and $125,000 on the negligent infliction of emotional distress claim.

The Ninth U.S. Court of Appeals, in February 1988, struck down the federal government's policy of requiring 200,000 railroad workers to submit to drug-testing (and alcohol-testing); the program was not justified simply because a railroad worker was on a train crew that got into an accident or was guilty of excessive speed in the movement of the train.[10] According to the court, "accidents, incidents or rule violations, by themselves, do not create reasonable grounds for suspecting that tests will demonstrate alcohol or drug impairment in any one railroad employee, much less an entire train crew. . . . There must be reasonable grounds for suspecting the search will turn up evidence that the employee has violated the industry rule and the federal regulations." The dissenting opinion argued that "locomotives in the hands of drug or alcohol impaired employees are the substantial equivalents of time bombs, endangering the lives of thousands." However, other federal appellate courts have recently upheld mandatory drug-testing of federal employees on the basis of safety concerns or particular conditions of the employment so as to justify an exception to the normal requirement that drug-testing is unreasonable without grounds to suspect an individual employee of wrongdoing.[11]

Drug-testing technology in 1988 required certification of many private laboratories by the National Institute on Drug Abuse, but the results from varied techniques of drug-testing are still uncertain. For example, poppy seeds contain traces of morphine, and eating three poppyseed bagels can produce enough morphine in the body to show a positive test for morphine![12] Similarly, drinking quinine water (used by drug dealers to dilute heroin) may be revealed in drug-testing! Another problem with drug-testing is that some illegal substances also have medical uses: marijuana, or the active chemical "delta-9-tetrahydrocannabinol," is used to treat nausea caused by some cancer therapies. Ibuprofen, used in over-the-counter headache preparations, can give a false reading for marijuana. Even cocaine is used in some kinds of surgery. None of the drug-testing techniques currently being used can determine positively when someone last took the drug, or prove whether the drug actually impaired a person's performance in the workplace.[13] Indeed, drug-testing requires both (a) screening tests (radioimmunoassay, using radioactive material to label the presence of a special drug in a sample; or enzyme immunoassay, using chemical reaction; or fluorescence polarization immunoassay, using fluorescence) and (b) confirmation testings with sophisticated laboratory techniques.[14]

It should be noted that the military began drug-testing in 1981, and that drug-testing is done by such national security units as the Central Intelligence Agency. The U.S. Department of Transportation began civilian testing in 1986. The U.S. Department of Health and Human Services, pursuant to a June 1987 law, formulated guidelines for testing that state that testing should be limited to sensitive jobs that affect the public safety and health and national security. Drug-testing must be truly random except for reasonable cause, like suspicion of drug use. A result indicating possible use must be confirmed by a second urine test using a method that is more expensive and more accurate. In most jobs offenders will be offered the chance to keep their jobs by entering drug rehabilitation programs, and offenders have the right to examine their records and data on the reliability of the testing laboratories.[15] Labor unions that represent government workers strongly oppose drug-testing on the grounds of the Fourth Amendment as an intrusive and unnecessary search and seizure.[16] Nevertheless, on December 14, 1988, the U.S. Department of Health and Human Services announced that 8,600 employees out of 118,000 would be subject to random drug-testing. These government employees are in health care and medical research, including those who provide direct patient care or who handle hazardous or sensitive materials. Security personnel and those who operate potentially hazardous equipment are also included.[17]

A federal district court in New York, in Fowler v. New York City Department of Sanitation,[18] upheld the preemployment and probationary drug-testing of a city sanitation worker who was fired for substance abuse: "Pre-employment physical examination, including urinalysis, is simply too familiar a feature on the job market on all levels to permit anyone to claim an objectively based expectation of privacy in what such analysis might disclose."[19] The court also rejected the defense argument that urine-testing violated the Fourth Amendment's ban on unreasonable searches and seizures. Indeed, "the government has a very real interest in preventing drug abuse outside work hours because of the direct and deleterious impact on performance during work hours."

A tangential issue of interest is whether it is constitutional to bar members of a church from drawing unemployment compensation when they are public employees who were discharged for using the hallucinogenic drug peyote. In Smith/Black v. Employment Division II the Oregon court[20] sustained plaintiff's claim, despite the personnel department policy concerning "misuse of alcohol and/or other mind-altering substances." The court upheld their free exercise claim to unemployment compensation (i.e., First Amendment rights):

The State's interest in denying unemployment compensation benefits to a claimant discharged for religiously motivated conduct must be found in the unemployment compensation statutes, not in the criminal statutes prohibiting the use of peyote. . . . The outright prohibition of good faith religious use of peyote by adult members of the Native American Church would violate the First Amendment directly and as interpreted by Congress. . . . The use of peyote is the kind of free exercise of religion that the First Amendment protects.

NOTES

1. See Note, A.B.A.J. (August 1, 1988) at 35.
2. See Freedman, The Right of Privacy in the Computer Age (Quorum Books, 1987) at Section 2.11 thereof.
3. 601 F. Supp. 482 (ND Ga., 1985).
4. Supra note 1.
5. 612 F. Supp. 1122 (SD Iowa, 1985).
6. 461 U.S. 138 (1983).
7. Supra note 1 at 34.
8. 849 F.2d 41 (1st Cir., 1988).
9. See 31 ATLA L. Rep. (October 1988) at 344–345.
10. See New York Times (February 12, 1988) at A16.
11. Id.
12. See New York Times (November 20, 1988) at E7.
13. Id.
14. Id.
15. See New York Times (December 18, 1988) at 41.
16. Id.
17. See New York Times (December 15, 1988) at A25.
18. 704 F. Supp. 1264 (SD N.Y., February 3, 1989).
19. See N.Y.L.J. (February 3, 1989) at 1 and 27.
20. 763 P.2d 146 (Or., 1988).

5.2 Constitutionality of Drug-Testing

The recent New York Court of Appeals decision in Matter of Caruso v. Ward[1] examined at length the constitutionality of New York's "periodic random urinalysis drug-testing program" affecting *certain* city police officers. The court dismissed the officers' challenge because it found that the drug-testing program "does not transgress State or federal constitutional safeguards and because it is otherwise premature." The thrust of the constitutional issue here was the Fourth Amendment's strictures against unreasonable searches and seizures,[2] and the relevancy of the prior New York case of Patchogue-Medford Congress of Teachers v. Board of Education[3] that plenary drug-testing of schoolteachers is constitutionally forbidden, absent reasonable suspicion.[4] The "diminished expectation of privacy"[5] was also delineated, as the majority of the court ruled: "In sum, we cannot say it is unreasonable to have the additional and exceptional random drug testing authorization for this special police unit as a deterrent as well as a device to discover unlawful drug users, particularly in view of the minimal expectation of privacy involved. The police commissioner's plan for random drug testing of members of the elite OCCB unit falls within the narrow exception to *Patchogue-Medford Congress of Teachers v. Board of Education* (70 N.Y.2d 57, 70, supra) and is sufficient to withstand a facial constitutional attack.'' The dissenting opinion contended that the Patchogue case[6] controls, and that the drug-testing program violated the Fourth Amendment against unreasonable searches and seizures.[7]

The U.S. Supreme Court on March 21, 1989, upheld the drug-testing program of the Reagan administration for the railroad industry in Skinner v. Railway Labor Executives.[8] The suit concerned a 1985 regulation of the Federal Railroad Administration subjecting all crew members of trains involved in serious accidents to mandatory blood and urine testing for drug use. A separate part of the regulation authorized, but did not require, railroads to test after less serious accidents. By a vote of 7–2 the highest court upheld the regulation as a reasonable and effective way to serve the government's ''surpassing safety interests'' in protecting both the traveling public and rail workers themselves from the consequences of operating rail equipment while impaired by drugs. The court balanced the ''diminished'' privacy interests of the workers against the government's ''compelling'' interest in detecting and determining drug use on the railroads. The dissenting opinion of Justice Marshall accused the majority of the court of allowing itself to be ''swept away by society's obsession with stopping the scourge of illegal drugs. . . . History teaches that grave threats to liberty often come in times of urgency, when constitutional rights seem too extravagant to endure. . . . There is no drug exception to the Constitution.''

NOTES

1. 520 N.Y.S.2d 551 (October 25, 1988).

2. According to the court, ''the petitioners' successful challenge in the lower courts rests on a claimed violation of state and federal constitutional guarantees against unreasonable search and seizure (U.S. Const., 4th Amend.; N.Y.S. Const., art. I, §12), directed essentially at the randomness feature. Heavy reliance is understandably placed on the rule and rationale of *Patchogue-Medford Congress of Teachers v. Board of Education* (70 N.Y.2d 57) that plenary drug testing of teachers is constitutionally forbidden absent reasonable suspicion.

''In *Patchogue* we considered the constitutionality of a public school's declared policy requiring across-the-board urinalysis drug testing of all probationary teachers as a condition to qualifying for tenure. The school district informed probationary teachers that those who refused to provide the test sample would not be recommended for tenure. We held that the mandatory production of a urine specimen was a search and seizure under both the federal and state constitutions and that testing for all those teachers, without reasonable suspicion, was forbidden.

"Our search and seizure analysis rests directly on the uniquely private nature of the act and the individual's privacy right, which we accorded a high priority of protection. 'Although [urine] is a waste product, it is not generally eliminated in public or in such a way that the public or government official can gain access to it in order to read its contents' (*Patchogue-Medford Congress of Teachers v. Board of Education*, 70 N.Y.2d 57, supra, at 67). Not only is it inherently private, the urine specimen and what it may reveal about the tested individual are also highly personal, e.g., pregnancy, diabetes, treatment for various medical problems including manic depression, epilepsy, heart disease and schizophrenia, etc. Indeed, the debate is over that urine samples extracted from governmental employees constitutes a search and seizure (see, 3 LaFave, Search & Seizure §10.3[e], at 41–42 [Supp. 1988]).

"The police commissioner, recognizing the impact of *Patchogue* (70 N.Y.2d 57, supra), concedes that the random drug testing announced in Interim Order #36 is a search and seizure. He contends, however, that unlike the probationary teachers subjected, across-the-board, to drug testing in *Patchogue*, the proposed testing of this high risk, highly sensitive, voluntary unit within the police force is reasonable and therefore constitutional.

"The constitutionality of a search conducted by a public employer for 'noninvestigatory, work-related purposes, as well as for investigations of work-related misconduct, should be judged by the standard of reasonableness under all the circumstances' as to 'both the inception and the scope of the [government] intrusion' (*O'Connor v. Ortega*, 107 S. Ct. 1492, 1502–1503; see also, *New Jersey v. T.L.O.*, 469 U.S. 325). In particular, a search by a public employer may be justified at its inception 'when there are reasonable grounds for suspecting that the search will turn up evidence that the employee is guilty of work-related misconduct, or that the search is necessary for a non-investigatory work-related purpose' (*O'Connor v. Ortega*, 107 S. Ct. 1492, supra, at 1502).

"The Supreme Court has not decided whether individualized suspicion is an 'essential element' of a valid work-related search (id., at 1503), nor has it ruled specifically on the constitutionality of employee drug testing programs conducted on a uniform or random basis (id., at 1504, n; but see, *Natl. Treasury Employees Union v. VonRaab*, 816 F.2d 170, 175–176 [5th Cir., 1987], cert. granted 108 S. Ct. 1072 [2-29-88] No. 86-1879] [to be argued 11-2-88]; *Railway Labor Executive Assn. v. Burnley*, 839 F.2d 575 [9th Cir., 1988], cert. granted 108 S. Ct. 2033 [6-6-88] [No. 87-1555] [to be argued 11-2-88]). Outside the area of public employment, however, the court has upheld the seizure of individuals in the absence of individualized suspicion only after first determining that the privacy interests at stake were minimal in nature (see, *United States v. Martinez-Fuerte*, 428 U.S. 543 [permitting brief questioning of vehicle occupants at border checkpoint]). The recognition that public employees might suffer a reduced expectation of privacy at the workplace has prompted one renowned authority, in discussing drug testing, to comment that: '[T]here are a few forms of public employment in which the hazards of even a momentary lapse of attention or judgment are so substantial in terms of the physical danger to fellow workers or the general public and in which the opportunities for preventative close supervisions are so limited that only random or blanket testing will suffice' (3 LaFave, Search & Seizure §10.3[e], at 47–48 [Supp. 1988], supra)."

3. 70 N.Y.2d 57 (1986).

4. "Of crucial significance in this case is that OCCB members have a very dimin-

ished expectation of privacy due to their pursuit of service in the elite unit based on conditions known in advance, including many unchallenged components of Interim Order #36 itself. All members enter this service informed, fairly and reasonably, that they will be held to the strictest standards of probity and purity, over and above those already imposed on the police force at large. They enter with professionally sophisticated eyes wide open to the reality that they will operate in fishbowl-like circumstances undreamed of by Calpurnia herself. The officers agree to undergo microscopic examinations of their personal lives, their financial affairs and their professional judgment calls. Realistically, the proposed random drug testing in these narrow circumstances is just another layer of an already heightened, persistent and employee-expected scrutiny. Notably, these special officers also enjoy job benefits they sought out, including greater promotional opportunity and exciting, challenging work.

"The essential error of the lower courts in the instant case is that they gave an absolutist reading to *Patchogue*'s holding and insufficient consideration to the complementary exception analysis. This case is very different from *Patchogue* where the school district's asserted interest in a drug-free teaching staff was limited to ensuring that 'its teachers are fit and that drug abuse does not impair their ability to deal with the students' (*Patchogue-Medford Congress of Teachers v. Board of Education, 70 N.Y.2d 57, supra* at 69). Here, unlike that case, these elite officers have significantly lowered their own expectations of privacy to a bare minimum level. With that privacy distinction established, we take note of the police department's assertion of a substantial state interest in ensuring that OCCB officers never take drugs. The commissioner wants to be sure public perception of the OCCB unit and the entire police department would not be seriously impaired by these officers taking drugs on or off duty because, in either case, they would be violating the law they have been sworn to uphold and enforce. In a very real sense, these officers are effectively on duty 24 hours a day.

"We believe that the department has established a justifiable interest and responsibility in the periodic testing of special officers constituting its main line offense and defense in the war against drug trafficking. Daily exposure to drug users and traffickers and to offers of drugs, staggering sums of money and other human temptations presents enormous and self-evident risks. The expense alone of maintaining unlawful drug use magnifies the susceptibility of OCCB members to traitorous exchanges of classified information in return for drugs and illegal diversions of seized drugs (see, *Natl. Treasury Employees Union v. VonRaab*, 816 F.2d 170, cert. granted 108 S. Ct. 1072, supra)."

5. "The central question for us persists whether a privacy intrusion that we characterized as being 'at least as intrusive as a strip search' may, on this record, be justified so as to permit random drug testing of OCCB members. Taken alone, the intrusion in this case would fail under *Patchogue*. But the analysis does not end so simply. There are factors here which take this case beyond *Patchogue* and render petitioners' privacy interests insubstantial, thus permitting this urine testing program to be authorized in the absence of reasonable suspicion.

"We observed in *Patchogue* that all public employees have some diminished expectations of privacy in respect to inquiries by the state into their physical fitness to perform on the job (*Patchogue-Medford Congress of Teachers v. Board of Education, 70 N.Y.2d* at 69, supra). The privacy expectations of police officers must be regarded as even further diminished by virtue of their membership in a paramilitary force, the integrity of which is a recognized and important state concern (see, *Morrisette v. Dilworth*, 59

N.Y.2d 449, 452; *Matter of Purdy v. Kreisberg,* 47 N.Y.2d 354, 361; *Flood v. Kennedy,* 12 N.Y.2d 345, 347). Indeed this court has held that 'it is well established that it is within the State's power to regulate the conduct of its police officers even when that conduct involves the exercise of a constitutionally protected right' (*Morrisette v. Dilworth,* 59 N.Y.2d at 452, supra). On the other hand, the special status of police officers does not alone reduce their expectation of privacy to 'minimal' level in respect to random drug testing. Rather, their status, considered with the substantial privacy intrusions to which these particular OCCB members and applicants already have subjected themselves, reduces their privacy interest to a minimal or insubstantial level such that the admittedly crucial state interest justifies the random testing.''

 6. Supra note 3.

 7. ''Today's decision is an abrupt about-face from *Patchogue-Medford Congress of Teachers v. Board of Education* (70 N.Y.2d 57), where only last year this court concluded that the proposed random urine testing of probationary teachers constituted a search, that having to urinate under the observation of another person was at least as intrusive as a strip search, and that—despite the teachers' diminished expectation of privacy, the public importance of unimpaired teachers, and the prevalence of drugs in schools—such searches were constitutionally prohibited in the absence of individualized reasonable suspicion. Now, the court upholds a program of random urine testing under the observation of another person without any individualized suspicion, and without any reviewable procedural safeguards yet in place, because this is an elite voluntary corps of police officers with access to narcotics, because of the strong public interest in the purity and integrity of these employees, and because of their diminished privacy interest.

 ''The criteria the court identifies are applicable to a wide array of public employees—even teachers, who are in an environment where drug use is particularly high. I disagree with the departure from *Patchogue* and with the new boundless test for permissible searches. The court should not approve this program on the present record, or in its present procedural posture. . . . The drug testing program before us is thus three steps removed from the warrant requirement. It does not fall within any of the carefully drawn exceptions to the warrant-preference rule involving probable cause, and it does not fall within the exceptional circumstances involving individualized reasonable suspicion. Although the court has hypothesized that searches might at times be permitted even without individualized suspicion, we have made it clear that such searches will be 'closely scrutinized, and generally only permitted when the privacy interests implicated are minimal, the government's interest is substantial, and safeguards are provided to insure that the individual's reasonable expectation of privacy is not subjected to unregulated discretion' (*Patchogue,* supra, at 70).

 ''Those prerequisites are not satisfied on this record.

 ''Most significantly, the commissioner has demonstrated no need in this case for surprise drug testing. The majority opinion incorrectly inverts and thus bypasses the proper order of analysis, reasoning from the premise that the OCCB officers have a reduced expectation of privacy to the conclusion that they therefore may be searched without cause. Unless at the outset the standard of reasonable suspicion is inadequate to allow identification of substance-abusing officers, the government lacks an interest that justifies departure from an individualized suspicion standard, and a random search is impermissible (see, 3 LaFave, Search & Seizure §10.3[e], at 47–48 [Supp. 1988]).

 ''The important goal of deterrence—to the extent that it is suggested as the object of this program—is not, without evidence of a pervasive problem among the persons to be tested, justification for this search. Many types of illegal conduct could be deterred were the state permitted to search everyone 'periodically in an all-inclusive dragnet. * * * By restricting the government to reasonable searches, the state and federal constitutions recognize that there comes a point at which searches intended to serve the public interest, however effective, may themselves undermine the public's interest in maintaining the privacy, dignity and security of its members' (*Patchogue, supra*, at 70).''

8. 109 S. Ct. 1726 (1989).

5.3 Penalties for Drug Dealers

The federal district court for the Southern District of New York, in United States v. Torres,[1] ruled that a mandatory life sentence without parole for drug dealers is not "cruel and unusual" punishment in violation of the Eighth Amendment.[2] The court noted that the crucial balancing was between "the gravity of the offense and the harshness of the penalty," and the court concluded: "The challenged statute (21 U.S.C. 848[b]) is aimed at combatting the devastating effect that the use of illegal narcotics is having on our society. . . . The purposes of imposing this penalty is evident: to deter individuals from heading such enterprises and to ensure that once convicted, such persons are never again given the opportunity to recommence their illegal activities." And the most important purpose of the law is "to limit the available supply of illicit narcotics."[3]

Simultaneous with the heavy penalties imposed on drug dealers has been the growth of drug treatment groups like Straight Inc., of Springfield, Virginia, and six other locations in the United States, with its tough regimen of intense discussions, separation from home and family, and severe penalties.[4] Unfortunately the drug treatment program has been marred by civil rights violations by the treatment centers, such as assault and battery, medical malpractice, and false imprisonment.[5]

NOTES

1. 683 F. Supp. 56 (S.D.N.Y., September 14, 1988).
2. See A.B.A.J. (December 1, 1988) at 98–99.
3. Interestingly, the court ordered that 40 percent of the forfeited property of the defendants here (about $10 million) be devoted to detoxification programs in Bronx, N.Y.
4. See Insight Magazine (December 5, 1988) at 18.
5. Id.

6

Roles of the Parties in Occupational Injury, Disease, or Death

6.1 Introduction

Of the countless people and entities involved in the occupational injury, disease, or death situation, focus hereinafter is placed on the plaintiff-claimant and his or her family,[1] defendant-employers and successors,[2] and the various third-parties, such as the federal government,[3] product manufacturers and suppliers,[4] technical experts,[5] the Social Security Administration,[6] the Occupational Safety and Health Administration,[7] the Superfund Act enforcement,[8] and insurance companies.[9]

NOTES

1. See section 6.2 hereinafter.
2. See section 6.3 hereinafter.
3. See section 6.4 hereinafter.
4. See section 6.5 hereinafter.
5. See section 6.6 hereinafter.
6. See section 6.7 hereinafter.
7. See section 6.8 hereinafter.
8. See section 6.9 hereinafter.
9. See section 6.10 hereinafter.

6.2 Plaintiff-Claimant and His or Her Family

It is obvious that the claimant and his or her family are at the heart of the occupational injury, disease, or death situation, since he or she is the injured worker in the workplace, and the immediate family is affected thereby.[1] Even more "physical" can be the injury to the household of the worker who, having been exposed to large concentrations of asbestos fiber in the workplace, for example, brings home significant amounts of asbestos fiber on his or her clothing. Inhalation of the asbestos fiber may initiate asbestosis, lung cancer, or mesothelioma in the immediate family of the worker.

When a number of workers in a given plant or office are exposed to a toxic substance, for example, the claim for occupational injury, disease, or death may take the form of a class action.[2] Class actions save substantial time and money, bolster the contention that the injury, disease, or death occurred in the workplace, and even toll the statute of limitations for all members of the class.[3] However, in Yandle v. PPG Industries,[4] the federal district court in Texas frowned on the class action as the instrumentality for mass tort occupational disease because of the inherent, individual differences among the members of the class. Class action status has generally been granted in personal injury cases,[5] and cases pending in different jurisdictions have readily been consolidated for multidistrict discovery and pretrial proceedings.[6]

NOTES

1. See Baron, Handling Occupational Disease Cases (Lawpress, 1981) at 44 et seq.
2. See Warren Freedman, Hazardous Waste Liability (Michie, 1987) at Section 5.6 thereof.
3. Note American Pipe & Construction Co. v. Utah, 94 S. Ct. 756 (1974).
4. 65 F.R.D. 566 (ED Tex., 1974).
5. See Hernandez v. M/V Skyward, 61 F.R.D. 558 (SD Fla., 1974), aff. 507 F.2d 1278 (5th Cir., 1975).
6. Note In Re "Agent Orange" Product Liability Litigation, 475 F. Supp. 928 (J.P.M.L., 1979).

6.3 Defendant-Employers and Successors

Occupational injury, disease, and death cases, when litigated, bring together as defendants the employers and their successors. Although workers' compensation is generally deemed to be the exclusive remedy, courts are prone to recognize many exceptions to the exclusivity rule. If the occupational disease actually was contracted outside the scope of employment, the injured, diseased, or dead employee may have a cause of action against the employer in the employer's capacity as an intentional tortfeasor.[1] Another exception is when the employer occupied a dual capacity vis-à-vis the employee, and is liable as a product manufacturer.[2] A third exception to the exclusivity rule of workers' compensation occurs when the employer, for whatever reason, failed to obtain workers' compensation insurance or to qualify under the self-insurance provisions of the state law on workers' compensation.[3] Note that the burden is on the defendant-employer to plead and prove, as an affirmative defense, that the workers' compensation act provides the exclusive remedy.[4] Officers and directors of the corporate employer are generally not clothed with immunity and are frequently sued as separate entities from the employer.[5] An employee is generally precluded from bringing suit against co-employees, supervisors, and others immediately involved in the employment relationship.[6] Yet in Hathcock v. Commercial Union Insurance Co.[7] the federal appellate court, applying Alabama law, sanctioned the suit by an employee against supervisory employees, alleging negligent supervision and negligence in failing to provide the injured employee with safety devices. The exclusive remedy provisions of the Federal Employees' Compensation Act,[8] which relates to civilian employees of the federal government,[9] have been held not to preclude suit by an injured employee against a co-employee.[10]

Parent companies of the employer are not immune from tort liability to employees of the subsidiary employer for the parent company's own independent acts of negligence. In Boggs v. Blue Diamond Coal Co.[11] the Sixth U.S. Court of Appeals observed:

The increasing concentration of discrete business entities in the hands of holding companies, regional, national and international . . . (have) a more subtle influence. . . . Implicit in these decisions is the suggestion that the tort system should not deny recovery in an increasingly concentrated economy to an injured employee due to the fortuitous circumstance that the tortfeasor is not a stranger but is controlled by the same business enterprise that controls his immediate employer.[12]

On the other hand, the subsidiary corporation may be liable as a third party to an employee of the parent corporation, as illustrated in Thomas v. Hycon.[13] Here the injured worker collected workers' compensation benefits from the employer–parent company for an accident in which he was operating a truck owned by defendant–subsidiary corporation. Subsequently the injured employee sued defendant, alleging that the truck had defective brakes. Although the two corporations had the same officers and the same directors, the court found that the subsidiary had real business functions with interests different from its parent corporation, and as a separate business entity was subject to common law tort liability.[14] A division of the employer is merely an extension of the employer and, therefore, is entitled to immunity from suit as "employer."[15]

Other potential third-party defendants include medical personnel of the employer, who are subject to liability for not informing the employee-patient of his state of health or disease, for example.[16] If a physician-patient relationship can be said not to exist, the physician may not have a duty to disclose the employee's condition to the employee.[17] In Hoover v. Williamson[18] a physician, retained by the employer to supervise annual x-ray examination of employees, was apparently negligent, and the injured employee was held by the Maryland court not to be liable for malpractice in the absence of a physician-patient relationship. Outside this professional physician-patient relationship the company doctor may have a duty to employees that he examines or treats under Section 324A of Restatement (Second) of Torts:

One who undertakes, gratuitously or for consideration, to render services to another which he should recognize as necessary for the protection of a third person or his things, is subject to liability to the third person for physical harm resulting from his failure to exercise reasonable care to protect his undertaking, if
    (a) his failure to exercise reasonable care increases the risk of such harm, or
    (b) he has undertaken to perform a duty owed by the other to the third person, or
    (c) the harm is suffered because of reliance of the other or the third person upon the undertaking.

The underlying theory for liability of the company doctor depends on whether or not the employer exercises the necessary control over "the means and manner of the performance" of the doctor; if the employer does not, then the doctor may be an independent contractor subject to his own tort liability.[19] In Lemonovich v. Klimoski[20] the physician was a "surgical liaison officer" whose duties included caring for all of the employer's hospitalized employees; he was paid on a fee-for-service basis, but the court described him as an independent contractor who was not immune from suit. Incidentally, a contract physician who provided inadequate medical care to a prison inmate was held, in West v. Atkins,[21] to have acted under color of law, and the prison inmate was authorized in a civil rights suit, under 42 U.S.C. 1983, to prove that his Eighth Amendment right against cruel and unusual punishment was violated. The U.S. Supreme Court, in 1988, pointed out that a prison inmate must rely on prison authorities to meet his medical needs, and the state has a constitutional obligation to meet those needs. If the defendant–contract physician was indifferent to plaintiff's needs, the resulting deprivation was caused by the state's exercise of its right to punish him by incarceration and to deny him a venue independent of the state to obtain needed medical care. It was irrelevant that the physician was part-time and under contract, for he was a public employee and subject to tort liability.

NOTES

1. For example, note Silkwood v. Kerr-McGee Corp., 485 F. Supp. 566 (Okla., 1979). See Freedman, International Products Liability (Kluwer, 1987) at Section 3.10.

2. See Douglas v. Gallo Winery, 137 Cal. Rptr. 797 (1977).

3. Note Hall v. Burton, 19 Cal. Rptr. 797 (1962).

4. See Baron, Handling Occupational Disease Cases (Lawpress, 1981) at 47.

5. Cf. Mier v. Staley, 329 N.E.2d 1 (Ill. App., 1975).

6. See Green v. Verven, 204 F. Supp. 585 (Conn., 1959), and Smith v. Liberty Mutual Insurance Co., 409 F. Supp. 1211 (N.C., 1976).

7. 576 F.2d 653 (5th Cir., 1978).

8. 5 U.S.C. 8101 to 8193.

9. See Freedman, Federal Statutes on Environmental Protection (Quorum Books, 1987) at 49.

10. See Bates v. Harp, 573 F.2d 930 (6th Cir., 1978); also supra note 4 at 66.

11. 590 F.2d 655 (6th Cir., 1979).

12. See Davis, "Workmen's Compensation: Using an Enterprise Theory of Employment to Determine Who Is a Third Party Tortfeasor," 32 U. of Pitt. L. Rev. 289 (1971).

13. 244 F. Supp. 151 (D.C., 1965).

14. Supra note 4 at 71.

15. See Miller v. United States, 307 F. Supp. 932 (ED Va., 1969).

16. See 49 A.L.R.3d 501 (1973).

17. See Murphy v. Godwin, 303 A.2d 668 (Del., 1973).

18. 203 A.2d 861 (Md., 1964).

19. See Hoffman v. Houston Clinic, 41 S.W.2d 134 (Tex. Civ. App., 1931); supra note 4 at 83.

20. 315 F. Supp. 1290 (WD Pa., 1970).

21. 108 S. Ct. 2250 (1988).

6.4 Federal Government As Third Party

Historically, the federal government is immune from suit for liability, except to the extent to which it consents to respond to judicial proceedings,[1] as evidenced by the Federal Tort Claims Act of 1946.[2] A 1988 study by the National Safe Workplace Institute[3] faulted the federal government on deaths in the workplace, especially in the construction industry, owing to federal and state laxity in criminal prosecution. The largest cities in states that depend on the federal government for safety prosecutions had 4.13 deaths for each billion dollars of construction. In civil litigation the right of an injured employee to recover against the federal government in occupational disease litigation, for example, requires a finding by the court that some negligent act or omission of a government employee or official, in the course of his or her employment, produced injury and damage to the injured employee. The problem of recovery of damages is acute, especially when the occupational disease, for example, does not manifest until the expiration of the applicable statute of limitations, as was the case in Yandle v. PPG Industries.[4] Here suit was instituted against nonemployer third parties.

The federal government generally retains its immunity under the "discretionary function" exception to liability under the Federal Tort Claims Act,[5] that is, when the federal employer was merely exercising a judgmental or policy-type function, even though that exercise constitutes an abuse of discretion or poor judgment. In Raymer v. United States[6] the "discretionary function" exception was held to be inapplicable when the federal agency "is engaged in actions and directing the actions of other employees in carrying out an already formulated policy."

NOTES

1. Note Ickes v. Fox, 300 U.S. 82 (1937).
2. See Freedman, International Products Liability (Kluwer, 1987) at Section 10.06.
3. See New York Times (July 17, 1988) at 15.
4. 65 F.R.D. 566 (ED Tex., 1974).
5. See Indian Towing Co. v. United States, 350 U.S. 61 (1955).
6. 482 F. Supp. 432 (WD Ky., 1979).

6.5 Product Manufacturers and Suppliers As Third Parties

Product manufacturers and suppliers are often third parties in the occupational injury, disease, or death picture, and the action by the injured employee then takes the form of a products liability suit.[1] In recent years new industries, in particular, have explored the incipiency of occupational injuries, diseases, and deaths in an effort to control undesired occurrences. For example, in the computer chip factory, although precautions are taken to eliminate tiny specks of dust that might destroy the ultrafine computer chips, the computer chip workers have experienced health problems "ranging from headaches to malaise to miscarriages and possibly cancer."[2] The making of tiny computer chips requires dozens of chemicals, including poisonous gases like arsine and cyanide, strong acids, and noxious solvents; exposure to these hundred or more chemicals have undoubtedly caused health problems that have not yet been identified. The injured employee, even after recovery under workers' compensation, seeks additional compensation from the manufacturers and distributors of all the chemicals and other products used in the computer chip factory!

In Ferebee v. Chevron Chemical Co.[3] an agricultural worker allegedly contracted a fatal lung disease as a result of long-term skin exposure to paraquat, an herbicide distributed by defendant. After losing at trial the defendant appealed, claiming that plaintiff's evidence of causation did not support the jury's verdict: all recognized ill effects of paraquat occur within a short time of exposure, and here plaintiff's illness did not develop until ten months after the last exposure to the herbicide. The District of Columbia Court of Appeals refused to probe the validity of the expert's reasoning: "Judges, both trial and appellate, have no special competence to resolve the complex and refractory causal issues raised by the attempt to link low level exposure to toxic chemicals with human disease. On questions such as these, which stand at the frontier of current medical and epidemiological inquiry, *if experts are willing to testify* that such a link exists, it is for the jury to decide whether to credit such testimony" (emphasis added).[4]

NOTES

1. See Freedman, International Products Liability (Kluwer, 1987) at Section 3.10.
2. See New York Times (January 10, 1988) at E5.

3. 736 F.2d 1529 (D.C. Cir., 1984), cert. den., 105 S. Ct. 545 (1984).
4. See The Brief (Fall 1988) at 8.

6.6 Technical Experts As Third Parties

The range of technical experts who become involved as third parties in the occupational injury, disease, or death claim extends from the expert-employee (who may be immune from liability as an employee of the defendant-employer) to the expert who is an independent entrepreneur (and generally not immune). Most large companies, for example, use full-time industrial hygienists and expert medical personnel, some of whom are directly employed by employers, some are indirectly employed by parent companies, and others are independent contractors.[1] Industrial hygienists help to identify the hazards of toxic chemicals in the workplace and evaluate other risks in the workplace. The liability of an industrial hygienist for negligently misrepresenting that a workplace is free from occupational hazards depends on the nature of the relation to the employer. The independent industrial hygienist is not protected by the immunity afforded co-employees by the workers' compensation statutes of the various states. The liability of the independent industrial hygienist is delineated under Section 311 of Restatement (Second) of Torts: "One who negligently gives false information to another is subject to liability for physical harm caused by action taken by the other in reasonable reliance upon such information, where such harm results . . . to such third persons as the actor should expect to be put in peril by the action taken."[2]

If a company physician negligently fails to disclose his knowledge of the state of an employee's health to the employee, the employer may be vicariously liable to the employee for any physical damage resulting from the technical expert's failure to disclose.[3] In Union Carbide & Carbon Corp. v. Stapleton[4] the Sixth U.S. Court of Appeals held that the employer had a duty to disclose its knowledge of an employee's health condition to the employee. The court compared the failure of the employer to disclose to the employee its knowledge of his health problems with a failure to warn of a premises or product defect: the duty to disclose is included within the employer's general duty to exercise ordinary care for the safety of its employees. This general duty does not require the employer to conduct physical examinations of employees; but once the employer does so, it must act carefully and responsibly and disclose the results of that physical examination to the employee.[5] The Ninth U.S. Court of Appeals, in Jines v. General Electric Co.,[6] may have gone too far in recommending that an employer conducting physical examinations of its employees has a duty to discover the occupational injury or disease!

NOTES

1. See Baron, Handling Occupational Disease Cases (Lawpress, 1981) at 85–86.
2. Note generally 39 A.L.R.3d 184.

3. See Betesh v. United States, 400 F. Supp. 239 (D.C., 1974).
4. 237 F.2d 229 (6th Cir., 1956).
5. Supra note 1 at 57; also see Hoover v. Williamson, 203 A.2d 851 (Md., 1964).
6. 303 F.2d 76 (9th Cir., 1962).

6.7 Social Security Administration As Third Party

The Social Security Administration disability system is a third party in many occupational injury, disease, or death claims.[1] Under 42 U.S.C. 423(d)(1) disability is defined as an "inability to engage in any substantial gainful activity by reason of any medically determinable physical or mental impairment which can be expected to result in death or which has lasted or can be expected to last for a continuous period of not less than 12 months." As pointed out in Stephens v. Heckler,[2] a claimant who can perform some type of work or activity is not considered disabled.

Title II of the Social Security Act benefits those workers who have worked and paid Social Security taxes for a specified period of time; that is, he or she is fully insured *and* is currently insured.[3] On the other hand, the Supplemental Security Income Program in Title XVI of the Act provides lesser benefits to the disabled worker, regardless of the worker's work history or payment of Social Security taxes. Title II benefits are computed as if the claimant were sixty-five years of age and had retired the year the disability commenced, whereas Title XVI benefits provide only a basic level of income. Three basic groups of workers are eligible for benefits: disabled adults under age sixty-five, people disabled since childhood who have a parent covered by Social Security, and disabled widows or widowers aged fifty to sixty whose spouses were eligible to receive Social Security.[4]

In Burnette v. Bowen[5] the federal district court for the Eastern District of New York hit the "injustices" in the Social Security Administration's handling of the claim. Ruling in the case of a printing press operator who claimed that he was disabled more than five years ago, the court stressed its finding that "case after case appearing before the court reveals a predetermined disposition" on the part of the Social Security Administration to rule against claimants "without any substantial evidence. . . . The instances are so numerous as to call into question the intellectual integrity of the entire program." The court concluded that "there is nothing" in the reports of three government physicians to refute the assertion of plaintiff's physician that if he stayed at his job, "he may get his hand caught and be pulled into the mechanism" because of his diabetic condition.[6]

More than 300,000 claims are filed annually against the Social Security Administration, and almost 700 administrative law judges hear appeals from people denied disability or health insurance benefits.[7] Unfortunately the federal agency frequently harasses its judges, who are supposed to be independent of the agency, whose salary is not subject to change, and whose term is secure.

In 1982 the Social Security Administration began to review the decisions of the judges who allowed benefits in 70 percent of their decisions; the agency warned them that if their performance did not change, "other steps" would be taken.[8]

NOTES

1. See McCormick, Social Security Claims and Procedures (1984), and DeBofsky, "Social Security Disability Law," Trial Magazine (June 1988) at 18 et seq.
2. 766 F.2d 284 (7th Cir., 1985).
3. See 20 C.F.R. 404.110, 404.120, 404.130, and 404.132 (1987).
4. Supra note 1: DeBofsky at 18.
5. ____ F. Supp. ____ (ED N.Y., December 27, 1988).
6. See N.Y.L.J. (December 27, 1988) at 1 and 29.
7. See New York Times (January 16, 1989) at 16.
8. Id.

6.8 Occupational Safety and Health Administration as Third Party

Undoubtedly the Occupational Safety and Health Administration (OSHA) is the most prominent third party involved in occupational injury, disease, or death cases. It was in 1970 that the federal government realized that the workplace had become the site for as many injuries, diseases, and deaths as occur on the battlefield, and Congress promptly enacted the Occupational Safety and Health Act of 1970,[1] designed to end decades of neglect by the states in the field of industrial safety and health.[2] The Act applies to all nonpublic employers who have employees in a business that affects interstate commerce, although employers subject to other federal legislation are excluded.[3] The Act states that "each employer shall furnish to each of his employees employment and a place of employment which are free from recognized hazards that are causing or are likely to cause death or serious physical harm to his employees."[4] Civil penalties may be imposed on employers who violate this general duty clause.[5] Employers must also comply with occupational safety and health standards promulgated by the secretary of labor;[6] the Act authorizes a compliance officer to enter any workplace at reasonable hours without notice and delay in order to inspect and investigate.[7] Of course, the inspection procedures "shall be implemented so as to avoid any undue and unnecessary disruption of the normal operations of the employer's plant."[8]

The standards promulgated by OSHA include consensus-type standards of private industry and associations, but all OSHA standards may be promulgated without complying with the public hearing and other procedural requirements of the Administrative Procedure Act[9] when employees are in "grave danger from exposure" to toxic substances, for example.[10] The National Institute of Occupational Safety and Health, which was established to conduct research and

draft standards, publishes annually a list of toxic substances for public information and consumption.[11] OSHA is not required to engage in a cost-benefit
analysis to demonstrate that the standard reflects a reasonable relation between
costs imposed on employers and the benefits to employees associated with the
standards because Congress, in enacting OSHA, weighed the costs and benefits
of protecting the health and safety of workers and decided that OSHA should
promulgate worker protection standards that prevent material health impairment
to the extent that this is capable of being done, when necessary to create a safe
and healthful working environment, even though such standards may impose
substantial costs on employers.[12] But OSHA, in imposing a fine or civil penalty
on a violating employer, must develop "substantial evidence" for the record,
if the court, in reviewing the record, is to uphold the violation; in National
Realty & Construction Co. v. OSH Review Commission[13] the court reversed
the imposition of the fine or civil penalty because OSHA failed to shoulder its
burden of proof that the workplace was indeed unsafe.[14]

The federal courts have generally held that no private cause of action exists
under OSHA for an employee to sue his or her employer for OSHA violations
by the employer.[15] However, a violation of OSHA may well support a claim
for gross negligence or malfeasance or provide other tort remedies as exten-
sions of workers' compensation.[16] Employees have substantial rights under OSHA
that are protected against employee discharge or discrimination, as illustrated
in Whirlpool Corp. v. Marshall,[17] in which employees refused to work on
aerial screens that had proved incapable of holding a man's weight, and the
U.S. Supreme Court upheld the actions of employees against discrimination by
the employer placing reprimands in their personnel files.[18] "Whistle-blowers"
are similarly protected from discharge or discrimination simply because the
employee made a complaint, testified in a proceeding against the employer, or
exercised any rights under OSHA.[19] On the other hand, in Industrial Union
Department, AFL-CIO v. OSH Review Commission,[20] the highest court the
same year declared that OSHA was "not designed to require employers to
provide absolutely risk-free workplaces whenever it is technologically feasible
to do so, so long as the cost is not great enough to destroy an entire industry.
. . . (Congress only) intended to require elimination, as far as feasible, of
significant risks of harm." Indeed, "employers and employees have separate
but dependent responsibilities and rights with respect to achieving safe and
healthful working conditions."

Federal, state, and local governments are not governed by OSHA[21] because
OSHA deals exclusively with private employers. Private employers are required to maintain records of work-related injuries, diseases, and deaths, and
employees, under OSHA's right-to-know provisions,[22] have a right of reasonable access to an employer's medical and hazard-exposure records pertaining
to employee exposure to toxic substances, for example.[23] (There is a curious
exclusion for situations in which the harmful physical substance is not present
in the workplace "in a manner different from typical non-occupational situa-

tions."[24] Thus employers have no statutory or regulatory duty to tell employees that employee X or Y or Z has acquired immunodeficiency syndrome[25] or other disease, or to maintain records that disclose that act, for example.)

OSHA does not authorize employees to leave the workplace because of potential unsafe work conditions; employees are required to inform their employer of the unsafe condition, or request an OSHA inspection of the workplace if no ameliorative action is taken by the employer.[26] But if the employee is confronted with a workplace condition presenting a real danger of serious injury, disease, or death, he may refuse "in good faith" to continue working.[27]

OSHA has in recent years promulgated a vast array of standards that run the gamut of hazards in the workplace. For example, OSHA expanded the scope of its Hazard Communication Standard,[28] which had applied only to manufacturers, to cover all employers with employees exposed to hazardous chemicals.[29] The revised standards were responsive to a court order in United Steelworkers of America v. Pendergrass.[30] After the destructiveness of explosions in grain-handling facilities in late 1977 and early 1978, resulting in almost sixty deaths and fifty injuries in 1977 alone, the existing OSHA general agricultural industry standards were modified to encompass the new situation. But the new regulations and new standards did not become effective until March 30, 1988![31]

Enforcement has not been one of OSHA's strong points for unfortunately "politics" seems to play a strong role in determining whether OSHA will take action toward enforcement of its standards, rules, and regulations. In February 1988 OSHA "took it on the chin time after time . . . as Democrats and Republicans alike criticized its poor enforcement record."[32] Specifically, the complaints centered about "its failure to push for higher budgets and more manpower, for the inconsistent penalties it imposes against employers for safety violations, for not listening to its construction safety advisory committee, for its inexperienced inspectors, and for reporting rules that allow potentially disastrous accidents to go unchecked."[33] On the other hand, in November 1987, OSHA slapped a $325,000 fine on Ford Motor Co. for violations in its injury and illness record-keeping at its plants in Georgia and Missouri, although the other seventy Ford plants were not involved.[34] Improperly maintained records can benefit the employer by making its record look good, thereby lessening the chances of an OSHA safety investigation at the plant.[35] Most recently OSHA took a bold step to inquire into assertions by workers of Lockheed Corp. in Burbank, California, that they are endangered by chemicals in making the top secret Stealth bomber aircraft![36]

But the trend of the Reagan years (and possibly the Bush years to follow) do not presage any concerted effort by OSHA to protect workers' safety.[37] The number of prosecutions by the U.S. Department of Justice has been minimal: between 1981 and 1988 only two indictments have been achieved. The lack of federal prosecution is enhanced by the argument of federal preemption[38] that is, the state cannot prosecute employers for workplace injuries.[39] Yet in December 1988 the U.S. Justice Department issued an opinion that employers whose employees are killed or injured on the job can be prosecuted for murder, manslaughter, or assault under state laws and cannot seek refuge under OSHA and other federal laws on workplace safety.[40] This indicates that the governmental opinion runs counter to state court rulings on federal preemption.[41]

The U.S. Labor Department, in mid-January 1989, broadened OSHA regulations of toxic and hazardous substances in the workplace, putting new limits on such substances as grain dust and gasoline fumes and strengthening existing limits on others.[42] The new regulation limits worker exposure on 164 substances for the first time and strengthens the limits on 212 substances that are already regulated. OSHA estimates that the new regulations could save 700 lives a year![43]

NOTES

1. 84 Stat. 1590 (1970), codified at 29 U.S.C. 651 et seq.

2. See Hornberger, "Occupational Safety and Health Act of 1970," 21 Cleve. St. L. Rev. 1 (January 1972).

3. 29 U.S.C. 652.

4. For example, Federal Coal Mine Health and Safety Act of 1969 (31 U.S.C. 801 et seq) and Federal Metal and Non-Metallic Mine Safety Act (30 U.S.C. 721 et seq).

5. 29 U.S.C. 654(a)(1). Note that the Longshoremen's and Harbor Workers' Compensation Act provides a similar requirement, 33 U.S.C. 941.

6. 29 U.S.C. 666.

7. See 29 C.F.R. 1903.3, for example.

8. See 29 C.F.R. 1903.6(c), for example.

9. 5 U.S.C. 6551 et seq. Also see Freedman, Federal Statutes on Environmental Protection (Quorum Books, 1987) at 6–10.

10. See 29 U.S.C. 655(c).

11. See 29 C.F.R. 1910.1000.

12. Note American Textile Manufacturers Institute, Inc. v. Donovan, 452 U.S. 490 (1981).

13. 489 F.2d 1257 (D.C. Cir., 1973).

14. According to the court, "the hearing record is barren of evidence describing, and demonstrating the feasibility and likely utility of, the particular measures which National Realty should have taken to improve its safety policy. Having the burden of proof, the Secretary must be charged with these evidentiary deficiencies. The Commission sought to cure these deficiencies *sua sponte* by speculating about what National Realty could have done to upgrade its safety program. These suggestions, while not unattractive, came too late in the proceedings. An employer is unfairly deprived of an opportunity to cross-examine or to present rebuttal evidence and testimony when it learns the exact nature of its alleged violation only after the hearing. As noted above, the Secretary has considered scope before and during a hearing to alter his pleadings and legal theories. But the Commission cannot make these alterations itself in the face of an empty record. To merit judicial deference, the Commission's expertise must operate upon, not seek to replace, record evidence. Only by requiring the Secretary, at the hearing, to formulate and defend *his own* theory of what a cited defendant should have done can the Commission and the courts assure even-handed enforcement of the general duty clause. Be-

cause employers have a general duty to do virtually everything possible to prevent and repress hazardous conduct by employees, violations exist almost everywhere, and the Secretary has an awesomely broad discretion in selecting defendants and in proposing penalties. To assure that citations issue only upon careful deliberation, the Secretary must be constrained to specify the particular steps a cited employer should have taken to avoid citation, and to demonstrate the feasibility and likely utility of those measures.''

15. See Rogers v. Frito-Lay, Inc., 611 F.2d 1074 (5th Cir., 1980).

16. See Freedman, International Products Liability (Kluwer, 1987) at Section 3.10.

17. 445 U.S. 1 (1980).

18. Id. at 14–19.

19. See 29 U.S.C. 660(c): ''No person shall discharge or in any manner discriminate against any employee because such employee has filed any complaint or instituted or caused to be instituted any proceeding under or related to this chapter or has testified or is about to testify in any such proceeding or because of the exercise by such employee on behalf of himself or others of any right afforded by this chapter.''

20. 448 U.S. 607 (1980) at 641.

21. See 29 U.S.C. 651(b).

22. See For the Defense (May 1988) at 7.

23. Id.

24. See 29 C.F.R. 1910.20.

25. See 29 U.S.C. 1910.20(c)(8).

26. Section 3.5 hereinbefore.

27. See 29 C.F.R. 1977.12(b)(2).

28. See 29 C.F.R. 1910.1200; see also Trial Magazine (November 1987) at 18–19.

29. Estimated at 35,000,000 workers.

30. 819 F.2d 1263 (3rd Cir., 1987); see also United Steelworkers of America v. Auchter, 763 F.2d 728 (3rd Cir., 1985).

31. See Trial Magazine (April 1988) at 69–71; also 29 C.F.R. 1910.272 (1987).

32. See Hartford Courant (February 3, 1988) at A2.

33. Id.

34. See Hartford Courant (November 10, 1987) at F9.

35. Note New York Times (January 10, 1988) at E5.

36. See New York Times (October 2, 1988) at 28.

37. Note Trial Magazine (December 1988) at 84.

38. See Section 8.5 hereinafter.

39. See People v. Chicago Magnet Wire Corp., 510 N.E.2d 1173 (Ill. App., 1987).

40. See New York Times (December 16, 1988) at D20.

41. Id., citing courts in Colorado, New York, Illinois, Texas, and Michigan.

42. See New York Times (January 14, 1989) at 1 and 6.

43. Supra note 2 at 1.

6.9 Superfund Act Enforcement As Third Party

The Superfund Amendments and Reauthorization Act of 1986 (SARA)[1] is important federal legislation for employees who work or live near Superfund sites.[2] SARA has radically increased the number of personal injury lawsuits over contamination from hazardous waste sites because it allows plaintiffs to establish their cases, at least in part, at the expense of defendants potentially responsible for cleanup of hazardous waste. SARA also makes compensation more readily available to the injured worker by developing medical causation evidence through health effects studies.[3] In addition, SARA created a duty to warn under the community right-to-know provisions of Title III of the Act,[4] and revived personal injury claims dating back to 1980 by preempting state statutes of limitations.[5]

Employees who work or live near hazardous waste sites listed on the National Priorities List can petition for a health assessment to determine dosage and exposure and for toxicological and epidemiological evaluations of short- and long-term health effects of not only the toxic substances found therein, but also their synergistic effects.[6] These reports or studies constitute "response costs,"[7] which are financed by the defendant or defendants deemed potentially responsible for the hazardous waste site. Other "response costs" include the expense of relocating homes or businesses and the establishment of public health advisories.[8]

Citizen-enforcement suits are promoted by SARA,[9] and the net result is greater enforcement activity on the part of the Environmental Protection Agency (EPA) and other concerned state and federal agencies. Citizen suits for violations of the Act are brought in the district court for the district in which the alleged violation occurred; suits to compel adherence to cleanup schedules or promulgation of toxicological profiles are brought in the federal district court for the District of Columbia.[10] But such citizen suits cannot be brought until a portion of the final remedy has been completed.[11] And citizen suits must await EPA action under the Superfund Act or under the Resource Conservation and Recovery Act.[12] SARA also established a discovery-based statute of limitations, preempting state statutes of limitations, thereby reviving old personal injury claims back to the year 1980.[13]

Most important, SARA, under Title III, requires disclosure of more information about the identity of chemicals, for example, at chemical manufacturing plants or facilities.[14]

NOTES

1. 100 Stat. 1613 (1986). See Freedman, Hazardous Waste Liability (Michie, 1987) at Section 3.24.
2. See Frank, "Superfund Changes: Recent Amendments Help Plaintiffs," Trial Magazine (October 1987) at 63–66.
3. Supra note 1: Freedman, Chapter 6 thereof.
4. Supra note 1: Freedman, Section 3.24.
5. Id. at Section 14.16.
6. Note 42 U.S.C. 9604(i)(6)(B)(F); also infra note 5 at Sections 1.20 and 1.21.
7. Supra note 5 at Section 9.13.
8. Supra note 2 at 63.

9. Supra note 5 at Chapter 5.
10. 42 U.S.C. 9659(b).
11. 42 U.S.C. 9613(h).
12. Supra note 5 at Section 3.20.
13. 42 U.S.C. 9658.
14. 42 U.S.C. 9658 and supra note 2 at 65.

6.10 Insurance Company As Third Party

Insurance companies have become involved in the occupational injury, disease, and death claims as more and more attempts are made by employees to hold the employer's workers' compensation carrier liable as a third party on the basis of the nature of the employer's intentional act[1] or the dual-capacity role of the employer.[2] Insurance companies have also been pulled into litigation on the basis of their own negligence, for example, in performing safety inspections or in rendering medical services. In Nelson v. Union Wire Rope Corp.[3] the Illinois appellate court, construing the Florida Workmen's Compensation Act, imposed liability on the insurer, not on the basis of the insurance policy itself, but on the basis of the insurer's gratuitous safety inspections of the employer's equipment and safety practices, which had been negligently performed.[4] In the instant case the insurer was held liable for its negligent performance that proximately caused the injuries and death to the employee. But the altruistic ruling of the Illinois appellate court was subsequently negated by the Illinois Supreme Court holding ten years later in Reid v. Employers Mutual Liability Insurance Co.,[5] ruling that the exclusive remedy provision of the Illinois Workmen's Compensation Act precluded an action by an injured employee against his employer's insurance company for failure to make safety inspections. Shortly thereafter the Illinois legislature amended the Act to remove insurers from third-party common law liability.[6] This immunity to insurers, however, is limited to a number of states that have accepted the basic premise that the insurer and the employer are but one defendant.[7]

NOTES

1. See Section 9.10 hereinafter.
2. See Section 9.9 hereinafter.
3. 199 N.E.2d 769 (Ill. App., 1964).
4. See Baron, Handling Occupational Disease Cases (Lawpress, 1981) at 93–94. Also see Freedman, Richards on Insurance (Lawyers Coop., 1989) at Chapter 9 thereof with respect to bad faith and unfair dealing situations.
5. 319 N.E.2d 769 (Ill., 1974).
6. See Ill. Rev. Stat., ch. 48, sec. 138.5.
7. Note Matthews v. Liberty Mutual Insurance Co., 238 N.E.2d 348 (Mass., 1968), and Bartolotta v. Liberty Mutual Insurance Co., 411 F.2d 115 (2nd Cir., 1969).

7

Theories of Liability and Remedies

7.1 Introduction

One of the great principles of the common law is that the existence of any right is defined by the existence of a remedy.[1] The right to a safe workplace is today being carved out not only by decisional court law, but also by federal, state, and local statutes and by agencies of the various units of government. However, there are still the basic theories of liability and corresponding remedies, as delineated hereinafter: negligence,[2] strict liability in tort,[3] trespass,[4] nuisance,[5] concerted action or conspiracy,[6] intentional conduct or behavior,[7] enterprise liability,[8] fraud, misrepresentation, and concealment,[9] violation of statute and regulations,[10] punitive damages,[11] emotional damages,[12] vicarious liability,[13] and wrongful death actions.[14] These theories of liability are not necessarily separate and independent, for they overlap under many circumstances. The corresponding remedies expand to encompass new conduct and retract only when the Congress or state or local legislature, or the appellate courts, overrule the utilization of a particular remedy for the particular right.

Relief under the various remedies may be found before federal, state, and local administrative agencies; in litigation before federal, state, and local courts; and, to the extent that the injury, disease, or death is work-related, before the employer and the labor union involved with plant safety.

Whatever the theory of liability or the particular remedy, the employee has the burden of proof; with respect to "toxic torts," for example, the employee might have to demonstrate by a preponderance of the evidence the following: (a) an actual exposure to the hazardous substance; (b) injury, disease, or death actually did result therefrom; (c) a definitive period of time elapsed between the exposure and the onset of the injury, disease, or death; (d) there is scientific and medical recognition of the hazardous substance as a toxin capable of causing the alleged harm; (e) there is a scientific and medical acceptance of the causal relation between the toxin and the specific injury, disease, or death; (f) the exposure to the particular dosage or amount of the toxin was medically and scientifically sufficient to cause the particular injury, disease, or death; (g) the exposure did in fact cause that injury, disease, or death; and (h) other possible or alternative causes of the specific injury, disease, or death have been eliminated.[15]

NOTES

1. See Ashby v. White, 92 Eng. Rep. 126 (1703) at 136.
2. See Greer and Freedman, The Law of Toxic Torts (Prentice-Hall, 1989).
3. See section 7.2 hereinafter.
4. See section 7.3 hereinafter.
5. See section 7.4 hereinafter.
6. See section 7.5 hereinafter.
7. See section 7.6 hereinafter.
8. See section 7.7 hereinafter.
9. See section 7.8 hereinafter.
10. See section 7.9 hereinafter.
11. See section 7.10 hereinafter.
12. See section 7.11 hereinafter.
13. See section 7.12 hereinafter.
14. See section 7.13 hereinafter.
15. See, generally, Tortora and Anagnostakos, Principles of Anatomy and Physiology (1984), and Patty, Industrial Hygiene and Toxicology (3rd ed.) at Secs. 4804–4807.

7.2 The Negligence Cause of Action

Section 282 of Restatement (Second) of Torts defines negligence as ''conduct which falls below the standard established by law for the protection of others against unreasonable risk of harm.'' And Prosser sets forth the elements of a cause of action in negligence in these terms: (1) a duty or standard of conduct imposed by law; (2) defendant's failure to comply with that duty or standard; (3) sufficient causal connection between defendant's conduct and plaintiff's injury for the law to impose liability; and (4) actual loss or damage to the plaintiff.[1] In analyzing a fact situation using these four elements the uniform standard of behavior is that of the ''reasonable man'' exercising ordinary care and skill *after* first assessing the probabilities that an accident will occur, the gravity of the resulting harm if the accident does occur, and the cost, financial or otherwise, of taking adequate precautions.[2]

In La Rossa v. Scientific Design[3] the defendant contracted with decedent's employer to design, engineer, and supervise the construction and initial operation of a plant for the manufacture of phthalic anhydride. Pellets coated with vanadium were loaded into a reactor, and plaintiff alleged that her husband-employee died of cancer occasioned by his exposure to vanadium dust. The Third Circuit Court of Appeals affirmed dismissal of the breach of warranty counts because "they who hire experts . . . are not justified in expecting infallibility, but can expect only reasonable care and competence." The negligence count was also dismissed because it was equally difficult to pinpoint the professional's act of negligence.[4] Indeed, in negligence, the standard of care owed to another is only reasonable care to protect against a foreseeable and unreasonable risk of harm.[5] Because the probability of the accident was analyzed from the perspective of the reasonable person at the time of defendant's conduct under all the circumstances and "not with the wisdom born of the event,"[6] the *first* victims of the particular toxic tort are left without a remedy.

The concept of the "reasonable man" pervades common law standards of liability, and is especially useful in assessing negligence in the toxic tort situation.[7] For a plaintiff to recover, proof must be established that the defendant behaved unreasonably in causing plaintiff's exposure to the hazardous substance in question.[8] Some courts have analyzed the reasonableness of defendant's behavior retrospectively; in New Jersey v. Ventron[9] the court opined: "While the discharge of mercury might be considered unreasonable, unwarranted, or unlawful by today's standards, the actions of the defendants must be measured as of the date they occurred." Also the "reasonable man" standard must be measured by the greater social interest, such as maintaining high employment and bringing in high tax revenues, which benefits might be lost if defendant's behavior is deemed unreasonable under the circumstances.[10] It is also difficult to quantify costs and benefits when plaintiff seeks to establish defendant's liability for acting unreasonably; assigning nonmonetary values to nonpecuniary costs and benefits poses great problems.[11] Courts, in establishing what a "reasonable man" would do, must weigh factors from the realms of science, business, and politics.[12]

The cost of precautions to prevent the toxic accident can be rendered minimal by giving adequate warning of the dangers of the hazardous substance. Duty to warn means that a defendant will be liable for his or her failure to provide adequate warnings if the defendant knew or had reason to know that the substance is or is likely to be dangerous, if the defendant had no reason to believe that the public would have realized the dangerous condition of the substance, or if the defendant failed to exercise reasonable care to inform the public of the dangerous condition of the substance or of facts that made it likely to be dangerous or hazardous.[13] In Ionmar Compania v. Central of Georgia Railroad Co.[14] a powerful oxidizing agent was loaded in bulk on a ship and later ignited, causing extensive damage to the ship and cargo. The substance carried a *general* warning, but evidence revealed that, as a consumer product, the label warned of the substance's combustible characteristics, which the general warning did not. The trial court held that the magnitude of the risk mandated the more adequate warning for those who handled the substance during transportation on a ship. In Tucson Industries, Inc. v. Schwartz[15] plaintiff-employee suffered eye injuries when toxic fumes entered her workplace through the building's air conditioning system. The Arizona court opined that an adequate warning would have stated that the fumes caused blindness even in rooms separated by closed doors, and therefore caution should be taken that ventilation of the use area did not contaminate other occupied areas. But when the inadequacy or failure of the warning was not the proximate cause of the injuries, liability cannot be predicated thereon.[16]

In Ellis v. Louisville & Nashville Railroad Co.[17] plaintiff-employee sued his employer under the Federal Employees' Liability Act (FELA)[18] for damages owing to silicosis, which he contracted, allegedly because the employer did not furnish him for twenty-five years with safe tools, safe equipment, and a safe workplace. The court found the employer not guilty of negligence because the record of trial "plainly shows that the practice by railroads generally throughout the nation was not to furnish masks or respirators to men doing the same character of work plaintiff performed for defendant."[19] On the other hand, the owner or operator of a toxic dump has a solemn duty to warn all people in the entire surrounding area, regardless of custom or practice in the area.[20]

In September 1988 the Connecticut appellate court, in Hartman v. Black & Decker Manufacturing Co.,[21] was concerned with an employee who was injured while operating a radial arm saw owned by his employer and manufactured by defendant B; the employee sued both his employer and the product manufacturer on the theory of negligence. At the time of his injury plaintiff-employee was using the saw for a personal project after working hours (with the permission of his employer). The trial court rendered judgment for the plaintiff-employee against his employer only; and the appellate court agreed that the employer owed a duty of reasonable care to the plaintiff-employee, that the use of the saw constituted a bailment for the mutual benefit of the employer and the employee, and the employer as bailor was therefore under a duty to use reasonable care to ensure that the saw was reasonably safe for its intended use by the plaintiff-employee. However, if the allegedly defective radial arm saw was found to be open and obvious, the employer could not be held liable, especially since the employee had apparently removed a certain safety device from the saw. (The product manufacturer's judgment in its favor at the trial level was affirmed.)

NOTES

1. Prosser, The Law of Torts (1971) at 143–144.
2. See 9 Hofstra L. Rev. 859 (1981) at 887.
3. 402 F.2d 937 (3rd Cir., 1968).
4. Id. at 943.
5. See Borel v. Fibreboard Paper Products Corp., 493 F.2d 1076 (5th Cir., 1973), cert. den., 419 U.S. 869 (1974).

6. See Greene v. Sibley, 177 N.E. 416 (N.Y., 1931) at 417.

7. See generally 7 Harv. Environ. L. Rev. 177 (1983) at 193 et seq.

8. See 33 Vand. L. Rev. 1281 (1981) at 1296–1298.

9. 436 A.2d 893 (N.J., 1983).

10. See 4 Harv. Environ. L. Rev. 191 (1980) at 196–198.

11. See 45 Geo. Wash. L. Rev. 901 (1977) at 906 et seq.

12. See 5 Harv. Environ. L. Rev. 1 (1981).

13. See Sec. 388 of Restatement (Second) of Torts.

14. 471 F. Supp. 942 (SD Ga., 1979).

15. 501 P.2d 936 (Ariz., 1972).

16. See Martinez v. Dixie Carriers, Inc., 521 F.2d 457 (5th Cir., 1976).

17. 251 S.W.2d 577 (Ky. App., 1952).

18. See Freedman, Federal Statutes on Environmental Protection (Quorum Books, 1987) at 49–50.

19. Cf. Sadowski v. Long Island Railroad Co., 55 N.E.2d 497 (N.Y., 1950).

20. See LaPlant v. duPont, 346 S.W.2d 231 (Mo. App., 1961).

21. 16 Conn. App. 1 (September 1988).

7.3 Strict Liability in Tort

Strict Liability in Tort is a theory of liability designed to make industry, in this technologically complex age, more responsive to the public welfare by allowing private individuals to recover damages against defendants without regard to fault. Its genesis stems from the 1868 English decision in Rylands v. Fletcher[1] and from Section 402A of the Restatement (Second) of Torts in the 1960s. The English case involved a situation in which plaintiff's mine was damaged by a flood that resulted from the fact that defendants had built a reservoir on their land with water brought onto the land. Unfortunately the reservoir was located above an old mine shaft, and so the water escaped down the abandoned mine shaft and into the adjoining mine belonging to the plaintiff. There was no evidence that defendants intentionally damaged plaintiff's mine, nor was there any evidence of negligence on the part of the defendants. The English court reasoned that "the person who, for his own purposes, brings on his lands and collects there anything likely to do mischief if it escapes, must keep it at his peril, and if he does not do so, is prima facie answerable for all the damage which is the natural consequence of its escape." Strict Liability was, in effect, imposed on the landowner, regardless of fault. Section 402A of the Restatement provides:

(1) One who sells any product in a defective condition unreasonably dangerous to the user or consumer or to his property is subject to liability for physical harm thereby caused to the ultimate user or consumer, or to his property, if

    (a) the seller is engaged in the business of selling such a product, and

    (b) it is expected to and does reach the user or consumer without substantial change in the condition in which it is sold.

(2) The rule stated in Subsection (1) applies although

    (a) the seller has exercised all possible care in the preparation and sale of his product, and

    (b) the user or consumer has not bought the product from or entered into any contractual relationship with the seller.

The Restatement imposes Strict Liability on sellers of products, which includes raw materials such as asbestos,[2] and the focus is not on the conduct of the defendant, but on the condition of the product or substance.[3] Strict Liability relates only to defective and unreasonably dangerous products or substances.[4]

A court favoring Strict Liability imposed liability on the oil company whose oil escaped and caused the expenditure of funds by a municipality to prevent the spread of the oil spill.[5] The New Jersey court hailed "the diminishing quantity and quality of our environment" and the "almost unchecked development of products whose misuse or improper employment lead to disfigurement and death. . . . The law is not, or ought not to be, so feeble as to exonerate those whose conduct causes harm to others by reason of such use or abuse."[6] And in Atlas Chemical Industries, Inc. v. Anderson[7] the Texas court applied Strict Liability when the defendant was found to have deliberately dumped industrial waste on sixty acres of plaintiff's land. In Salt River Project v. Westinghouse Electric Corp.[8] plaintiff had purchased from defendant in 1970 a gas turbine generator unit. Six years later the rotating blades of one unit were destroyed in an accident, and plaintiff-project experienced damages in excess of $1.9 million. The Arizona court ruled that personal injuries suffered by an engineer at the plant were recoverable under Strict Liability, for the defect in the unit was unreasonably dangerous to person or property. And in New Jersey v. Ventron Corp.[9] the owner and operator of a mercury processing plant was held liable under Strict Liability for damages caused by mercury that flowed from the plant site to a nearby creek. Similarly, Strict Liability was applicable for pollution of a freshwater well caused by leakage of crude oil and salt water[10]; for property damage and pollution of water supply caused by spillage of a toxic chemical[11]; for pollution of creek and river caused by escape of phosphate lime[12]; for pollution of a well caused by seepage of gasoline from an underground tank;[13] and for dumping hazardous substances on plaintiff's land.[14]

Another aspect of Strict Liability pertains to "abnormally dangerous or ultrahazardous activities," as delineated in Sections 519 and 520 of the Restatement (Second) of Torts. Section 519 provides:

1   One who carries on an abnormally dangerous activity is subject to liability for harm to the person, land or chattels of another resulting from the activity, although he has exercised the utmost care to prevent the harm.
2   This strict liability is limited to the kind of harm, the possibility of which makes the activity abnormally dangerous.

Liability is not predicated on intent to do harm or on negligence; liability arises out of the nature of the activity, and Section 520 spells out the factors to be considered in determining whether an activity is abnormally dangerous or ultra-hazardous:

(a) existence of a high degree of risk of some harm to the person, land or chattels of others;

(b) likelihood that the harm that results from it will be great;

(c) inability to eliminate the risk by the exercise of reasonable care;

(d) extent to which the activity is not a matter of common usage;

(e) inappropriateness of the activity to the place where it is carried on; and

(f) extent to which its value to the community is outweighed by its dangerous attributes.

The determination lies within the province of the court and not the jury; in Doundoulakis v. Town of Hempstead[15] the New York Court of Appeals opined that defendant's hydraulic dredging and landfill operations were an abnormally dangerous activity, but remanded the case for further evidence on the factors (a), (b), and (c) of Section 520 of the Restatement. In Chavez v. Southern Pacific Transportation Co.[16] the California court ruled that the activity of transporting bombs was an ultrahazardous activity, and the railroad, as a common carrier, was not exempt from Strict Liability, although acting pursuant to a public duty at that time.

NOTES

1. L. R. 3 H.L. 330 (1868).
2. See Neal v. Carey Canadian Mines, Ltd., 548 F. Supp. 357 (ED Pa., 1982).
3. See Dougherty v. Hooker Chemical Corp., 540 F.2d 174 (3rd Cir., 1976).
4. See Greeno v. Clark Equipment Co., 237 F. Supp. 427 (Ind., 1965).
5. See City of Bridgeton v. BP Oil, Inc., 146 N.J. Super. 169, 369 A.2d 49 (1976).
6. Id. at 177–178 and 54.
7. 514 S.W.2d 309 (Tex. Cir. App., 1974).
8. 694 P.2d 198 (Ariz., 1984).
9. 182 N.J. Super. 210, 440 A.2d 455 (1981).
10. See Mowrer v. Ashland Oil & Refining Co., 518 F.2d 659 (7th Cir., 1975).
11. See Indiana HB Railroad Co. v. American Cyanamid Co., 517 F. Supp. 314 (ND Ill., 1981).
12. See Cities Service Co. v. State, 312 So.2d 799 (Fla. App., 1975).
13. See Yommer v. McKenzie, 255 Md. 220, 257 A.2d 138 (1969).
14. See Kassouf v. Harpe, 20 E.R.C. 1751 (D Fla., 1983).
15. 42 N.Y.2d 440, 368 N.E.2d 24 (1977).
16. 413 F. Supp. 1203 (ED Cal., 1976).

7.4 Trespass

At common law Trespass was a direct intrusion on another's land or property, an unauthorized entry by a person or thing or substance or pollutant resulting from a volitional act. The interest protected was the exclusive possession of the land or property in question, and the resulting liability of the trespasser was for all the harm caused by such invasion, even if such invasion was unforeseeable. There was no moral or culpability issue in the action for trespass, only a form of strict liability. By the end of the sixteenth century the English courts had fully developed the action "trespass on the case" for *indirect* invasions or entries on another's land or property.[1] But, for the indirect invasion, the landowner or property owner had to show that the invasion or entry was committed either intentionally or negligently and that the invasion or entry actually caused harm. But today that distinction has largely disappeared, as have the common law forms of action, so that the *intentional* invasion or intrusion that causes a third person or thing or pollutant to enter the land or property is liable in trespass, irrespective of whether the actor caused actual harm or whether the actor made a mistake not induced by the possessor of the land. The *unintentional* invasion or intrusion is liable in trespass only if the actor was reckless or negligent or was engaged in ultrahazardous activity; liability for the unintentional entry or invasion is limited to the harm actually caused by the entry or invasion. It would appear that modern Trespass is predicated on fault, not the protection of legal title to the land or property, when unintentional entry or invasion occurs. On the other hand, modern Trespass for intentional entry or invasion provides many excuses or nonconsensual privileges that condone intentional entry or invasion. The Restatement (Second) of Torts recognizes no fewer than twenty-one separate privileges of this sort,[2] two of the more obvious being Section 196 on Public Necessity and Section 197 on Private Necessity.[3] But there is no broadly based privilege to enter the land of another simply because, on balance, the social benefit of doing so appears to outweigh the risks of harm to the land or property of another.

There are two major considerations in determining whether an action in Trespass will lie for injury, disease, or death or for property damage or economic loss owing to the hazardous substance, to wit: (1) intent and (2) the size or mass of the intruding substance. Obviously the requisite intent is met when the actor purposely causes the consequences or when the actor knows that the consequences will occur.[4] Intent is established when plaintiff has given the defendant notice of the contamination[5] or when defendant has received constructive notice of the damage.[6] If, despite notification, the person responsible continues to allow waste to be dumped and seepage to flow from his land onto another's land, the necessary intent has been shown.[7] The second major consideration means that some courts will not allow recovery for trespass based on the invasion of "invisible particles."[8] But the majority view today, as illustrated by Martin v. Reynolds Metals Co.,[9] favors recovery even for minute particles of matter. Here plaintiffs sued in trespass, alleging that gaseous and particulate fluoride compounds from defendant's aluminum reduction plant became airborne and settled on plaintiff's farm. The Oregon Supreme Court, in 1959, after observing the poisoning of plaintiff's cattle caused by their consuming forage and water contaminated with fluoride, reflected on the holdings of other courts to the effect that causing shot from a gun to fall on the land, depositing soot and carbon from defendant's mill on the land, and causing a vibration of the soil or even the concussion of air over the land were all instances of trespass. Judge O'Connell concluded:

In this atomic age even the uneducated know the great and awful force contained in the atom and what it can do to a man's property if it is released. In fact, the now famous equation $E = mc^2$ has taught us that mass and energy are equivalents and that our concept of "things" must be reframed. If these observations on science in relation to the law of trespass should appear theoretical and unreal in the abstract, they become very practical and real to the possessor of land when the unseen force cracks the foundation of his house. The force is just as real if it is chemical in nature and must be awakened by the intervention of another agency before it does harm.

If, then, we must look to the character of the instrumentality which is used in making an intrusion upon another's land we prefer to emphasize the object's energy or force rather than its size. Viewed in this way we may define trespass as any intrusion which invades the possessor's protected interest in exclusive possession, whether that intrusion is by visible or invisible pieces of matter or by energy which can be measured only by the mathematical language of the physicist. We are of the opinion, therefore, that the intrusion of the fluoride particulates in the present case constituted a trespass.

The same Oregon court, in 1968, in Davis v. Georgia-Pacific Corp.,[10] ruled that the emanation from defendant's pulp and paper plant of "vibrations, offensive odors, fumes, gases, smoke and particulates which damage the residence and plant life" constituted Trespass, entitling plaintiff to both compensatory and punitive damages. A contrary view was taken by the New York Court of Appeals, in 1954, in Phillips v. Sun Oil Co.,[11] when, even though the defendant may have intentionally discharged pollutants on his land, no liability ensued in the absence of knowledge that subterranean currents or other conditions would carry the contaminants onto plaintiff's property or land.

In tort law the lowest duty is owed to a trespasser, who is defined as "a person who enters or remains upon land in the possession of another without a privilege to do so created by the possessor's consent or otherwise."[12] The duty owed to the trespasser is, however, far greater than simply refraining from intentional, willful, or wanton infliction of injury or damage.[13] The duty to the trespasser varies from jurisdiction to jurisdiction, and depends on such factors as whether the presence of the trespasser is known, whether he or she is an adult or child, and whether the Trespass is on a limited portion of the land frequently trespassed by a number of people.[14]

NOTES

1. See 31 Columbia L. Rev. 778 (1931) and 46 Yale L.J. 1142 (1937).

2. *"Privileges Arising Irrespective of Any Transaction Between the Parties:*

191. Use of premises of public utility

192. Use of public highway

193. Use of navigable stream . . .

195. Deviation from public highway

196. Public necessity

197. Private necessity

198. Entry to reclaim goods on land without wrong of actor

199. Entry on another's land to relieve actor's land of goods without his wrong

200. Entry to reclaim, or to relieve land of, goods which are where they are by wrong of actor

201. Entry to abate private nuisance

202. Abatement of public nuisance by public official

203. Abatement of public nuisance by private person

204. Entry to arrest for criminal offense

205. Entry to recapture or to prevent crime and in related situations

206. Forcible entry of dwelling to arrest, recapture, prevent crime, and related situations

207. Entry to assist in making arrest or other apprehension

208. Entry to execute civil process against occupant of land

209. Entry to execute civil process against non-occupant of land

210. Entry pursuant to order of court

211. Entry pursuant to legislative duty or authority."

3. "§196. Public Necessity. One is privileged to enter land in the possession of another if it is, or if the actor reasonably believes it to be, necessary for the purpose of averting an imminent public disaster.

"§197. Private Necessity

(1) One is privileged to enter or remain on land in the possession of another if it is or reasonably appears to be necessary to prevent serious harm to
   (a) the actor, or his land or chattels, or
   (b) the other or a third person, or the land or chattels of either, unless the actor knows or has reason to know that the one for whose benefit he enters is unwilling that he shall take such action.

(2) Where the entry is for the benefit of the actor or a third person, he is subject to liability for any harm done in the exercise of the privilege stated in Subsection (1) to any legally protected interest of the possessor in the land or connected with it, except where the threat of harm to avert which the entry is made is caused by the tortious conduct or contributory negligence of the possessor."

4. Note Section 825 of Restatement (Second) of Torts.

5. See Curry Coal Co. v. Arnoni Co., 439 Pa. 114, 266 A.2d 678 (1970).

6. See Furrer v. Talest Irrigation District, 258 Ore. 494, 466 P.2d 605 (1971).

7. Supra note 5 at 119 or 683.

8. See Prosser on Torts (4th ed., 1971) at 66.

9. 221 Or. 86, 342 P.2d 790 (1959), cert. den., 362 U.S. 918 (1960).

10. 251 Or. 239, 445 P.2d 181 (1968).

11. 307 N.Y. 328, 121 N.E.2d 249 (1954) at 331 and 251.

12. Section 329 of Restatement (Second) of Torts.

13. See 63 Yale L.J. 144 (1953).

14. See IMRE v. Riegel Paper Corp., 24 N.J. 438, 132 A.2d 505 (1957).

7.5 Nuisance

Like Trespass, Nuisance focuses on the invasion of plaintiff's property rights rather than on the nature of defendant's activities; but unlike Trespass, Nuisance, at least private nuisance, delineates not the invasion of the possessory interest in the land, but the use and enjoyment of one's land. Nuisance covers a broader range of invasions than Trespass; Nuisance requires that the invasion or intrusion, or entry, be negligent, unreasonable, or intentional[1]: in Associated Metals & Minerals Corp. v. Dixon Chemical & Research Inc.[2] the defendant was found to have intentionally allowed sulfur dust to escape from its property, and in Worthen & Aldrich v. White Spring Paper Co.[3] the defendant was held to be negligent in discharging cotton fiber into a stream. The apparently conflicting elements of negligence and intentional conduct (as well as operation of an ultrahazardous activity[4]), which constitute the basis of Nuisance, prompted Dean Prosser to remark: "There is perhaps no more impenetrable jungle in the entire law than that which surrounds the word 'nuisance.' "[5] And, furthermore, the private nuisance must be distinguished from the public nuisance, for the latter, as defined by Section 821B of the Restatement (Second) of Torts is "an unreasonable interference with a right common to the general public," while "the essence of a private nuisance is an unreasonable interference with the use and enjoyment of land."[6]

The private nuisance is by far a more important body of law than public nuisance, for both toxic torts (and hazardous waste disposal) have their roots in the protection of private interests in the use and enjoyment of one's land or property.[7] Private nuisance is defined in Section 821D of the Restatement (Second) of Torts as "a non-trespassory invasion of another's interest in the private use and enjoyment of land"; that is, private nuisance does not require a physical entry like Trespass. An early English decision, William Aldred's Case,[8] dated 1611, illustrates the function of the private nuisance in the legal system: here plaintiff brought an action on the case against the defendant, alleging that the stench from defendant's hog sty next door constituted a substantial interference with plaintiff's use and enjoyment of his land. On appeal from a judgment in favor of the plaintiff, the defendant argued that "the building of the house for hogs was necessary for the sustenance of man; and one ought not to have so delicate a nose that he cannot bear the smell of hogs." King's Bench then affirmed judgment for the defendant by balancing the utility of defendant's conduct with the mild discomfort of plaintiff in the use and enjoyment of his land. Reaching a similar conclusion was the 1977 decision of the New York Court of Appeals in Copart Industries Inc. v. Consolidated Edison Co.[9]: here a firm engaged in a new-car preparation business sued the utility because its emissions into the air pitted and discolored the new paint on the automobiles, and the jury found in favor of the utility, which verdict the court affirmed, finding that private nuisance based on negligence permitted a defense of contributory negligence.[10]

The negligence element in the law of private nuisance is also illustrated by St. Louis–San Francisco Railway Co. v. Wade,[11] which involved the encroachment of a rockslide on a railroad's right of way; judgment in favor of the quarry operator whose dynamiting caused the slide was reversed because "the reasonableness of a plaintiff's expectation to be free from the interference with the use and enjoyment of his land" must be respected.[12] In Gabaldon v. Sanchez[13] defendant allegedly caused the stripping of natural vegetation from the land with the resultant blowing of sand and dirt onto plaintiff's property. The New Mexico court found that the defendant was not acting unlawfully in attempting to improve the land for subdivision purposes, for defendant has the "legal right to remove brush and vegetation . . . and was not negligent in removing them." The court, in finding the defendant not negligent, remarked that the defendant as a "landowner does not know which way the wind blows."[14]

When the private nuisance is said to involve the element of intent, plaintiff must show that defendant created or continued the nuisance condition with full knowledge that harm to plaintiff's use and enjoyment of his land was almost certain to follow.[15] In Waschak v. Moffat,[16] in which gas or fumes from culm banks, the refuse of a coal breaker, damaged the paint on plaintiff's dwelling, the Pennsylvania court found no such intent to harm, and concluded that the utility of defendant's conduct clearly outweighed the gravity of the harm thereby caused:

In applying [the law of nuisance] it is evident the invasion of plaintiff's land was clearly *not intentional.* And even if it were, for the reasons above stated, it was not unreasonable. On the contrary, since the emission of gases was not caused by an act of defendants and arose merely from the normal and customary use of their land without negligence, recklessness or ultrahazardous conduct, it was wholly *unintentional,* and no liability may therefore be imposed upon the defendants.[17]

In Wright v. Masonite Corp.[18] the Fourth Circuit Court of Appeals pointed out that where a dump site owner knew nothing of the harm that a plaintiff suffered after the dumping occurred and where the dump site owner received no prior complaints, the plaintiff had little chance of establishing that defendant's acts were intentional; therefore, the alleged private nuisance was actionable.

Because private nuisance cases have equity origins, courts have used equitable remedies in balancing the harm against the use and enjoyment of the land.

In Boomer v. Atlantic Cement Co.[19] a bare majority of the New York Court of Appeals balanced the harms to plaintiff's property caused by the dirt, smoke, and vibration emanating from defendant's cement plant against the value of defendant's activities which represented an investment in excess of $45 million and gave employment to more than 300 persons. The court refused to grant a permanent injunction, although it awarded plaintiff the sum of $185,000 in permanent damages. The court reviewed the technological, economic, and political facets of the problem, and emphasized the difficulties courts had in coming to grips with issues of air pollution in private litigation:

Effective control of air pollution is a problem presently far from solution even with the full public and financial powers of government. In large measure adequate technical procedures are yet to be developed and some that appear possible may be economically impracticable. It seems apparent that the amelioration of air pollution will depend on technical research in great depth; on a carefully balanced consideration of the economic impact of close regulation; and on the actual effect on public health. It is likely to require massive public expenditure and to demand more than any local community can accomplish and to depend on regional and interstate controls. A court should not try to do this on its own as a by-product of private litigation and it seems manifest that the judicial establishment is neither equipped in the limited nature of any judgment it can pronounce nor prepared to lay down and implement an effective policy for the elimination of air pollution. This is an area beyond the circumference of one private lawsuit. It is a direct responsibility for government and should not thus be undertaken as an incident to solving a dispute between property owners and a single cement plant.[20]

A Pennsylvania court the very next year, in Folmar v. Eliot Coal Mining Co.,[21] held that an actor's conduct will lack utility if it is economically and technically feasible to correct the harm and such action is not taken.[22] In the case of illegal dumping there is obviously a complete absence of social utility,[23] so that the private or public nuisance is actionable.

To maintain an action for private nuisance there must be a substantial interference with the use and enjoyment of the land, which finding must attest to the fact that plaintiff suffered physical effects as a result of the odors or leachate from a chemical dump site.[24] Some courts require that the action creating the private nuisance be continuing and not simply a "one-shot" or single incident.[25] Indeed, the duration and recurrence of the interference is a factor in determining the substantiality of the damage.[26] The Restatement (Second) of Torts recognizes the importance of the gravity of the harm and delineates at least five factors involved in assessing the gravity of harm from an intentional invasion of another's interest in the use and enjoyment of land.[27] The unreasonableness of the intentional invasion[28] and the utility of conduct factors[29] are also delineated in the Restatement; the invasion of the plaintiff's interest will be found to be unreasonable when the defendant's conduct is malicious or indecent,[30] when the resulting invasion could have been avoided by the defendant's relatively easy conduct,[31] or when the plaintiff's use of his land is, and the defendant's conduct is not, suited to the locality in which the invasion occurred.[32] A new Section 829A spells out "gravity v. utility," and sanctions liability on the independent ground that the plaintiff cannot financially afford to go without a remedy.

The *public* nuisance, in contrast to the private nuisance, is "an unreasonable interference with a right common to the general public."[33] Public nuisance had its origins in criminal interferences with the rights of the Crown, and therefore, it need not necessarily involve interference with interests in land.[34] Section 821C of the Restatement (Second) of Torts provides for individual suits based on a public nuisance,[35] as illustrated by actions for the pollution of both ground and surface waters,[36] although plaintiff must prove some "particular, direct and substantial injury" apart from that suffered by the public as a whole, if plaintiff is to recover individual damages.[37] In Burgess v. M/V Tamano[38] the federal district court in Maine found that commercial fishermen and clam diggers had alleged sufficiently particular damages resulting from an oil spill to support a private action for a public nuisance, but the court denied recovery to local businessmen on the ground that their losses were common to all businesses and residents of the area. In Bishop Processing Co. v. Davis[39] a Maryland court ruled that the operation of a plant processing chicken feathers, offal, viscera, blood, heads, feet, beef bones, and other similar by-products into poultry feeds and fertilizers was a public nuisance, and that plaintiffs who owned adjoining realty had shown sufficient discomfort to themselves and injury to their property to entitle them to injunctive relief and damages; also, the court ruled that it was not necessary for plaintiffs to prove that their damages were different in character from that sustained by the public generally.

The federal common law of nuisance was, in effect, created by the U.S. Supreme Court to resolve interstate water pollution and interstate air pollution disputes in the absence of a relevant federal statutory scheme.[40] In 1972 the Court applied a federal common law of nuisance in Illinois v. City of Milwaukee (Milwaukee I)[41] in which Illinois sued defendant for discharging inadequately treated sewerage into Lake Michigan; the Court ruled that the remedy sought was not within the scope of 1972 federal water pollution laws, and remanded the case for consideration of the federal common law of nuisance. But in 1981 in City of Milwaukee v. Illinois (Milwaukee II),[42] the Court held that the Federal Water Pollution Control Act (FWPCA) preempted the federal common law of nuisance in the area of interstate water pollution. Here the appellate court had applied the federal common law of nuisance to enjoin the discharge of raw sewerage into Lake Michigan, but the U.S. Supreme Court insisted that the use of the federal common law of nuisance was "peculiarly inappropriate."[43] In Middlesex County Sewerage Authority v. National Sea Clammers Assn.[44] the highest court again reiterated that the federal common law of nuisance in the area of ocean pollution had been fully preempted by various federal statutes that afforded no private remedies. However, in Weinberger v. Romero-Barcelo,[45] the U.S. Supreme Court, in 1982, allowed the federal district court to balance the equities as if the federal common law of nuisance was applicable, with the result that the U.S. Navy's discharge of ordnance without a permit was allowed to continue, without monitoring or reporting requirements. A pivotal point not to be overlooked is the typical "savings clause," such as Section 505(e) of the FWPCA,[46] which states that "nothing in this section shall restrict any right which any person (or class of persons) may have under any statute or common law . . . or to seek any other relief." One possible solution to resurrect the federal common law of nuisance in such situations in which federal statutes allegedly preempt the field is for the state, under the parens patriae doctrine,[47] to bring suit; a state's interest in protecting its natural resources has long been recognized.[48] The concept of a parens patriae claim is closely analogous to the notion of public nuisance, for it usually involves the health and welfare of the community as a whole.[49] It should be noted that the U.S. Supreme Court, in 1984, in Silkwood v. Kerr-McGee Corp.,[50] held that the Atomic Energy Act did not preempt a state-authorized award of punitive damages for injuries arising out of the escape of plutonium from a nuclear facility that was licensed by and subject to regulation by the Nuclear Regulatory Commission under the Act. More broadly, the Act did not preempt remedies that a person has under state law.[51]

NOTES

1. See Section 822 of Restatement (Second) of Torts: "§822. General Rule. One is subject to liability for a private nuisance if, but only if, his conduct is a legal cause of an invasion of another's interest in the private use and enjoyment of land, and the invasion is either

(a) Intentional and unreasonable, or
(b) Unintentional and otherwise actionable under the principles controlling liability for negligent or reckless conduct, or for abnormally dangerous conditions or activities."

2. 82 N.J. Super. 281, 197 A.2d 569 (1964).
3. 74 N.J. Eg. 647, 70 A. 468 (1908), aff.
4. 75 N.J. Eg. 624, 78 A. 1135 (1909).
5. See generally 12 Rutgers L. Rev. 117 (1980) at 126–127.
6. Prosser, Law of Torts (4th ed., 1971) at 571.
7. See Sans v. Ramsey Golf & Country Club, Inc., 29 N.J. 438, 149 A.2d 599 (1959).
8. 9 Co. Rep. 57, 77 Eg. Rep. 816 (1611).
9. 41 N.Y.2d 564, 362 N.E.2d 968 (1977).
10. Id. at 565 and 571, and 969 and 973.
11. 607 F.2d 126 (5th Cir., 1979).
12. Id. at 132.
13. 92 N.M. 224, 585 P.2d 1105 (1978).
14. Id. at 228 and 1109.
15. Infra note 22 at 574.
16. 379 Pa. 441, 109 A.2d 310 (1954).

17. Id. Justice Musmanno's dissent concluded: "If there were no other way of disposing of the coal refuse, a different question might have been presented here, but the defendants produced no evidence that they could not have deposited the debris in places removed from the residential districts in Taylor. Certainly, many of the strip-mining craters which uglify the countryside in the areas close to Taylor could have been utilized by the defendants. They chose, however, to use the residential sections of Taylor because it was cheaper to pile the culm there than to haul it away into less populous territory. This was certainly an unreasonable and selfish act in no way indispensably associated with the operation of the breaker. It brought greater profits to the defendants but at the expense of the health and the comfort of the other landowners in the town who are also entitled to the pursuit of happiness."

18. 368 F.2d 661 (4th Cir., 1966), cert. den. 87 S. Ct. 957 (1967).

19. 26 N.Y.2d 219, 257 N.E.2d 870 (1970).

20. Id.

21. 441 Pa. 592, 272 A.2d 910 (1971).

22. Id. at 596 and 912.

23. See Benton v. Kernan, 130 N.J. Eg. 193, 21 A.2d 755 (1941), and 12 Rutgers L. Rev. 117 (1980) at 127.

24. See, for example, Wood v. Picillo, 433 A.2d 1244 (R.I., 1982).

25. See Snellie v. Continental Oil Co., 127 F. Supp. 508 (D Colo., 1954).

26. Supra note 6 at 580.

27. "§827. Gravity of Harm—Factors Involved. In determining the gravity of the harm from an intentional invasion of another's interest in the use and enjoyment of land, the following factors are important:

(a) the extent of the harm involved;
(b) the character of the harm involved;
(c) the social value which the law attaches to the type of use or enjoyment invaded;
(d) the suitability of the particular use or enjoyment invaded to the character of the locality;
(e) the burden on the person harmed of avoiding the harm."

28. "§826. Unreasonableness of Intentional Invasion. An intentional invasion of another's interest in the use and enjoyment of land is unreasonable if

(a) the gravity of the harm outweighs the utility of the actor's conduct, or
(b) the harm caused by the conduct is serious and the financial burden of compensating for this and similar harm to others would not make the continuation of the conduct not feasible."

29. "§828. Utility of Conduct—Factors Involved. In determining the utility of conduct that causes an intentional invasion of another's interest in the use and enjoyment of land, the following factors are important:

(a) the social value that the law attaches to the primary purpose of the conduct;
(b) the suitability of the conduct to the character of the locality; and
(c) the impracticability of preventing or avoiding the invasion."

30. Section 829 thereof.

31. Section 830 thereof.

32. Section 831 thereof.

33. "§821B. Public Nuisance

(1) A public nuisance is an unreasonable interference with a right common to the general public.

(2) Factors conducing toward a determination that an interference with a public right is unreasonable, include the following:

(a) the circumstance that the conduct involves the kind of interference with the public health, the public safety, the public peace, the public comfort or the public convenience which sufficed to constitute the common law crime of public nuisance,

(b) the circumstance that the conduct is proscribed by a statute, ordinance or administrative regulation, or

(c) the circumstance that the conduct is of a continuing nature or has produced a permanent or long-lasting effect, that its detrimental effect upon the public right is substantial, and that the actor knows or has reason to know of that effect.''

34. Cf. City of Miami v. City of Coral Gables, 233 So.2d 7 (Fla. Ct. App., 1970).

35. ''§821C. Who Can Recover for Public Nuisance

(1) In order to recover damages in an individual action for a public nuisance, one must have suffered harm of a kind different from that suffered by other members of the public exercising the public right which was the subject of interference.

(2) In order to maintain a proceeding to enjoin or abate a public nuisance, one must

(a) be qualified to sue for damages, as indicated in subsection (1)

(b) have authority as a public official or public agency to represent in such matters the state or a political subdivision, or

(c) have standing to sue as a representative of the general public, or as a citizen in a citizen's action, or as a member of a class in a class action.''

36. See Anstee v. Monroe Light & Fuel Co., 171 Wis. 291, 177 N.W. 26 (1920), and Bouquet v. Hackensack Water Co., 90 N.J. L. 203, 101 A. 379 (1917).

37. Supra note 16, Bouquet case at 204 and 379.

38. 370 F. Supp. 247 (D Me., 1973), aff. 559 F.2d 1200 (1st Cir., 1977).

39. 213 Md. 465, 132 A.2d 445 (1957).

40. See Missouri v. Illinois, 200 U.S. 496 (1906) on water pollution, and note Texas v. Pankey, 441 F.2d 236 (10th Cir., 1971).

41. 406 U.S. 91 (1972).

42. 451 U.S. 304 (1981).

43. Id. at 325.

44. 453 U.S. 1 (1981).

45. 456 U.S. 305 (1982).

46. 33 U.S.C. 1365(e).

47. See Wyoming v. Colorado, 286 U.S. 494 (1932) at 509, for example.

48. See New York v. New Jersey, 256 U.S. 296 (1921) at 301–302.

49. See generally 34 Syracuse L. Rev. 619 (1983) at 646 et seq. Note Committee for the Consideration of the Jones Falls Sewerage System v. Train, 375 F. Supp. 1148 (D Md., 1974).

50. 104 S. Ct. 615 (1984).

51. See generally 12 Environ. Law 1059 (1982).

7.6 Conspiracy or Concerted Action

Still another theory of liability in the toxic tort situation is Conspiracy or Concerted Action. According to Prosser, ''all those who, in pursuance of a common plan or design to commit a tortious act, actively take part in it, or further it by cooperation, or who lend aid or encouragement to the wrongdoer, or ratify and adopt his acts done for their benefit"[1] are jointly and severally liable. When plaintiff cannot trace pollutants from the defendant's factories to the atmosphere in his area, or when plaintiff is unsure how persuasive his evidence will be in doing so, plaintiff can set forth a Conspiracy or Concert of Action theory of liability because under this theory, plaintiff need not prove which defendant's products was the cause in fact of the harm: "Liability is imposed on all because all have joined in breaching their duty of care to the plaintiff."[2] Indeed, a common plan or design may be implied from the conduct of the defendants; even negligent conduct in the form of advice or encouragement to act can make one defendant a member of the conspiracy or concerted action, and therefore liable for the consequences.[3] In Wright v. Tudor City[4] all people involved in contamination of groundwater, including the person who owned the pollutants and the owner of the land through which the pollutants passed, may be jointly liable under the doctrine of having acted in concert. It was no defense that they had provided the chemical wastes to an independent contractor for disposal or had merely leased the land for a dump.

Related to the liability for Conspiracy or Concert of Action is the concept of Alternative Liability, to wit: if two or more persons each act tortiously, independently of another, and one of them causes injury to the plaintiff but the plaintiff cannot identify which person did so, joint and several liability will be imposed on all tortfeasors except those who can absolve themselves.[5] Plaintiff must join in the action all the tortfeasors and show that each acted tortiously toward him.

Enterprise Liability, or Industrywide Liability (which is in reality an amalgam of Concert of Action and Alternative Liability theories), was proposed but not imposed in Hall v. du Pont,[6] probably because the exploding caps industry was not closely regulated nor a tight-knit industry composed of a small number of members.[7] Enterprise Liability imposes liability on businesses for those risks generated by the operation of the business; the federal district court in New York, in the Hall case, mentioned water pollution and air pollution as areas in which the risks could be foreseen and guarded against on an industrywide level.[8] Acid rain, for example, is a risk generated by the operation of power plants and smelters, and Enterprise Liability conceivably can be applicable because acid rain is the result of a business-generated risk. The risk is best ascertained by the industry working together, and the risk is best resolved or avoided by the industry working together.[9]

Several mills that polluted a stream were held, in 1926, jointly liable,[10] an early recognition of Enterprise Liability. But Market Share Liability, as epitomized by Sindell v. Abbott Laboratories,[11] is probably the most popular example of liability on defendants acting together: each defendant is liable for a percentage of plaintiff's damages equal to that defendant's share of the market of that particular hazardous substance.

Applying Conspiracy or Concerted Action or any of the theories of liability above has one distinct advantage, in that theory of liability shifts the burden of proof to the defendants. Such theories of liability are comparable to res ipsa loquitur, which establishes an inference of negligence subject to rebuttal by the defendant affirmatively showing that his conduct was not negligent.

From the viewpoint of the occupational injury, disease, and death complaint, the plaintiff-employee might allege that the defendants conspired to hide the hazardous character of their machinery or products. It might be shown that the employer conspired with a trade association or another employer, and that such occupational injury, disease, or death was freely discussed.[12]

NOTES

1. Note Section 876 of Restatement (Second) of Torts.
2. See Abel v. Eli Lilly & Co., 94 Mich. App. 59, 289 N.W.2d 20 (1979) at 72 and 25.
3. Note Bichler v. Eli Lilly & Co., 55 N.Y.2d 571, 436 N.E.2d 182 (1982).
4. 276 N.Y. 303 (1938).
5. See Summers v. Tice, 33 Cal. 2d 80, 199 P.2d 1 (1948).
6. 345 F. Supp. 353 (ED N.Y. 1972).
7. Id. at 378.
8. Id. at 377–378.
9. Id. at 376–378.
10. See Moses v. Town of Morgantown, 192 N.C. 102, 133 S.E. 421 (1926).
11. 26 Cal. 3d 588, 607 P.2d 924 (1980), cert. den., 449 U.S. 912 (1980).
12. See Baron, Handling Occupational Disease Cases (Lawpress, 1981) at 121.

7.7 Intentional Conduct or Behavior

Intentional conduct or behavior by employers, even in the course of employment will generally furnish a basis for the injured employee to avoid the exclusivity of workers' compensation.[1] As stated in Richardson v. The Fair,[2] "an employer cannot correct and punish with whips the mistakes of his employees committed in the course of employment, and protect himself against civil liability for the results of his assaults under the coverage of our Workmen's Compensation Act." When the employer intentionally injures the employee or subjects the employee intentionally to an exposure resulting in an occupational disease, the employer cannot logically or truthfully label the injury, disease, or death as an "accident," and therefore covered by the workers' compensation law.[3] More basically, an intentional tort does not constitute the risk of employment so as to be included within the exclusive remedy provision of the workers' compensation statutes. In Barnes v. Chrysler Corp.[4] the employees in 1945 were beaten up after being imprisoned for hours by plant guards of the employer; there was no way that their injuries could be covered by workers' compensation!

Negligence of the employer does not amount to intentional conduct or behavior, unless the negligence is found to be gross, wanton, and willful misconduct.[5] Yet, in Santiago v. Brill Monfort Co.,[6] the New York court ruled that allegations that the employer had intentionally removed safety guards from machinery to increase production and profits did not constitute such gross, wanton, and willfull behavior as to overcome the exclusivity of workers' compensation. The employer's behavior was not a conscious indifference to the physical safety of employees; it was not so outrageous that an intent to injure employees could be inferred.[7] But when the employer willfully and deliberately allowed the decedent to work under an overhanging bank that the employer knew was about to, and did in fact, collapse, the West Virginia court ruled that the employer's conduct was sufficient to overcome the exclusivity of workers' compensation.[8] The spiteful conduct of an employer requiring an employee to immerse his hands in an acid bath was held, in Fowler v. Southern Wire & Iron Co.,[9] believe it or not, to be shielded by the Georgia Workmen's Compensation Act!

For an interesting example of a case in which the exclusivity of workers' compensation did not preclude a suit for intentional wrongs, see Millison v. du Pont,[10] decided by the New Jersey Supreme Court in 1985.

NOTES

1. See Baron, Handling Occupational Disease Cases (Lawpress, 1981) at 48.
2. 124 S.W.2d 885 (Tex. Civ. App., 1939) at 886.
3. See Readinger v. Gottschall, 191 A.2d 694 (Pa., 1963).
4. 65 F. Supp. 806 (ND Ill., 1946).
5. See Larson, Workers' Compensation Section 68.13.
6. 176 N.E.2d 835 (N.Y., 1961), aff., 205 N.Y.S.2d 266 (1962).
7. Note 4 B.C. Ind. & Comp. L. Rev. 555 (1963) at 563–564.
8. See Collins v. Dravo Contracting Co., 171 S.E. 757 (W. Va., 1933); also supra note 1 at 51.
9. 122 S.E.2d 157 (Ga. App., 1961).
10. 501 A.2d 505 (N.J., 1985).

7.8 Enterprise Liability

When the employee sustains occupational injury, disease, or death from some unidentified source or unidentified substance, as in the case of a long-term exposure to asbestos or chemicals, liability against the employer and others might be predicated on the theory of Enterprise Liability. In Hall v. du Pont[1] the injured plaintiffs joined the entire blasting industry plus its trade association as defendants. There was evidence that the defendants had adhered to an industrywide standard concerning the safety features in the manufacture and design of blasting caps that caused the injuries to the employees. The federal court in New York ruled that if plaintiffs could establish that the blasting caps were manufactured by one of the defendants, the burden of proof as to causation would immediately shift to all defendants. The industrywide standard itself, therefore, became the cause of the injuries to the plaintiffs.[2] Thus, since each industry member had adhered to the standard, each member contributed to the injuries of the plaintiffs. It therefore becomes "more probable than not that the caps involved in the accident were the products of the named defendant manufacturers." In Bichler v. Eli Lilly & Co.[3] the New York court accepted the Enterprise Liability theory of liability to relieve the plaintiff of the difficult burden of identifying the product that allegedly caused the injury.

NOTES

1. 345 F. Supp. 353 (ED N.Y., 1972).
2. See Warren Freedman, International Products Liability (Kluwer, 1987) at Section 1.17.
3. 436 N.Y.S.2d 625 (New York County, 1979); see also 55 N.Y.2d 571, 436 N.E.2d 182 (1982).

7.9 Fraud, Misrepresentation, and Concealment

Another theory of liability, as well as remedy, turns about the varying shades of fraud misrepresentation (i.e., fraudulent or deceitful, negligent, and innocent or nonfault and concealment or nondisclosure).[1] The essence of such tort liability is that one who commits fraud, misrepresents, or conceals and thereby harms another must respond in damages. Courts must trace the fine line that separates hard, effective bargaining or negotiation from actionable fraud, misrepresentation, and actionable concealment. This task is made more difficult by the unreliability of morality as a guide, for there are situations in which courts impose liability even when the fraud, misrepresentation, or concealment was innocent, and there are situations in which recovery is denied even when the plaintiff can show that he was willfully misled. Misrepresentation and concealment overlap a number of other bases of tort liability as well as contract liability: the writ of deceit, out of which the modern law of misrepresentation and concealment developed, was an English remedy in the thirteenth century that later became the general common law remedy for fraudulent acts of any kind resulting in actual harm.[2] Many of the early cases on deceit were actions based on breach of contract warranties, and not until 1789 did English courts allow recovery by third persons not in privy with the tortfeasor.[3]

The basic elements today of the tort of Fraudulent Misrepresentation, or deceit, are set forth by the Utah Supreme Court in Pace v. Parrish[4] as follows:

This being an action in *deceit* based on fraudulent misrepresentations, the burden was upon plaintiffs to prove all of the essential elements thereof. These are: (1) That a representation was made; (2) concerning a presently existing material fact; (3) which was false; (4) which the representor either (a) knew to be false, or (b) made recklessly, knowing that he had insufficient knowledge upon which to base such representation; (5) for the purpose of inducing the other party to act upon it; (6) that the other party, acting reasonably and in ignorance of its falsity; (7) did in fact rely upon it; (8) and was thereby induced to act; (9) to his injury and damage.[5]

Sections 526 and 557A of the Restatement (Second) of Torts abbreviate the elements of Fraudulent Misrepresentation as (1) a misrepresentation of fact; (2) defendant's knowledge or belief that his or her representation is false or the absence of belief that his or her representation is true (i.e., scienter); (3) defendant's intention to induce the plaintiff to act or refrain from action in reliance on the misrepresentation; (4) plaintiff's justifiable reliance on the misrepresentation; and (5) damage or loss caused by such reliance. It would appear that the definition of Fraudulent Misrepresentation by the Utah Supreme Court put greater emphasis on the "materiality" of the fact and the requisite finding that the misrepresentation was indeed false. In Chatham Furnace Co. v. Moffat[6] the fraudulent misrepresentation was defendant's statement that there was a large quantity of iron ore in his land "uncovered and ready to be taken out and visible when the ore bed was free from water and debris," in order to induce plaintiff to lease the land. Defendant's survey report had not been verified, and the Supreme Judicial Court of Massachusetts, in 1888, ruled that "if under the circumstances he chose to take it upon himself to say that he knew that the mass of ore which had been discovered was in his ore bed, in reliance upon a plan which he knew was not fully verified, it might properly be found that the charge of fraudulent misrepresentation was sustained."[7] In 1982 a federal district court in Pennsylvania authorized punitive damages for fraudulent misrepresentation, on the grounds that the defendant continually failed to warn users of hazards associated with the inhalation of asbestos fibers for the purpose of inducing plaintiffs to continue to use the asbestos fibers.[8]

Negligent Misrepresentation consists of the failure to use reasonable care in ascertaining the accuracy of information or in the manner of communicating that information. Plaintiff must show reliance on that false or misleading information to have been reasonable[9]; in English v. Lehigh City Authority[10] reliance on a list of hazardous work omitting sewerage sampling was not only not established, but even if it were, the reliance would not have been reasonable. In United States v. Aretz[11] the court ruled that the United States could be held liable for negligent misrepresentation in reclassifying an illuminant from a fire hazard to an explosive and then failing to communicate the reclassification to its defense contractor. As a result of the negligent misrepresentation, twenty-nine employees of the contractor were killed and fifty employees of the contractor were injured when a fire broke out in a building in which loose illuminant material exploded.

Innocent or Nonfault Misrepresentation is a counterpart of the commercial law theory of express warranty; it is delineated under Section 402B of the

Restatement (Second) of Torts as a liability against sellers of chattels, despite the absence of contractual privity, for misrepresentation of a material fact that engenders consumer reliance, even though the representation is not fraudulent or negligent.[12] The innocent misrepresentation requires no culpability and is actionable if it turns out to be false or misleading in fact, so long as the plaintiff has reasonably relied thereon.[13] One example is the totally inadequate warning, as illustrated by Borel v. Fibreboard Paper Products Corp.,[14] in which the Fifth Circuit Court of Appeals observed that the label on asbestos products conveyed "no idea of the extent of the danger"[15] of fatal mesothelioma or asbestosis from inhalation of asbestos fibers. However, in Berkebile v. Brantly Helicopter Corp.,[16] the court refused to impose liability for nonfault or innocent misrepresentation, finding that references in a brochure to a "safe, dependable helicopter" were only "puffing."[17] And in Adkins v. Ford Motor Co.[18] the Sixth Circuit Court of Appeals denied a Section 402B claim because plaintiff's evidence about defendant's sales materials and other dealings concerning the truck revealed "no evidence of any assurance of quality in any particularity."[19]

Concealment and nondisclosure are also theories of liability, and can be illustrated by such asbestos decisions as Pitts v. Unarco Industries,[20] in which the Seventh Circuit Court of Appeals held that "passive silence . . . is insufficient to trigger the fraudulent concealment doctrine, absent allegations that the defendants were in a continuing fiduciary relationship with the plaintiff."[21] In Teklinsky v. Ottawa Silica Corp.[22] the court ruled that defendant's deliberate concealment of the plaintiff's medical condition, including the results of the company physician's examination and x-rays, constituted actionable concealment as a separate cause of action that was not barred by the exclusive remedy provisions of the Workers' Compensation Disability Act. And in Johns-Manville Products Corp. v. Contra Costa Superior Court[23] the court ruled that the injury resulting from the aggravation of the disease caused by defendant's fraudulent concealment of the employee's condition stated a separate cause of action in tort. In Delamotte v. Unitcast Division[24] the plaintiff, who had been employed by defendant for thirty years, alleged that x-rays taken by defendant as part of periodic physical examinations of employees revealed the existence of pneumoconiosis, but defendant fraudulently concealed that fact from plaintiff. The trial court in Ohio granted summary judgment for the defendant on the exclusivity of the workmen's compensation statute, but the appellate court reversed, holding that such fraudulent concealment or nondisclosure was an intentional tort by the employer that did not fall within the exclusivity provisions of the statute.

Harm to an employee resulting from the employer's fraud, misrepresentation, or concealment is not the type of "accident" arising out of and in the course of employment that should be remedied exclusively by workers' compensation.[25] In Johns-Manville Products Corp. v. Superior Court[26] the California court permitted recovery directly from the employer when the employer had deceived the employee into believing that the workplace was safe and that there was no risk, when in fact the workplace was unsafe and the employee was at substantial risk. The theory on which recovery was based was simply that the contract of employment was violated, and therefore the remedy of workers' compensation does not provide protection to the employee.

NOTES

1. See Warren Freedman, The Business Tort of Fraud and Misrepresentation (Butterworth, 1988).
2. See 1 Street Foundations of Legal Liability (1906) at 375–376.
3. See Pasley v. Freeman, 100 Eng. Rep. 450 (1789).
4. 122 Utah 141, 247 P.2d 273 (1952).
5. Id. at 144–145 and 274–275.
6. 147 Mass 403, 18 N.E. 168 (1888).
7. Id.
8. See Neal v. Carey Canadian Mines, Ltd., 548 F. Supp. 357 (ED Pa., 1982); also note Starling v. Seaboard Coast Line Railroad Co., 533 F. Supp. 183 (SD Ga., 1982).
9. See Section 311 of the Restatement (Second) of Torts.
10. 286 Pa. Super. 312, 428 A.2d 1343 (1981).
11. 248 Ga. 19, 280 S.E.2d 345 (1981), and 635 F.2d 485 (5th Cir., 1981).
12. See Ford Motor Co. v. Lonon, 217 Tenn. 400, 398 S.W.2d 240 (1966).
13. See 60 Va. L. Rev. 1109 (1974) generally.
14. 493 F.2d 1076 (5th Cir., 1973), cert. den., 419 U.S. 869 (1974).
15. Id. at 1104.
16. 462 Pa. 83, 337 A.2d 893 (1975).
17. Id. at 103–104 and 903.
18. 446 F.2d 1105 (6th Cir., 1971).
19. Id. at 1108.
20. 712 F.2d 276 (7th Cir., 1983).
21. Id. at 279.
22. 583 F. Supp. 31 (ED Mich., 1984).
23. 165 Cal. Rptr. 858, 612 P.2d 948 (1980).
24. 69 Ohio App. 2d 159, 411 N.E.2d 814 (1978).
25. See Baron, Handling Occupational Disease Cases (Lawpress, 1981) at 52.
26. 612 P.2d 948 (Cal. 1980).

7.10 Violation of Statute and Regulations

Violation of statute and regulations has historically been a successful theory of liability for plaintiffs, for a great majority of courts have held that if the statute is applicable (i.e., designed to protect the class of people of which plaintiff is a member against a specific risk of harm that in fact occurred as a result of the violation of the statute), the violation of the statute conclusively establishes negligence and liability.[1] Some states, like California, have legislatively provided that a presumption of negligence arises from violation of a statute or regulation when that violation proximately causes the harm of the type that the statute or regulation was designed to prevent for the benefit of a person for whose protection the statute or regulation was promulgated.[2] The California Evidence Code also gives rise to a "presumption affecting the burden of proof," requiring the defendant to come forward and prove that it is more probable than not that the violation of the statute or regulation was reasonable and justifiable under the circumstances.[3] The contrary view is that a violation of statute or regulation is only evidence of negligence for the jury to consider.[4] Yet, in Marsden v. Patane,[5] the Fifth Circuit Court of Appeals held that the violation of a state traffic statute was "not negligence per se but merely prima facie evidence of negligence" that gave rise to "a mandatory rather than a permissive presumption of negligence," thereby granting plaintiff's motion for summary judgment on the issue of liability.[6]

Courts have generally been cautious about holding that a statute itself is the source of legal rights when the statute does not expressly create those rights. Courts have generally accepted the concept that safety legislation defines standards of conduct, and that violation of a safety statute without excuse is "negligence per se" or negligence as a matter of law.[7] But the plaintiff must be a member of the class that the safety statute was intended to benefit. In Williams v. Hill Manufacturing Co.[8] an employee used a cutting torch on a drum that exploded owing to vapors retained in the drum after it had been emptied; the labeling of the chemical drum, in violation of government regulations, was deemed not to be "negligence per se" because the labeling requirements were designed only for the actual process of shipment, and the consignees could remove the labels immediately on receipt without violating government regulations. However, even if violation of a statute is evidence of negligence, compliance with the statute is not always due care; for example, a defendant cannot avoid liability by arguing that he complied with a statute requiring the packaging of the hazardous substance in an aluminum container when he was otherwise negligent by failing to adhere to another statute that forbid shipment of that hazardous substance.[9]

Violation of administrative regulations and agency standards is another theory of liability, and such violation, under Section 288B(1) of the Restatement (Second) of Torts, is deemed "negligence in itself." Compliance with agency standards is evidence of due care,[10] and violation is evidence of negligence.[11] In Arthur v. Flota Merchante Gran Centro Americana[12] the trial court had instructed the jury that a violation of Occupational Safety and Health Administration (OSHA) standards was negligence per se because the purpose of the agency standard or regulation was to promote safety and establish an unambiguous standard for measuring industrial safety. But four years later the same Fifth Circuit Court of Appeals overruled that determination and held that safety and health standards and regulations of OSHA do not automatically impose a duty on people unless they are acting as employers.[13]

There are innumerable federal statutes like those of OSHA[14] that do not provide for a private cause of action or a citizen's suit; but an employer's violation of OSHA regulations may be admitted as evidence of the lack of reasonable care on the part of the employer.[15] The Toxic Substances Control Act[16] subjects violators to both civil and criminal penalties.[17] And the Federal Hazardous Substances Act[18] authorizes the Consumer Product Safety Commission to specify labeling requirements for hazardous substances that may cause substantial injury through reasonable foreseeable use.[19]

NOTES

1. See Harris v. Hendrixson, 155 S.W.2d 876 (Tenn. App., 1941).
2. See California Evidence Code, Section 669.
3. Id.
4. Note Duby v. Columbia County, 215 N.W. 819 (Wis., 1927).
5. 380 F.2d 489 (5th Cir., 1967).
6. Id. at 491–492.
7. Cf. Lowe v. General Motors Corp., 624 F.2d 1373 (5th Cir., 1980) at 1380.
8. 489 F. Supp. 20 (S.C., 1980).
9. See generally Curtis v. Perry, 171 Wash. 542, 18 P.2d 840 (1933).
10. See generally 28 Texas L. Rev. 143 (1949) at 159 et seq.
11. See Buhler v. Marriott Hotels, Inc., 390 F. Supp. (ED La., 1974), dealing with OSHA.
12. 487 F.2d 501 (5th Cir., 1973).
13. See Gay v. Ocean Transport & Trading Co., 546 F.2d 1233 (5th Cir., 1977), and Brown v. Mitsubishi Shintaku Ginko, 550 F.2d 331 (5th Cir., 1977).
14. 29 U.S.C. 651 to 678.
15. See Buhler v. Marriott Hotels, 390 F. Supp. 999 (ED La., 1974).
16. 15 U.S.C. 2601 to 2629.
17. 15 U.S.C. 2614(a)–(b).
18. 15 U.S.C. 1261 to 1274.
19. See Baron, Handling Occupational Disease Cases (Lawpress, 1981) at 124.

7.11 Vicarious Liability

Often vicarious liability may be imposed on an individual or a company for the tortious act of another in his or its service or employment, even though the individual or company did not participate in the tortious act or even try to prevent the occurrence. An occupational injury is such an occurrence that can hold the "master" liable for the torts of his employees committed while the employees are acting within the scope of their employment.[1] Often referred to as the principle of "respondeat superior," its origins may be traced to ancient Greek and Roman law.[2] It is a principle of accountability that also reaches beyond the spectrum of employment relations, as where the tortfeasor is an independent contractor.[3] The rules for determining when the tortfeasor is a "servant" or "employee" are delineated in Section 220 of the Restatement of

Agency, and the factors identifying the "kind of conduct within scope of employment" are set forth in Section 229 of the Restatement of Agency.[4]

The employee need not be performing precisely the activity for which he was hired in order to expose the employer to liability.[5] But liability can be imposed on the state for torts committed by state officials in prosecuting violations of state laws.[6] Even intentional torts may be within the scope of employment and impose vicarious liability on the employer.[7] In Becker v. Interstate Properties[8] the Third Circuit Court of Appeals concluded that a developer's failure to engage a "properly solvent and adequately insured subcontractor" was a violation of its duty to the injured plaintiff. But negligence of an employer in selecting, instructing, or supervising an independent contractor does not generally impose vicarious liability on the employer.[9] The same negligence with respect to an employee results in vicarious liability.[10] Vicarious liability will be imposed on the employer or tortfeasor with respect to nondelegable duties and work that is especially dangerous.

When two or more persons join together in an enterprise in which each has an equal right to control the other's conduct, a "joint enterprise" or "joint venture" has been created. The negligence of each participant is generally imputed to every other participant, assuming that the acts of negligence were committed in the course of the enterprise. In Shell Oil v. Prestidge[11] the plaintiff, an employee of Rocky, was injured at an oil drilling site maintained and operated by Rocky that had contracted with Shell to conduct oil exploration on land controlled by Shell. Judgment was obtained against both companies, and the Ninth Circuit Court of Appeals upheld the judgment on the grounds that there was a "joint venture."

In Woodburn v. Standard Forgings Corp.[12] the employer was held vicariously liable for false and fraudulent misrepresentations by its company doctor that were apparently made to deceive the employee as to the nature of his injury and to prevent the timely filing of a workers' compensation claim. However, in Bevis v. Armco Steel Corp.[13] the employee brought an action for deceit, alleging that his employer had intentionally misrepresented the results of medical examinations and x-rays taken by the company doctor. The Ohio court took the view that workers' compensation was the employees' exclusive remedy: the deception of not informing plaintiff of his silicosis and further inducing him to work did not deprive him of a right of action in damages because he never had that right!

In Chasnoff v. Port Authority[14] the New York court refused to dismiss as a third-party defendant the employer of a person who was injured while working on a construction site. The employer of the injured employee had argued that since the injury was caused by fellow employees, the only remedy was with workers' compensation. It should be noted that the New York Labor Laws give the "workman in the hazardous employment of construction . . . added protection, *other than workmen's compensation,* in the form of non-delegable duties cast upon the owner and general contractor with ensuing liability for breach of those duties." The New York court rejected the employer's argument that those vicariously or derivatively responsible for the negligence of the fellow employee also have the benefit of the workers' compensation: according to the court, they have "no relationship with plaintiff's co-employees who were employed by . . . the third-party defendant (employer)."

In D'Alessandro v. Alfaro Motors[15] the employer of a pugnacious trucker was held vicariously liable. Here the injured plaintiff sued the defendant trucking company for assault, battery, and negligent hiring in that he was shot by a passenger in a truck owned by defendant. The injured plaintiff had had a series of quarrels with the employee-driver. The New York Supreme Court dismissed the claims of direct liability and negligent hiring,[16] but not those of vicarious liability under the theory of respondeat superior, finding that it was for the jury to decide whether the employee was acting within the scope of his employment at the time of the altercation.[17]

NOTES

1. See generally Section 219 of the Restatement of Agency:
"§219. When Master Is Liable for Torts of His Servants.

(1) A master is subject to liability for the torts of his servants committed while acting in the scope of their employment.

(2) A master is not subject to liability for the torts of his servants acting outside the scope of their employment, unless:

(a) the master intended the conduct or the consequences, or

(b) the master was negligent or reckless, or

(c) the conduct violated a non-delegable duty of the master, or

(d) the servant purported to act or to speak on behalf of the principal and there was reliance upon apparent authority, or he was aided in accomplishing the tort by the existence of the agency relation."

2. See 4 Harv. L. Rev. 345 (1891). See Section 40 of the Restatement of Agency: "§220. Definition of Servant.

(2) In determining whether one acting for another is a servant or an independent contractor, the following matters of fact, among others, are considered:

(a) the extent of control which, by the agreement, the master may exercise over the details of the work;

(b) whether or not the one employed is engaged in a distinct occupation or business;

(c) the kind of occupation, with reference to whether, in the locality, the work is usually done under the direction of the employer or by a specialist without supervision;

(d) the skill required in the particular occupation;

(e) whether the employer or the workman supplies the instrumentalities, tools, and the place of work for the person doing the work;

(f) the length of time for which the person is employed;

(g) the method of payment, whether by the time or by the job;

(h) whether or not the work is a part of the regular business of the employer;

(i) whether or not the parties believe they are creating the relation of master and servant; and

(j) whether the principal is or is not in business."

"§229. Kind of Conduct Within Scope of Employment

(1) To be within the scope of the employment, conduct must be of the same general nature as that authorized, or incidental to the conduct authorized.

(2) In determining whether or not the conduct, although not authorized, is nevertheless so similar to or incidental to the conduct authorized as to be within the scope of employment, the following matters of fact are to be considered:

(a) whether or not the act is one commonly done by such servants;

(b) the time, place and purpose of the act;

(c) the previous relations between the master and the servant;

(d) the extent to which the business of the master is apportioned between different servants;

(e) whether or not the act is outside the enterprise of the master or, if within the enterprise, has not been entrusted to any servant;

(f) whether or not the master has reason to expect that such an act will be done;

(g) the similarity in quality of the act done to the act authorized;

(h) whether or not the instrumentality by which the harm is done has been furnished by the master to the servant;

(i) the extent of departure from the normal method of accomplishing an authorized result; and

(j) whether or not the act is seriously criminal."

3. See Riviello v. Waldron, 47 N.Y.2d 297, 391 N.E. 1278 (1979).

4. See Orser v. State of Montana, 582 P.2d 1227 (Mont., 1978).

5. See generally 45 Chi.-Kent L. Rev. 1 (1968).

6. 569 F.2d 1203 (3rd Cir., 1977), cert. den., 98 S. Ct. 2237 (1977).

7. See generally 10 Rut.-Cam. L. J. 226 (1978).

8. See generally 53 Chi.-Kent L. Rev. 717 (1972).

9. See Dixie Stage Lines v. Anderson, 222 Ala. 673, 134 So. 23 (1931), and Misiulis v. Milbrand Maintenance Corp., 52 Mich. App. 494, 218 N.W.2d 68 (1974).

10. 249 F.2d 413 (9th Cir., 1957).

11. ____ F.2d ____ (9th Cir., ____).

12. 112 F.2d 271 (7th Cir., 1940).

13. 93 N.E.2d 33 (Ohio, 1949), cert. den., 340 U.S. 810 (1950).

14. 499 N.Y.S.2d 338 (1986).

15. ____ N.Y.S.2d ____ (Queens County, December 6, 1988).

16. According to the court, "the evidence adduced at the examination before trial fails to establish a cause of action for direct liability by the employers and for negligent hiring. There is no evidence that Mr. Arcanone's employer ever expressly ordered him to use physical force or violence, or to make any threats against Mr. D'Alessandro, or any other tow truck driver employed by its competitors. Moreover, there is no evidence which establishes that any such direct orders were given to Mr. Arcanone by Alfaro Motors following the series of incidents between Alfaro's drivers and Metro's drivers. It is well established that where as here the moving party has demonstrated that it is entitled to summary judgment, the opposing party must demonstrate, by admissible evidence, the existence of factual issues requiring a trial of the action or tender an acceptable excuse for the failure to do so (Zuckerman v. City of New York, 49 N.Y.2d 557). In the case at bar, plaintiff has failed to present any evidence which establishes that he was shot by an accomplice of Mr. Arcanone pursuant to Alfaro Motor's express orders. Counsel's conclusory assertions of direct liability are insufficient to warrant the denial of partial summary judgment on that part of plaintiff's first cause of action which alleges direct liability.

The evidence adduced at the examination before trial also fails to establish a cause of action for negligent hiring. Plaintiff in opposition to the motion for summary judgment has failed to come forward with any evidence which establishes that Mr. Arcanone was a person with vicious or dangerous propensities which his employer knew, or in the exercise of reasonable care, should have known, was dangerous (see, 52 N.Y. Jur. Employment Relations §355; Francella v. 2465 Crotona Ave. Corp., 44 A.D.2d 660). Rather, Mr. Alfaro testified that prior to hiring Mr. Arcanone, he knew him to be a hard worker, and that he never received any complaints concerning Mr. Arcanone's behavior during the course of his employment. Summary judgment dismissing the second cause of action against Alfaro Motors therefore is warranted.''

17. And the New York court concluded: ''Defendant's request for summary judgment dismissing that part of plaintiff's first cause of action for damages based on vicarious liability is denied. The doctrine of respondeat superior renders a master vicariously liable for a tort committed by his servant while acting within the scope of his employment (Riviello v. Waldron, 47 N.Y.2d 297, 302). Intentional torts as well as negligent acts may fall within the scope of employment and the employer need not have foreseen the precise act or the exact manner of injury so long as the general type of conduct may have been reasonably expected. Since the determination of whether a particular act was within the scope of the servant's employment is so heavily dependent on factual consideration, the question is ordinarily one for the jury (Riviello v. Waldron, supra; Quadrozzi v. Norcem, Inc., 125 A.D.2d 559). Summary judgment, therefore, is inappropriate, as Mr. D'Alessandro and Mr. Arcanone presented conflicting versions of the facts regarding the shooting as well as their prior conflicts.''

7.12 Wrongful Death Actions

One of the peculiarities of the common law was the effect of a plaintiff's death on the right to recover damages in a tort action: there was no cause of action for death itself,[1] and any cause of action to recover for physical injuries tortiously caused by defendant's conduct terminated with plaintiff's death.[2] Fortunately this state of law has changed in England and in every state in the United States principally by statute, either a ''survival statute'' preventing the abatement of existing causes of action owing to death, or ''wrongful death statutes'' creating causes of action that allow recovery when tortious conduct of the defendant causes plaintiff's death.[3]

The measures of recovery under these two types of statutes differ, to wit: under ''survival statutes'' the measure of recovery is what the plaintiff's decedent would have been able to recover for his injuries had he survived, whereas under ''wrongful death statutes'' the basic measure of recovery is the harm caused to the decedent's family by the defendant's conduct. But the amount of recovery under ''wrongful death statutes'' varies from state to state: Alabama measures wrongful death by the degree of defendant's fault;[4] New Jersey follows Lord Campbell's Act[5] and measures recovery by the loss suffered by the surviving family members and next of kin of the decedent; and few states measure recovery by the loss suffered by the decedent's estate.[6]

In Sea Land Services v. Gaudet[7] a longshoreman suffered personal injuries while working aboard a vessel, and recovered $140,000 for his permanent disability, physical agony, and loss of earnings. But he died shortly thereafter, and his widow instituted a wrongful death action for damages that she suffered. Based on her husband's prior recovery the court dismissed her suit for failure to state a claim and on the grounds of res judicata. The Fifth Circuit Court of Appeals reversed,[8] holding that her cause of action for wrongful death was separate and apart from his cause of action for personal injury. The U.S. Supreme Court affirmed, holding that the maritime wrongful death action based on unseaworthiness could be maintained even though the decedent, before his death, had recovered from the shipowner in a personal injury action, since the wrongful death remedy involved a different cause of action; the court also opined that under the maritime wrongful death remedy, the decedent's dependents could recover damages for their loss of support, services, and society as well as funeral expenses. The court declared that the doctrine of collateral estoppel precluded recovery in the wrongful death action of damages for loss of support insofar as such damages would overlap the decedent's prior recovery in his personal injury action for loss of future wages.[9]

The family of a deceased worker who was exposed to toxic substances before a 1976 amendment to the Louisiana workers' compensation law may proceed with an intentional tort claim falling outside the scope of the state statute.[10]

"Wrongful life" is a relatively new term assigned to a new element of damages, and was recognized as a new tort by the California Supreme Court in Turpin v. Sortini,[11] in which the parents of a handicapped baby alleged that the child would not have been born but for the negligence of the health care provider. The parents recovered damages for their child's special medical care until the age of majority.[12] Only the states of Washington[13] and New Jersey[14] have joined California in recognizing an action for "wrongful life."

NOTES

1. See Baker v. Bolton, 170 Eng. Rep. 1033 (1808).

2. See generally 13 Vand. L. Rev. 605 (1960).

3. Note that Massachusetts holds that the action for wrongful death has a basis in common law, Gaudette v. Webb, 362 Mass. 60, 184 N.E.2d 222 (1972).

4. See Hughes v. Southern Haulers, Inc., 379 So.2d 601 (Ala. App., 1980).

5. 9 & 10 Vict., c 93 (1846).

6. 414 U.S. 574 (1974).

7. 463 F.2d 1331 (5th Cir., 1972).

8. Note the 1970 decision of the U.S. Supreme Court in Moragne v. States Marine Lines, 398 U.S. 375 (1970).

9. 414 U.S. 574 (1972) at 609–610.

10. See Trupiano v. Swift & Co., 755 F.2d 442 (5th Cir., 1985).

11. 643 P.2d 954 (Cal., 1982).
12. See A.B.A.J. (April 1, 1986) at 47.
13. See Harbeson v. Parke-Davis Co., 656 P.2d 483 (Wash., 1983).
14. See Procanik v. Cillo, 478 A.2d 755 (N.J., 1984).

8

Defenses to Employee's Claim

8.1 Introduction

To examine all the defenses to the employee's claim is beyond the scope of this chapter. It will suffice to touch base only with respect to statutes of limitations, the state of the art, compliance with government specifications or industry standards, proximate cause, dual capacity, federal preemption, and diversity jurisdiction.

The infinite variations of defenses can be seen in Patton v. Klingon,[1] in which the New York court ruled that a treating physician cannot request a fee from the workers' compensation claimant. Here the physician sued the claimant for a $300 fee for medical services rendered before the claimant received workers' compensation benefits. The court found that the New York statute requires a physician who treats a compensation claimant to seek payment of his fee only from the claimant's employer. Of course,

a physician may refuse to examine a workers' compensation claimant, but once the doctor agrees to treat a claimant, he or she must look only to the employer for payment. Defendant claims that he had no knowledge that this was a workers' compensation case when he agreed to examine Bader and that he considered this a normal neurological consult, not specifically related to Bader's injury. While it appears that defendant was aware that this was a compensation case (see exhibits H and L to moving papers), it is not clear when defendant became aware of that fact and in his opposing papers defendant specifically denies such knowledge during the initial course of treatment. Therefore, summary judgment must be denied.

One interesting defense to an employee's claim was involved in Mental Hygiene Legal Service v. Surles,[2] in which "the underlying action raises significant constitutional questions, including what role a parent may properly play in regard to the psychiatric care to be provided to his or her minor child, and under what circumstances, if any, should a court become involved if the child disagrees with his physician and his parent as to what constitutes appropriate treatment.'' The decision of the New York court was that "society has long acknowledged the right of a parent to determine the medical care and treatment to be afforded to his or her minor child.'' Citing Planned Parenthood of Missouri v. Danforth,[3] the court reiterated that "constitutional rights do not mature and come into being magically only when one attains the State-defined age of majority. Minors, as well as adults, are protected by the Constitution and possess constitutional rights.'' The court went on:

However, those rights are not necessarily co-extensive with the rights enjoyed by those who have reached majority. Bellotti v. Baird, supra, at p. 634 ("We have recognized three reasons justifying the conclusion that the constitutional rights of children cannot be equated with those of adults: the peculiar vulnerability of children; their inability to make critical decisions in an informed, mature manner; and the importance of the parental role in child rearing").

Similarly, it is well established that minors are empowered to make important decisions—independent of parental control—in such matters as abortion and access to contraceptive devices. Planned Parenthood of Missouri v. Danforth, supra at p. 75 ("Any independent interest the parent may have in the termination of the minor daughter's pregnancy is no more weighty than the right of privacy of the competent minor mature enough to have become pregnant"); and Carey v. Population Services International, 431 U.S. 678, 97 S. Ct. 2010, 2013 (1977). But plaintiff's reliance on reproductive right cases is misplaced, for those decisions are sui generis as a class—unique unto themselves. Bellotti v. Baird, supra, at p. 642, and Parham v. J.R., supra, 61 L. Ed. 2d at p. 119 (Supreme Court rejected argument that its holding in the abortion decision of Danforth, supra, required conclusion that Georgia's psychiatric commitment procedures for children under the age of 18—which placed such power in the parent—were unconstitutional.) Those who endeavor to reconcile the autonomy provided to minors in such areas, with the basic common law tenet that a parent speaks for his or her child in medical matters, are entering an intellectual quagmire. The concepts may not be dovetailed. Rather, it must be recognized that a limited exception has been created by the courts, which exception does not apply to this case. Accordingly, Planned Parenthood of Missouri v. Danforth, supra, and Carey v. Population Services International, supra—both cited by plaintiff—lend little, if any support to his argument.

NOTES

1. _____ N.Y.S.2d _____ (New York County, November 17, 1988).
2. _____ N.Y.S.2d _____ (Suffolk County, December 28, 1988).
3. 428 U.S. 52 (1976) at 74.

8.2 Statutes of Limitations

Generally, a cause of action accrues and the statute of limitations begins to run at the time of injury. But in some occupational injuries, diseases, or deaths the commencement of the cause of action and the running of the statute of limitations is shrouded in different fact situations, especially when the symptoms do not occur until many years later. The injured worker may not even know that he was injured or diseased or that a cause of action exists. Most states, therefore, have used the "time of discovery" rule; that is, the statute of limitations does not begin to run until the worker discovers or should have discovered the injury, disease, or death.[1] There are many guidelines for determining when the statute of limitations begins to run, to wit: time of negligent act, time of last exposure to the particular offending substance,[2] time the occupational injury or disease manifested itself, time injured worker first learned or should have known of the presence of the occupational disease or injury, time that medical diagnosis was communicated to the worker, time the worker received an informal diagnosis, time the disability began, and time the worker discovered the causal relation between the injury or disease and the offending substance.[3]

In Pobieglo v. Monsanto Co.[4] the Massachusetts court held, inter alia, that because the state legislature had specifically provided that wrongful death claims must be brought within a specified period of time, it would be inappropriate for the courts to vitiate that legislative determination by permitting the application of a discovery rule.[5] The discovery rule is used to determine when a statute of limitations begins to run! The traditional view is seen in Cadieux v. International Telephone and Telegraph Co.,[6] in which the First U.S. Court of Appeals affirmed the dismissal of wrongful death claims brought on behalf of an electronics technician who had allegedly died as a result of exposure to x-rays and other sources of radiation, which exposure his representative did not learn about until after the two-year "from death" statute of limitations had expired. The court held that discovery rule did not apply: "The doctrine that suit must be brought within two years of death leaves . . . no room."

Concomitant with statutes of limitations are statutes of repose, which bar suits after a definitive period of years from the initial sale or first use of the offending substance or product.[7] Statutes of repose can pose constitutional issues,[8] as demonstrated in Saylor v. Hall,[9] which involved challenges under the Fifth and Fourteenth Amendments. The Kentucky court observed that the statute of repose was neither a due process violation nor a violation of the equal protection clause, even when holding that certain causes of action were time-barred before they ever actually arose!

NOTES

1. Note Bonney v. Upjohn Co., 487 F. Supp. 486 (WD Mich., 1980).
2. See Harrell v. Koppers Company, Inc., 499 N.Y.S.2d 968 (App. Div. 2, 1986), in which the court opined: "The plaintiff's cause of action could not be time-barred before it accrued, and prior manifestations allegedly caused by his extended exposure did not operate to create a 'discovery' accrual date. Rather, the plaintiff's cause of action for personal injury accrued upon his last exposure to the allegedly deleterious substance, and there is no authority for a 'discoverability exception to the date of last

exposure rule' (see Bradley v. Burroughs Wellcome Co., _____ A.D.2d _____ [2d Dept., Jan. 13, 1986]; Ward v. Desachem Co., 771 F.2d 663, 666).''

3. See Baron, Handling Occupational Disease Cases (Lawpress, 1981) at 165–168.

4. 521 N.E.2d 728 (Mass., 1988).

5. See Kasowitz, "Massachusetts High Court Decision Rejects Liberal Limitations Rulings," N.L.J. (July 18, 1988) at 18 and 19.

6. 593 F.2d 142 (1st Cir., 1979).

7. Note Davis v. Whiting, 674 P.2d 1194 (Or., 1984), and Barwick v. Celotex Corp., 736 F.2d 946 (4th Cir., 1984).

8. See Prosser and Keeton on Torts (5th ed., 1984) at 168.

9. 497 S.W.2d 218 (Ky., 1973).

8.3 State of the Art

The defense of state of the art is highly controversial, as the product manufacturer generally contends with the injured worker who argues that the product was outdated and defective, and should have been ameliorated or withdrawn from the market. The product manufacturer points out that the state of the art was such that it had no reason to believe that the product, when first marketed, would cause the type of injury that occurred to the employee. But, as stated in Dudley Sports Co. v. Schmitt,[1] even though the manufacturer's evidence demonstrated that the product met and exceeded the state of the art in the industry when the product was first marketed, "the fact that a particular product meets or exceeds the requirements of the industry is not conclusive proof that the product is reasonably safe. In fact, standards set by an entire industry can be found negligibly low if they fail to meet the test of reasonableness." And in Sturm Ruger & Co. v. Day[2] the Alaskan court concluded that, although state of the art was not a defense, it may be considered in determining whether a product is defective.

One of the few cases accepting state of the art as a defense is Basko v. Sterling Drug Co.,[3] but it simply does not make sense to allow the defense in strict liability actions in which the focus on care or the conduct of the manufacturer is irrelevant because strict liability focuses on the nature of the product, not the conduct of the product manufacturer. The product manufacturer has a duty to see that the product in the market is reasonably safe, even though at the time of the initial marketing of the product the state of the art deemed the product to be safe. As explained by the Connecticut court in Hartman v. Black & Decker Manufacturing Co.:

Bertolett's testimony that it was "possible" at the time of manufacture in 1966 to place warnings directly on the saws established the feasibility of placing such warnings. The jury was, therefore, aware that such warnings were feasible, and any evidence of a practice at Emerson Electric from 1976 to 1980 for the purpose of demonstrating feasibility was cumulative. Furthermore, the proffered evidence regarding procedures at Emerson Electric ten to fourteen years after the manufacture of the saw in question was remote in time as to the issue of the defectiveness of the saw as manufactured in 1966 by Black & Decker. Such evidence, moreover, was not critical to the plaintiff's demonstration of defectiveness. The plaintiff presented ample expert testimony on the issue of defectiveness, which testimony was emphasized by the trial court in its charge to the jury. In light of the concession of feasibility by Black & Decker, the remoteness in time of the proffered evidence and the ample evidence presented by the plaintiff on the issue of defectiveness, the trial court could have in its discretion concluded that any prejudice and confusion stemming from the proffered testimony outweighed its probative value. "The introduction of evidence about subsequent changes in the product or its design threatens to confuse the jury by diverting its attention from whether the product was defective at the relevant time to what was done later" (*Sanderson v. Steve Snyder Enterprises, Inc.*, supra, 145 n. 8, quoting *Grenada Steel Industries* v. *Alabama Oxygen Co.*, 695 F.2d 883, 888 [5th Cir., 1983]). Under these circumstances, the trial court did not abuse its discretion in excluding from evidence safety measures taken by Emerson Electric ten to fourteen years following the manufacture of the saw in question. *Schenck* v. *Pelkey*, supra (admissibility of safety measure taken by other manufacturers subsequent to manufacture of product in question to demonstrate feasibility within discretion of trial court); *Lolie* v. *Ohio Brass Co.*, 502 F.2d 741, 744–45 (7th Cir., 1974).[4]

NOTES

1. 279 N.E.2d 266 (Ind. App., 1972).
2. 594 P.2d 38 (Alaska, 1979).
3. 416 F.2d 417 (2nd Cir., 1969).
4. 16 Conn. App. 1 (September 6, 1988).

8.4 Compliance with Government Specifications or Industry Standards

The defense that the employer has complied with government specifications or industry standards does not establish the exercise of due care by the employer. In Westinghouse Electric Corp. v. Nutt[1] the federal appellate court opined that "it is axiomatic . . . that compliance with legislative or industry standards 'does not prevent a finding of negligence where a reasonable man would take additional precautions.' " However, the employer or product manufacturer may stand behind the government by invoking the "government contract" defense, as delineated in In Re "Agent Orange" Product Liability Litigation[2]; the essential elements of the defense embrace proof that the government established the specifications for the product and that the product manufactured by the defendant met the government's specifications in all material respects; in addition, the defendant must prove that the government knew as much or more than defendant about the hazards to people that accompanied use of the product.[3]

On the other hand, in Berkebile v. Brantly Helicopter Corp.,[4] the Pennsylvania court removed consideration of a question of defectiveness from the jury by ruling that a Federal Aviation Administration regulation should be the stan-

dard in judging whether the helicopter was defective and unreasonably dangerous, and that the manufacturer should be able to rely on the federal regulatory
standard. But the appellate court reversed, stating that "failure of the manufacturer to comply with the regulations would be negligence per se," but compliance with the regulations "does not establish as a matter of law that due care
was exercised."

Indeed, industry standards and customs are generally the minimum standards, and therefore compliance therewith should not be allowed as a defense.
However, as viewed in Wallner v. Kitchens of Sara Lee, Inc.,[5] evidence of
industry standards and customs is admissible.

NOTES

1. 407 A.2d 606 (D.C. Cir., 1979).
2. 534 F. Supp. 1046 (ED N.Y., 1982).
3. See Warren Freedman, Hazardous Waste Liability (Michie, 1987) at Section 14.2.
4. 281 A.2d 707 (Pa., 1971).
5. 419 F.2d 1028 (7th Cir., 1969).

8.5 Federal Preemption

Federal Preemption is a recognized defense, as illustrated in People v. Pymm,[1]
in which the jury convicted the owner of a thermometer factory of assault for
exposing employees to unsafe levels of mercury fumes; but the judge set aside
the verdict on the grounds that federal safety statutes preempted the state's
jurisdiction. In the cigarette products liability case of Cippolone v. Liggett Group[2]
the defendants asserted the defense that the Federal Cigarette Labeling and
Advertising Act[3] preempted common law tort liability:

The Act pre-empts those State law damage actions relating to smoking and health that
challenge either the adequacy of the warning on cigarette packages or the propriety of
the party's actions with respect to the advertising and promotion of cigarettes. . . .
Where the success of a State law damage claim necessarily depends on the assertion
that a party bore the duty to provide a warning Congress has required on cigarette
packages, such claims are pre-empted as conflicting with the Act.[4]

A contrary view is seen in Ferebee v. Chevron Chemical Co.,[5] in which the
defendant claimed that compliance with an Environmental Protection Agency
(EPA)-approved and -mandated pesticide warning insulated it from tort liability
on an inadequate warning theory. The federal statute provided that "a state
shall not impose or continue in effect any requirements for labeling . . . in
addition to or different from those required under this subchapter." Despite the
congressional policy of national uniformity of warnings, the District of Columbia Court of Appeals held that state remedies were not incompatible with the

federal program. The opinion noted that "the purposes of the [act] and those of state law may be quite distinct and that state law may have broader compensatory goals." The court further held that compliance with both federal and state law is not impossible, since the manufacturer can continue to use an EPA-approved label and can, at the same time, pay damages to tort plaintiffs or can petition the EPA to allow the labels to be made more comprehensive.

And in Thrift v. CSX Transportation, Inc.[6] the federal district court ruled that a railroad employee's claim under Federal Employees' Liability Act (FELA) for monetary damages resulting from work-related dermatitis was not preempted by the Railway Labor Act or barred by FELA's three-year statute of limitations. The employee here was exposed by his employer to solvent fumes and other toxic substances while he worked for twelve years. In McGowan v. General Dynamics Corp.[7] the Connecticut court held that since the plaintiffs had received under the federal act awards that exceeded the total benefits under Connecticut law, the additional awards were improper. The court opined:

The plaintiffs contend, however, that Connecticut's interest in compensating injured employees to the fullest extent possible (Simaitis v. Flood, 182 Conn. 24, 32, 437 A.2d 828 [1980]) compels our adoption of the category by category credit system. It is disingenuous to argue that our holding today infringes upon the state's legitimate interest in securing maximum compensation for claimants when the plaintiffs' awards under the LHWCA far exceed that available under the Connecticut act. The state's interest in compensating claimants for disfigurement or scarring is not infringed upon in any meaningful way under the facts of this case. Regardless of where an employee first seeks an award of benefits, he or she is entitled to the maximum amount allowed to an individual under either comprehensive legislative scheme.

It has been argued that courts should not find that Congress has preempted common law liability, absent an explicit statement of federal preemption.[8] The U.S. Supreme Court, in Silkwood v. Kerr-McGee Corp.,[9] ruled that plaintiff's common law punitive damages claim was not preempted by the Atomic Energy Act and the Atomic Energy Commission regulations. In Raymond v. Riegel Textile Corp.[10] the First U.S. Court of Appeals had also declared: "The evident solicitude of Congress for the plight of burn victims who are most often the very young and the aged must be taken into consideration when interpreting the 'supremacy clause.' We hold, therefore, that New Hampshire's application of its strict liability standard in tort actions involving injury from burning clothing is not 'inconsistent with [the] provisions' of the Flammable Fabrics Act."

The diphtheria-pertussis-tetanus (DPT) vaccine was used to vaccinate children against whooping cough, but its side effects have caused injury to many children. DPT manufacturers, in resisting suits, contend that federal regulations of the vaccine are so comprehensive and pervasive as to preempt state lawsuits.[11] In Hillsborough County v. Automated Medical Laboratories, Inc.[12] the highest court opined that federal regulation did not preempt county ordinances that imposed additional restraints on sellers:

We are even more reluctant to infer pre-emption from the comprehensiveness of regulations than from the comprehensiveness of statutes. As a result of their specialized functions, agencies normally deal with problems in far more detail than does Congress. To infer pre-emption whenever an agency deals with a problem comprehensively is virtually tantamount to saying that whenever a federal agency decides to step into a field, its regulations will be exclusive. Such a rule, of course, would be inconsistent with the federal-state balance embodied in our Supremacy Clause jurisprudence [cite omitted].

Moreover, because agencies normally address problems in a detailed manner and can speak through a variety of means, including regulations, preambles, and responses to comments, we can expect that they will make their intentions clear if they intend for their regulations to be exclusive. Thus, if an agency does not speak to the question of pre-emption, we will pause before saying that the mere volume and complexity of its regulations indicate that the agency did in fact intend to pre-empt. Given the presumption that state and local regulations related to matters of health and safety can normally coexist with federal regulations, we will seldom infer, solely from the comprehensiveness of federal regulations, an intent to pre-empt in its entirety a field related to health and safety.

An interesting variation on the theme of federal preemption is seen in the Federal Employees Liability Reform and Compensation Act of 1988,[13] which restored the absolute immunity from personal liability that government workers were believed to have always enjoyed. The new law removes the exception for "government discretion" and states that all claims against federal employees acting in official capacities must be litigated exclusively against the United States.[14] Thus federal employees, in effect, enjoy a federal preemption from civil lawsuits claiming that they were negligent on the job.[15]

NOTES

1. _____ N.Y.S. 2d _____ (1987). See New York Times (November 14, 1987) at 31.

2. 789 F.2d 181 (3rd Cir., 1986).

3. Pub. L. No. 89-92, 79 Stat. 282 (1965) (codified as amended by Pub. L. No. 91-222, 84 Stat. 87 (1970), at 15 U.S.C. §§1331–1340 [1982]). Congress amended certain provisions of the Act by the Public Health Cigarette Smoking Act of 1969, Pub. L. No. 91-222, 84 Stat. 87 (1970) (hereinafter "the 1969 Act"), and again by the Comprehensive Smoking Education Act, Pub. L. No. 98-474, 98 Stat. 2200 (1984) (hereinafter "the 1984 Act"). The Act does not prohibit cigarette companies from providing additional information regarding the health hazards of their product. Note this excerpt: "No statement relating to smoking and health, other than the statement required by section 1333 of this Title shall be required on any cigarette package. (b) No requirement or prohibition based on smoking and health shall be imposed under state law with respect to the advertising or promotion of any cigarettes the packages of which are labeled in conformity with the provisions of this chapter."

4. See McSorley v. Philip Morris, Inc., _____ N.Y.S. 2d _____ (Queens County, January 27, 1989), ruling in favor of the cigarette manufacturer that the Federal Ciga-

rette Labeling and Advertising Act preempted state tort claims that challenged the inadequacy of warnings on packages of cigarettes: "As set forth in the Federal Cigarette Labeling and Advertising Act (hereinafter 'the Labeling Act'), (15 U.S.C. §1331 et seq) the declared purpose of the program is to adequately inform the public of the hazards of cigarette smoking by including a warning on each package and to protect against diverse, nonuniform and confusing cigarette labeling, section 1334 specifically provides:

'(a) No statement relating to smoking and health, other than the statement required by section 1333 of this title, shall be required on any cigarette package.

'(b) No requirement or prohibition based on smoking and health shall be imposed under State law with respect to the advertising or promotion of any cigarettes the packages of which are labeled in conformity with the provisions of this chapter.'

"A clear reading of the foregoing evidences that the Labeling Act preempts state tort claims which challenge the inadequacy of warnings on packages if the warning is in compliance with statutory mandates. (Palmer v. Liggett Group, Inc., 825 F.2d 620). To impose any further or different duty upon manufacturers would result in a direct conflict with the Labeling Act (Cipollone v. Liggett Group, Inc., 789 F.2d 181)."

5. 736 F.2d 1529 (D.C. Cir., 1984), cert. den., 105 S. Ct. 545 (1984).

6. ____ F. Supp. ____ (SD Ga., July 19, 1988).

7. 15 Conn. App. 615 (August 23, 1988).

8. See Cohen, "Federalism in Product Liability: Courts Should Be Slow to Find Pre-emption," Trial Magazine (November 1987) at 67 et seq.

9. 104 S. Ct. 615 (1984).

10. 484 F.2d 1025 (1st Cir., 1973).

11. Note Wilson and McKowne, "Federal Pre-Emption in DPT Cases: The Courts Should Reject This Defense," Trial Magazine (January 1988) at 59 et seq.

12. 105 S. Ct. 2371 (1984).

13. See Insight Magazine (December 19, 1988) at 49.

14. Id.

15. Id.

8.6 Proximate Cause

Lack of proximate cause is the factual defense, but the issue is complicated by the recognition given by the courts to the argument that the wrongful act need not be the sole cause; it is sufficient if the negligence of the tortfeasor concurs with the negligence of another, for example.[1] A negligent act or omission may be the proximate cause of injury or disease or death when it concurs with other causes acting at the same time and in the same combination.[2] The South Carolina court, in LaCount v. General Asbestos & Rubber Co.,[3] found that the employee's death was caused by pneumoconiosis or asbestosis contracted in the course of employment because of the employer's negligence in providing improper and unsafe workplace. The employer argued that the death resulted from an idiosyncrasy of the employee to lipiodol, a chemical injected to better outline the small tracts in the chest during x-rays. The physician who signed the death certificate refused to state that lipiodol was the sole cause of the employee's death. The court held that the jury could reasonably infer that the employee's sensitivity to the drug was the only concurring cause of death, and this was properly a question of fact for the jury. Indeed,

an injury is held to be the proximate cause of death where disease intervenes, when it is shown that the injury caused the disease from which death resulted; or, if the injury did not cause the disease, that it concurred with the disease as a direct agent in producing death, and without which death would not then have resulted; provided, in either case, there was no intervening act or neglect of the decedent or a third person which contributed to the fatal result. Annotation, "Injury as proximate cause of death where disease intervenes" (79 A.L.R. 351 [1932]).

Chemical injury cases are difficult to evaluate, especially when the workplace is not easily defined, for employees may be transferred from one job to another with varying exposures.[4] On the other hand, a court might not have any interest in spelling out the proximate cause, as seen in Houck v. State of New York,[5] in which the New York court allowed recovery "from whatever source she suffered from physical symptoms which prevent her from teaching. . . . As such, the Board's determination (that she should not receive benefits) is clearly inappropriate and arbitrary." The claimant here was allergic to her environment, making her allergic to practically every substance in typical workplaces.[6]

One writer[7] has simplified his approach to proximate cause by asserting that proof of causation involved but two elements: (1) proof that the chemical can cause the condition at issue, and proof of this should render relevant and admissible competent evidence of epidemiological studies and other scientific information about the chemical, even though the employee was not part of the study[8]; and (2) proof that the toxin indeed caused the injury.

NOTES

1. See Bobbe v. Camato, 272 N.Y.S.2d 475 (1966). Also, see Baron, Handling Occupational Disease Cases (Lawpress, 1981) at 179.

2. See Section 432 Restatement (Second) of Torts.

3. 192 S.E. 262 (1937).

4. See Hawes and Chu, "Proximate Cause in Toxic-Tort Cases," Trial Magazine (October 1987) at 68 et seq.

5. ____ N.Y.S.2d ____ (Albany County, 1987).

6. See McMahon, "Teacher's Allergy to School Rules Disabling," N.Y.L.J. (November 24, 1987) at 3.

7. Bell, "Proving Causation: Thorough Preparation Is Crucial in a Toxic Tort Case," Trial Magazine (October 1988) at 50 et seq.

8. See Marsee v. U.S. Tobacco Co., 639 F. Supp. 466 (WD Okla., 1986).

8.7 Exclusivity of Workers' Compensation

The exclusivity of workers' compensation constitutes a defense to the employer, as illustrated in the New York case of Chouinard v. Clare Rose, Inc.[1] Here plaintiff was injured working on property owned by defendant corporation, which, although owned in common with plaintiff's employer, was a separate entity. After plaintiff prevailed in the workers' compensation claim against both entities, the plaintiff sued the defendant as landowner. But the court dismissed the suit,[2] finding defendant's status irrelevant, since plaintiff had chosen workers' compensation as the remedy:

Plaintiff having elected to proceed against defendant under the guise of an employer and having received, accepted and retained such benefits is now estopped from pursuing an alternative remedy of a civil action at law against the defendant (Werner v. State of New York, 79 A.D.2d 873 [4th Dept. 1980], aff'd., 53 N.Y.2d 346 [1981]; Johnson v. Razor Realty Corp., 25 A.D.2d 632 [1st Dept. 1966]; Hulis v. Foschi & Sons, 123 Misc. 2d 567, 572 [1984]).

Finally, it should be pointed out the court rejects the arguments advanced by defendant that plaintiff is precluded from maintaining a lawsuit against him under the rationale of Heritage v. VanPatten, 90 A.D.2d 931 (3rd Dept. 1988), aff'd., 59 N.Y.2d 1017 (1983). The fact that Reliance Fuel Oil Inc. and defendant Clare Rose, Inc. have a common ownership underlying the corporate form does not give either corporation the status of a co-employee with an employee of the other commonly owned corporation (Thomas v. Maigo Corp., 37 A.D.2d 754 [4th Dept. 1971]). Each corporation is distinct from the other and not true "alter egos" of each other (Shine v. Duncan Petroleum, 60 N.Y.S.2d 672 [1983]).

In Panaro v. Electrolux Corporation[3] plaintiff and his wife sought damages from both his employer and a nurse employed by the employer at a medical facility maintained by the employer. Plaintiffs contended that the nurse's failure to exercise reasonable professional care had increased the severity of and the risk of harm from a stroke which plaintiff suffered at the company facility. The trial court granted defendant's motion for summary judgment, and the Connecticut appellate court affirmed, pointing out that the exclusive remedy was provided by the workers' compensation law under which plaintiff had previously been awarded benefits. In another Connecticut case, Sharp v. Mitchell,[4] the court ruled that the exclusivity provisions of the workers' compensation law did not deprive plaintiffs of the right of access to the courts guaranteed by the Connecticut constitution:

Although our interpretation of our own constitution is dispositive on this issue, we also recognize that the workers' compensation scheme has been sustained against attack on constitutional grounds, including access to the courts, in many jurisdictions throughout the country. See, e.g., Kandt v. Evans, 645 P.2d 1300, 1306 (Colo., 1982); Young v. O.A. Newton & Son, Co., 477 A.2d 1071, 1078 (Del. Super., 1984); Acton v. Fort

Lauderdale Hospital, 440 So.2d 1282, 1284 (Fla., 1983); *Boyd v. Barton Transfer & Storage, Inc.*, 2 Kan. App. 2d 425, 430, 580 P.2d 1366 (1978); *Schmidt v. Modern Metals Foundry, Inc.*, 424 N.W.2d 538, 542 (Minn. 1988); *Linsin v. Citizens Electric Co.*, 622 S.W.2d 277, 281 (Mo. App., 1981); *Roberts v. Gray's Crane & Rigging, Inc.*, 73 Or. App. 29, 35, 697 P.2d 985, review denied, 299 Or. 443, 702 P.2d 1112 (1985); *Kline v. Arden H. Verner Co.*, 503 Pa. 251, 255, 469 A.2d 158 (1983); *Edmunds v. Highrise, Inc.*, 715 S.W.2d 377, 379 (Tex. Civ. App., 1986); *Messner v. Briggs & Stratton Corporation*, 120 Wis. 2d 127, 134, 353 N.W.2d 363 (1984). A leading commentator has noted: "Exclusiveness clauses have consistently been held to be constitutional, under the equal protection and due process clauses of both federal and state constitutions. Attacks based on specific state constitutional provisions, such as those creating a right of action for wrongful death, have fared no better." 2A A. Larson, Workmen's Compensation Law (1988) §65.20, pp. 12–18–12–20.

We conclude that since an action for wrongful death was not a constitutionally incorporated right at the time of the constitution of 1818, we need not reach the issue of whether the Workers' Compensation Act provides a reasonable alternative remedy.

In Mermelstein v. City of New York[5] the plaintiff, a psychiatric resident, was attacked by a patient and she thereupon sued the city hospital for negligence. Defendant moved to amend its answer to add the defense of exclusivity of workers' compensation. Plaintiff objected, asserting that the employer had not been the city hospital, but an affiliated university medical center. The court ruled that plaintiff could prevail if she could prove that she was not an employee at the time of the incident of the city hospital.

In sharp contrast to the foregoing is Blancato v. Feldspar Corp.,[6] in which the Connecticut court observed that the employer had illegally hired a minor to work in hazardous employment as a sand operator at defendant's mining facility. The Connecticut Supreme Court ruled that the minor's estate could avoid the illegal contract of employment and sue the employer in tort for the wrongful death, despite the exclusivity of workers' compensation.

NOTES

1. ____ N.Y.S.2d ____ (Suffolk County, October 6, 1988).

2. According to the court, "Workers' Compensation Law Section 11 provides in part: 'The liability of an employer . . . shall be exclusive and in place of any other liability whatsoever to such employee.'

"Thus, Section 11 mandates that workers' compensation shall be the exclusive remedy in place of any other liability whatsoever, to an employee, his personal representatives, or any other person entitled to recover damages, at common law or otherwise on account of an injury or a death to the employee if occurring within the scope of his employment (Belinson v. Town of Amherst, 65 A.D.2d 812, 913 [4th Dept., 1978]).

"This provision along with Workers' Compensation Law Section 29(6) precludes an employee from maintaining a separate civil action against his employer. Further, it has been held that a plaintiff may not bring an action against his employer in his capacity as a property owner (Cipriano v. FYM Associates, 117 A.D.2d 770, 771 [2nd Dept.,

1986]). This 'dual capacity' theory in which an employee may proceed against his employer in another capacity, such as the property owner, has been specifically rejected in New York (Billy v. Consolidated Machine Tool Corp., 51 N.Y.2d 152, 158–159 [1980])."

3. 208 Conn. 589 (August 16, 1988).
4. 209 Conn. 59 (September 6, 1988).
5. ____ N.Y.S.2d ____ (New York County, August 8, 1988).
6. 522 A.2d 1235 (Conn., 1987).

8.8 The Dual Capacity Doctrine

The defense of exclusivity of workers' compensation is overcome by the dual capacity doctrine, which describes the situation in which an employer has two capacities or legal persons; in short, the employer may become a third person, vulnerable to tort suit by the employee if, and only if, the employer possesses a "second persona" so completely independent from and unrelated to his status as employer that by established standards the law recognizes it as a separate legal person.[1] In the case of Duprey v. Shane[2] a chiropracter's employee was injured in the course of employment, and she was treated negligently by her employer himself. Although the chiropracter normally acted in the capacity of an employer with respect to the injured employee, by treating the employee here he was held to have been acting in the capacity of a doctor, and thus was "a person other than an employer" with respect to the injured employee. And the U.S. Supreme Court, in Reed v. The Yaka,[3] ruled that a charterer of a ship who also hired longshoremen directly was liable for injuries resulting from the unseaworthiness of the vessel as well as for compensation benefits under the Longshoremen's and Harbour Workers Compensation Act. A Texas court, in Cohn v. Spinks Industries, Inc.,[4] however, rejected the dual capacity doctrine: "We do not believe that the creation of a new ground of recovery for employees covered by workers' compensation is a proper judicial function." The Michigan appellate court, in Bednarski v. General Motors Corp.,[5] ruled that the worker's disability compensation act does not bar actions against an employer if the employment relationship was only incidentally related to another relationship between the parties that forms the basis for the claim. In this case, a wrongful death action was brought against the employer, alleging that the physicians employed by the corporation failed to detect or reveal decedent's lung cancer during a series of physical and x-ray examinations. The case was remanded to circuit court to be held in abeyance pending a decision by the Workmen's Compensation Board on whether the injury was compensable under the compensation act. If the injury arose from decedent's working condition, the court indicated that it agreed with defendants that compensation benefits should be the exclusive remedy. If the injury was found not to be compensable under the act, plaintiff would then be free to pursue a common law tort action.[6]

To the contrary is Panaro v. Electrolux Corporation,[7] in which the court opined:

The reasons given for rejecting the dual capacity or independent contractor theory are varied but include the fact that company health providers are bona fide regular employees, who have annual salaries, fixed hours and work under the employer's supervision; see, e.g., *Babich v. Pavich*, supra; that the health providers are furthering the primary business interests of the employer; see, e.g., *Proctor v. Ford Motor Co.*, supra; that the health service is limited to employees and not the general public; see, e.g., *Garcia v. Iserson*, supra, 423; and that carving out exceptions to a workers' compensation act is a legislative function; see, e.g., *Boyle v. Breme*, supra, 133. The decision of the Indiana court in *McDaniel v. Sage*, supra, was severely criticized by a leading authority in the field of workers' compensation as follows: "The short answer to the Indiana approach is that company doctors, and nurses, like salaried lawyers, interns, and other professional persons, are now routinely held to be employees for purposes of compensation benefits, and it is unthinkable that a legislature should intend that a given person should be an employee under the act for one purpose and an independent contractor for another." 2A A. Larson, Workmen's Compensation Law (1983) §72.61 (b), pp. 14–228.48-228.49.

A variation on the dual capacity doctrine is the "dual injury" doctrine; that is, instances in which the injury is clearly compensable under workers' compensation but the employer inflicted, with respect to the initial injury, a second and separate injury on the employee outside the scope of workers' compensation.[8] A third-party complaint against the employer for the second injury will be valid.

A successor corporation can be the actor in a dual capacity, as illustrated in Robinson v. KFC National Management Co.,[9] holding that the successor corporation was liable to the injured employee. The Illinois appellate court observed that the successor corporation was obligated to assume the responsibilities and liabilities of its predecessor.

NOTES

1. See 2A Larson, Workmen's Compensation Law (1983) at 14-229.
2. 249 P.2d 8 (Cal., 1952).
3. 373 U.S. 410 (1963).
4. 602 S.W.2d 102 (Tex. Civ. App., 1980).
5. 276 N.W.2d 624 (Mich. App., 1979).
6. See Baron, Handling Occupational Disease Cases (Lawpress, 1981) at 62.
7. 208 Conn. 589 (August 1988) at 597.
8. See Delamotte v. Unicast of Midland Ross Corp., 411 N.E.2d 814 (Ohio App., 1974). See generally Harvey, "Insuring and Defending Employer Liability in a Blankenship/Jones Action: A Contemporary Analysis of Workplace Intentional Torts in Ohio," Def. Counsel J. (April 1987) at 226 et seq.
9. 525 N.E.2d 1028 (Ill. App., 1988).

9

Some Procedural and Other Aspects of Litigation

9.1 Introduction

It should be evident that within the bounds of this volume no effort to delineate the many procedural aspects of occupational injury, disease, and death claims can suffice. Accordingly, focus is placed only on injunctive relief and equitable remedies generally, protective orders, expert testimony, settlement practices, forum non conveniens, res judicata, and collateral estoppel, all of which aspects can play a prominent role in occupational injury, disease, and death claims.

9.2 Injunctive Relief and Equitable Remedies

Equitable remedies developed historically in the English Court of Chancery to counter the rigidity of the common law; they are discretionary in nature and tailored to meet the needs of the particular situation. But injunctive relief is not readily forthcoming, for the traditional rule of equity is that injunctive relief will not be granted when the legal remedy of compensatory damages would be complete and adequate.[1] In more recent days injunctive relief may be granted so long as the legal remedy is not as adequate as the equitable remedy would be.[2]

Restraining orders leading to temporary or permanent injunctions are valuable tools in litigation. In Casoc v. Gotbaum[3] the New York court held that allegations of malicious pollution or contamination of the environment supported the suit for injunctive relief as well as both compensatory and punitive damages. Rule 64 of the Federal Rules of Civil Procedure (FRCP) authorizes the provisional remedy before trial to preserve the status quo, while Rule 65 of FRCP delineates the preliminary injunction granted after notice and hearing, based on the threat to the plaintiff, the hardship on the defendant, the probability that plaintiff will succeed, and the public interest.[4] In Environmental Defense Fund, Inc. v. Lamphier[5] state environmental agencies and private environmental groups sought injunctive relief against the owner-operator of an industrial waste disposal facility, ordering him to comply with the applicable hazardous waste regulations and to make his facility accessible for the purpose of monitoring the wastes. The Fourth Circuit Court of Appeals upheld the injunctive relief as proper when the plaintiff is a state and when the activity may endanger the public health; a state is not bound to conform with the requirements of private litigation, for the state must protect the public interest.

In general, courts have issued injunctive relief without a need of balancing the equities when important public policy is at stake.[6] Irreparable harm is said to occur when a decision to which National Environmental Policy Act (NEPA) obligations attach is made without the informed environmental consideration that NEPA requires, and therefore injunctive relief is in order.[7] But there are numerous cases that uphold the necessity for balancing the equities before a preliminary injunction is validated.[8] In Environmental Defense Fund, Inc. v. Marsh[9] the Fifth Circuit Court of Appeals expounded:

When a court has found that a party is in violation of NEPA, the remedy should be shaped so as to fulfill the objectives of the statute as closely as possible, consistent with the broader public interest. An injunction of the federal action at issue is often appropriate, but the injunction should be limited by general equity principles. One beneficial effect of such injunction is to maintain the *status quo* so that the relevant decision makers and the public may still have the opportunity to choose among alternatives, as required by NEPA. Another purpose is to provide the agency with an incentive to comply with NEPA in as rapid and thorough a manner as is reasonably possible. The court should tailor its relief to fit each particular case, balancing the environmental concerns of NEPA against the larger interests of society that might be adversely affected by an overly broad injunction.

Because the majority of environmental civil actions are equitable, and the characteristic relief sought is injunction, or declaratory judgment or other equitable remedies, the defense of laches can be an important defense. But courts generally frown on that defense, and have repeatedly held that laches is not a bar to relief, as illustrated by Citizens Committee Against Interstate Route 675 v. Lewis,[10] in which laches were held not a bar to an action challenging the adequacy of the environmental impact statement, and Jicarilla Apache Tribe v. Andrus,[11] in which the Tenth Circuit Court of Appeals held that laches is not dependent on when plaintiff becomes aware of the possible legal claim. But in Citizens and Landowners Against the Miles City New Underwood Powerline v. U.S. Secretary of Energy,[12] the Eighth Circuit Court of Appeals found that plaintiffs were aware of state action for an extended period before filing suit, and their unreasonable delay prejudiced the federal government, so that laches was a proper defense.

NOTES

1. See 68 Mich. L. Rev. 1254 (1970) at 1278–1282.
2. Id. at 1279.
3. 323 N.Y.S.2d 742 (1971).
4. Note Lundgrin v. Claytor, 619 F.2d 61 (10th Cir., 1980).
5. 714 F.2d 331 (4th Cir., 1985).
6. See Lathan v. Volpe, 455 F.2d 1111 (9th Cir., 1971).
7. See Massachusetts v. Watt, 19 E.R.C. 1745 (1st Cir., 1983).
8. See Allison v. Froehlke, 470 F.2d 1123 (5th Cir., 1972).
9. 651 F.2d 983 (5th Cir., 1981).
10. 542 F. Supp. 496 (SD Ohio, 1982).
11. 687 F.2d 1324 (10th Cir., 1982).
12. 683 F.2d 1171 (8th Cir., 1982).

9.3 Expert Testimony

In occupational injury, disease, and death litigation expert testimony is mandatory owing to the complex scientific and medical nature of the claim. Should a court rely on the most credible expert, although the expert's opinion is inconsistent with the opinion of the scientific or medical community, or should the court rely on the preponderance of evidence in the scientific or medical community as presented by a party's chosen expert?[1] In Ferebee v. Chevron Chemical Co.[2] an agricultural worker had been exposed in the workplace to the chemical paraquat, and he subsequently contracted pulmonary fibrosis. The employer's defense was based on the statement that paraquat's known effects are acute, not chronic, and that plaintiff-employee had not been exposed in the workplace to a sufficient quantity of the chemical to cause such an illness or disease. The employer's views were generally supported by the scientific and medical communities. But the District of Columbia Court of Appeals refused to reverse the trial court's finding of liability, based, as it were, on the testimony of plaintiff's two examining experts, who were convinced that paraquat exposure had indeed caused his occupational disease. In short, what the federal appellate court had done was supportive of the view favoring preponderance of the evidence as opposed to holding inadmissible an expert's testimony if that testimony did not stand in concert with the general scientific and medical community.

Among the experts in the typical occupational injury, disease, or death litigation are epidemiologists, who study medical statistics. Epidemiology has been recognized in medical science and is generally credited with providing the basis for determining which chemical substances are potentially carcinogenic, for example.[3] As an expert in the science of health statistics and probabilities, an epidemiologist is able to determine, with a high degree of accuracy, the likelihood of certain workers exposed to certain hazards in the workplace to contract occupational injuries, diseases, or death. The epidemiologist is used to testify that, based on available statistics, the probabilities are such that plaintiff-employee's exposure to a certain substance in the workplace did in fact cause the physical injury, disease, or death. As stated in Sulesky v. United States,[4] epidemiological studies "attempt to address the causative line between a disease and a given variable . . . by comparing the incidence of the disease in the population exposed to that given variable . . . with the incidence of the disease in the unexposed population." Epidemiological evidence is deemed more scientific than evidence from animal studies because epidemiological studies are performed on the same "biological species" in order to show "an association between exposure and disease."[5] Unfortunately epidemiological evidence is still inconsistent and sporadic, and a court may instruct the jury to ignore such evidence on a case-by-case basis when the opinion of a treating physician or a similar expert is recognized as being more valuable.[6] The court in the Sulesky case[7] had concluded:

Necessarily and appropriately, the court highly values the testimony of these treating and evaluating physicians. Thus, their expert testimony is more relevant and it is accorded greater weight by the court than that of the epidemiologists who made diagnostic findings in regard to the cause of plaintiff's GBS [Guillain-Barre syndrome] merely by comparing her single occurrence of GBS to a huge statistical universe of GBS incidents and swine flu immunizations.

Yet in Allen v. United States[8] the federal district court in Utah had completely relied on the statistical significance of the relation between ionizing radiation and various cancers, notably leukemia and breast cancer.[9]

Another expert called on to attest to the occupational injury, disease, or death is the toxicologist,[10] who analyzes physical evidence such as tissue samples taken from the employee to establish that plaintiff's condition was caused or was not caused by exposure to workplace conditions.[11] The toxicologist generally speaks in scientific terminology as to how the exposure in the workplace operated so as to cause harm to the employee. The testimony of the toxicologist goes to the establishment of a claim by a preponderance of the evidence; that is, it is more likely than not that a given substance or exposure is the causative agent of the occupational injury, disease, or death. The toxicologist testifies as to probabilities, not possibilities.

The industrial hygienist is the chemical or environmental engineer whose job is to maintain a safe and healthful workplace.[12] His or her testimony is valuable to explain to the jury what type of controls could have been used to prevent the type of occupational injury, disease, or death.

NOTES

1. See generally Jones, "Problems of Causation in Toxic Torts," Def. Counsel J. (July 1988) at 282 et seq.

2. 736 F.2d 1529 (D.C. Cir., 1984): "A cause-effect relationship need not be clearly established by animal or epidemiological studies before a doctor can testify that, in his opinion, such a relationship exists. As long as the basic methodology employed to reach such a conclusion is sound, such as use of tissue samples, standard tests, and patient examination, products liability law does not preclude recovery until a 'statistically significant' number of people have been injured or until science has had the time and resources to complete sophisticated laboratory studies of the chemical. In a courtroom, the test for allowing a plaintiff to recover in a tort suit of this type is not scientific certainty but legal sufficiency; if reasonable jurors *could* conclude from the expert testimony that paraquat more likely than not caused Ferebee's injury, the fact that another jury might reach the opposite conclusion or that science would require more evidence before conclusively considering the causation question resolved is irrelevant" (at 1535–1536).

3. See Baron, Handling Occupational Disease Cases (Lawpress, 1981) at 281–282.

4. 545 F. Supp. 426 (SD W. Va., 1982).

5. See in re "Agent Orange" Product Liability Litigation, 611 F. Supp. 1223 (ED N.Y., 1985) at 1241.

6. Supra note 1 at 286.

7. Supra note 4 at 431.

8. 588 F. Supp. 247 (Utah, 1984).

9. Evaluation of epidemiological evidence must first pass the barrier of whether the particular factor or substance is related to the disease, for example; and the answer is obtained from the famous ten postulates of Henle-Koch-Evans of the nineteenth century, to wit:

1. The prevalence rate of the disease should be significantly higher in those exposed to the hypothetical cause than in controls not so exposed (the cause may be present in the external environment or as a defect in host responses).

2. Exposure to the hypothesized cause should be more frequent among those with the disease than in controls without the disease when all other risk factors are held constant.

3. Incidence of the disease should be significantly higher in those exposed to the cause than those not so exposed, as shown by prospective studies.

4. Temporarily, the disease should follow exposure to the hypothesized causative agent with the distribution of incubation periods on a log-normal-shaped curve.

5. A spectrum of host responses should follow exposure to the hypothesized agent along a logical biologic gradient from mild to severe.

6. A measurable host response following exposure to the hypothesized cause should have a high probability of appearing in those lacking this response before exposure (e.g., antibody, cancer cells) or should increase in magnitude if present before exposure; this response pattern should occur infrequently in persons not so exposed.

7. Experimental reproduction of the disease should occur more frequently in animals or man appropriately exposed to the hypothesized cause than in those not so exposed; this exposure may be deliberate in volunteers, experimentally induced in the laboratory, or demonstrated in a controlled regulation of natural exposure.

8. Elimination or modification of the hypothesized cause or of the vector carrying it should decrease the incidence of the disease (e.g., control of polluted water, removal of tar from cigarettes).

9. Prevention or modification of the host's response on exposure to the hypothesized cause should decrease or eliminate the disease (e.g., immunization, drugs to lower cholesterol, specific lymphocyte transfer factor in cancer).

10. All of the relationships and findings should make biological and epidemiologic sense. The

second portion of the test is whether the 'attributable risk' is greater than .50. Although derived from a mathematical formula, the concept of attributable risk is simple and straightforward. It is the risk the exposed population can attribute to the exposure, taking into account the number of cases that would have occurred in the absence of the exposure. If this risk is greater than .50, it means that more than half the cases of a disease in an exposed population can be attributed to the exposure. Another way to state the ratio is: If the number of cases in the exposed population is at least two times greater than the number of cases in the unexposed population, then the attributable risk is equal to or greater than .50. This also has been defined as the percentage decline in the population disease incidence that would occur if the population's exposure to the factor were eliminated.''

See Nace, ''Epidemiological Evidence: Its Uses and Misuses in Toxic Tort Cases,'' Trial Magazine (October 1988) at 62 et seq.

10. See Freedman, Hazardous Waste Liability (Michie, 1987) at Section 1.22; also note Section 1.19 on the role of the physician, Section 1.20 on the roles of the industrial hygienist and the chemist, and Section 1.21 on the roles of the epidemiologist and the biostatistician.

11. Supra note 3 at 282.

12. Id. at 283.

9.4 Protective Orders

Claiming confidentiality and even competitive harm, employers often use protective orders as a first line of defense against occupational injury, disease, or death claims by employees.[1] The motion for a protective order, if successful, means that the employer will have the responsibility for determining what documents and what information is "confidential"; the employer can even bar disclosure of such documents or information to anyone other than the employee's consulting experts or testimonial experts. As the court in Thayer v. Liggett & Myers Tobacco Co.[2] so well expressed it,

the protective order was serving defendant well in areas unrelated to the protection of its trade secrets or legitimate procedural rights. These indirect benefits, which were unclear to all but defendant when the order was granted, may have been the most important reason for seeking 30(b) protection the [protective order].

. . . .

Plaintiff's attorneys were prohibited from disclosing, discussing or referring to, with any other person, any material, privileged or not, which was furnished by defendant. Fruitful consultation between plaintiff's attorneys with similar cases in other areas was thus effectively throttled. . . . Defendant thus succeeded, to a very significant degree, in isolating plaintiff from outside assistance and advice.

. . . .

The court was somewhat puzzled by the failure of either the discovered material in the court's file or the evidence presented to reveal anything approaching a trade secret.

. . . .

From the first day of the trial approximately a half dozen to a dozen defense attorneys, involved in similar cases around the country, were in constant attendance in the courtroom. These attorneys took notes, conferred with each other and conferred with defendant's counsel. By way of contrast, the breadth of defendant's protective order had effectively prohibited plaintiff from similar consultations.

. . . .

In addition, the order prevents discovery, in future cases, of documents which would normally be public records. This, too, serves defendant well. It makes future discovery for other individual plaintiffs more difficult, more time consuming, and more expensive. It insulates data that could be used for impeachment or other evidentiary purposes. In overall effect, it magnifies the burden any plaintiff will face in the trial of a similar lawsuit. It is calculated to do so. It has already been used for this purpose.

. . . .

The court is convinced that the magnitude of the impact of the disparity of resources between these parties, plus the sophisticated and calculated exploitation of the situation by the defendant, approaches a denial of due process.

NOTES

1. See generally Gilbert and Neumann, "Protective Orders: How to Counter Them," Trial Magazine (November 1987) at 54 et seq.
2. Unreported _____ F. Supp. _____ (WD Mich., 1970).

9.5 Settlement Practices

Settlement practices are so varied as to defy classification, but it is well to observe some of these settlement practices in action. In some states settling with one tortfeasor disposes of the entire case[1], whereas in other states settlement with some tortfeasors is treated as a pro rata offset of the entire settlement amount.[2] The Uniform Contribution Among Joint Tortfeasors Act[3] states that a settlement acts only as a numerical offset from the total amount of the judgment received.

Settlement can frequently result by the utilization of a "Mary Carter" agreement[4]; that is, an agreement between plaintiff-employee and one or more of the defendants who secretly agree to settle the claim in exchange for a lesser amount, or in exchange for defendant's or defendants' financial interest in the favorable outcome of the litigation. In practice, the settling defendant or defendants become a "friend" of the plaintiff in a collusive manner. Although a number of states appear to invalidate the "Mary Carter" agreement,[5] the majority of states hold that such settlement agreements are valid if there is full disclosure of contents to the court and jury.[6] Assume that plaintiff-employee has sustained an occupational injury, disease, or death and sues his employer, the parent company, and the various suppliers of raw materials, and seeks $150,000 in damages. If plaintiff-employee enters into a "Mary Carter" agreement with his employer and the parent company to settle for $100,000, both the plaintiff and his two employers can convivially join forces against the various suppliers. The settling defendants might even retain a financial interest in the outcome of the continuing litigation, and eventually pocket some proceeds in "repayment" from the employee, assuming that the employee is successful in his continuing suit against the various suppliers. The settling defendants will also be called on to furnish evidence, perhaps to attest to the fact that the suppliers knew of the hazards and demonstrated indifference or even callousness toward possible injury, disease, or death of employees.

NOTES

1. See Warren Freedman, Joint and Several Liability: Allocation of Risk and Apportionment of Damages (Butterworth, 1987) at Chapter 4 and Appendix D therein.

2. See Baron, Handling Occupational Disease Cases (Lawpress, 1981) at 267 et seq. Also note 73 A.L.R.2d 403 (1960).

3. See Section 4, 12 Uniform Laws Ann 98: "When a release or a covenant not to sue or not to enforce judgment is given in good faith to one of two or more persons liable in tort for the same injury or the same wrongful death: (a) It does not discharge any of the other tortfeasors from liability for the injury or wrongful death unless its terms so provide; but it reduces the claim against the others to the extent of any amount stipulated by the release or the covenant, or in the amount of the consideration paid for it, whichever is the greater; and, (b) It discharges the tortfeasor to whom it is given from all liability for contribution to any other tortfeasor."

4. See Freedman, International Products Liability (Kluwer, 1987) at Section 3, 02.

5. See Cullen v. Atchison, T. & S.F. Ry., 507 P.2d 353 (Kan., 1973); Lumm v. Stinnett, 87 Nev. 402, 488 P.2d 347 (1971); Alder v. Garcia, 324 F.2d 483 (10th Cir., 1963); Cox v. Kelsey-Hughes Co., 594 P.2d 354 (Okla., 1978); Monjay v. Evergreen School Dist., 13 Wash. App. 654, 537 P.2d 825 (1975); and Trampe v. Wisconsin Tel. Co., 214 Wis. 210, 252 N.W. 675 (1934).

6. See Johnson v. Moberg, 334 N.W.2d 411 (Minn., 1983).

9.6 Forum Non Conveniens

Plaintiff-employee, a resident of Pennsylvania, sustained injuries in Massachusetts while employed by the Pennsylvania employer; he brought his suit in New York, and the employer moved to dismiss on grounds of forum non conveniens.[1] In Anderson v. Consolidated Rail Corp.[2] the New York court granted the motion, finding that the only connection of the lawsuit with the state of New York was that "two of Conrail's employees who witnessed the accident reside in this State, though in counties hundreds of miles from New York County," (where the instant suit was brought). The court opined that "while it is clear that jurisdiction in New York is proper, it is likewise clear that there is no substantial nexus between the action and this State. New York may be convenient for its general accessibility to residents of surrounding States, but the overburdened courts of this State cannot retain jurisdiction in the absence of any nexus with the action simply by reason of New York's accessibility."

A similar approach has been seen in maritime injury cases, like Cruz v. Maritime Company of the Philippines,[3] holding that, even if a crew member may have a claim against the employer-shipowner under the Jones Act, the suit may still be sent to a foreign country under the doctrine of forum non conveniens. Here the Filipino seaman was injured in New Jersey and received treatment in the United States; his employers were Philippine citizens, and the principal base of operations of the vessel was the Philippines. The vessel flew the Philippine flag. Accordingly, the federal district court dismissed the suit, even though U.S. law would apply to the fact of injury and U.S. law had permitted alien crew members to sue foreign shipowners in U.S. courts.[4]

NOTES

1. See generally Freedman, Foreign Plaintiffs in Products Liability Actions: The Defense of Forum Non Conveniens (Quorum Books, 1988).
2. _____ N.Y.S.2d _____ (New York County, November 23, 1988).
3. 702 F.2d 47 (2nd Cir., 1983).
4. Note Karvelis v. Constellation Lines, S.A., 608 F. Supp. 866 (SD N.Y., 1985), aff., 806 F.2d 49 (2nd Cir., 1986).

9.7 Res Judicata

In Mancuso v. Celotex Corp.[1] plaintiff-employee decedent had brought action for personal injury (i.e., asbestosis caused by inhalation of asbestos fibers in the workplace) against various defendants, some of whom he had sued previously in a suit that was terminated with prejudice by a stipulation of discontinuance. These defendants defended on the ground of res judicata, and the New York court granted their motion, since they were parties to the prior action. As the court explained:

Consequently, the court holds that the plaintiff's causes of action against defendants H. K. Porter Co., Inc.; Pittsburgh-Corning Corporation; and Owens-Corning Fiberglass Corporation are barred by the doctrine of res judicata. These defendants were parties to the prior action brought by the plaintiff and were signatories to the stipulation of discontinuance. Therefore, the causes of action against these defendants shall be severed and dismissed.

The plaintiff's contention that the stipulation does not bar this action because of the "revival statute" is without merit. The revival of the limitations period has no effect upon the stipulation of discontinuance which terminated the prior action. The plaintiff's remedy is to bring a plenary action to set aside the stipulation, if so advised (see Teitelbaum Holdings v. Gold, 48 N.Y.2d 51, 54–56; Yonkers Fur Dressing Co. v. Royal Ins. Co., 247 N.Y. 435, 446).

Additionally, the court notes that while the complaint in the discontinued action asserted two causes of action and the complaint in this action asserts four causes of action (albeit the claim for punitive damages is not a separate cause of action, see Collision Plan Unlimited v. Bankers Trust Co., 63 N.Y.2d 827), the doctrine of res judicata "sees a claim or cause of action as coterminous with the transaction regardless of the number of substantive theories or variant forms of relief . . . available to the plaintiff"

(Smith v. Russell Sage College, 54 N.Y.2d 185, 192). Thus, all of the plaintiff's present claims against these defendants are barred.

This cross-motion is, however, denied insofar as it seeks the dismissal of the complaint as against the ACF defendants who were not parties to the prior action (i.e., The Celotex Corporation; Armstrong World Industries, Inc.; Fibreboard Corporation; Owens-Illinois, Inc.; AC and S, Inc.; and GAF Corporation). These defendants cannot rely upon the stipulation of discontinuance and the doctrine of res judicata.

In contrast thereto, note Utter v. South Brookhaven Obstetric and Gynecologic Associates,[2] in which plaintiff-employee, while pregnant, fell at her place of work, and she sued her employer in a representative capacity for the injuries that her child might have suffered in utero! Once that suit against her employer was settled, she turned about and sued the physician who delivered the infant. The physician defended on the ground of res judicata, contending that the plaintiff had recovered for all injuries in the suit against her employer. But the New York Appellate Division, 2nd Dept., refused to dismiss the suit:

The terms of the release given to the employer of the infant plaintiff's mother do not expressly provide for the release of other tortfeasors and there is nothing, short of sheer speculation, to warrant the conclusion that the amount of the settlement is equal to the total amount of the infant plaintiff's loss (see, *Ott v. Barash,* supra, at 263). Moreover, although the infant plaintiff will bear the burden at any hearing conducted pursuant to CPLR 4533-b (*Hill v. St. Clare's Hospital,* supra), it will not be necessary to hold that hearing unless and until one of the defendants is found liable to the infant plaintiff and unless the amount of the verdict exceeds the settlement amount (see, *Manginaro v. Nassau County Med. Center,* 123 A.D.2d 842).

The court took the position that the physician might still be liable for the aggravation of the original injuries to the fetus![3]

NOTES

1. _____ N.Y.S.2d _____ (Nassau County, August 23, 1988).
2. 135 A.D.2d 811 (App. Div. 2nd, 1987).
3. See generally Kramer and Moore, "Joint and Successive Tortfeasors," N.Y.L.J. (July 5, 1988) at 3 and 4.

10

Miscellaneous Occupational Injuries, Diseases, or Deaths and Their Problems

10.1 Physical Injury from Computer Software Error

Admittedly, physical injury caused by computer software error is a new phenomenon,[1] but an increasing number of severe patient harm caused by defective computer software has recently been reported.[2] Recently a patient died, another became partially paralyzed, and a third suffered nerve damage and lost the use of her arm, all from massive overexposure to radiation owing to a flaw in the computer software.[3]

Probably the most prominent "expert system" is "Mycin," designed at Stanford University in the mid-1970s to assist doctors with the diagnosis of bacterial infections and to recommend antibiotic therapy. The doctor supplies "Mycin" with a patient's history, symptoms, and laboratory test results, and "Mycin" recommends a drug treatment according to rules that have been supplied by doctors experienced in infection disease therapy.[4] The risk of catastrophic personal injuries resulting from malfunctioning software is well recognized; computer programs have caused near-misses in the air between passenger jets, the closing of nuclear plants, the false alert of another world war, and the wrong diagnosis by the computer of a person's physical condition.[5] However, as of 1989, the courts seem to have refused to apply strict liability in tort standards to defective software causing injuries, diseases, or death.[6] In Independent School District v. Statistical Tabulating Corp.,[7] however, the federal district court for the Northern District of Illinois had no trouble predicating liability for economic losses sustained when the insured property was damaged by fire; the computer software had made mathematical miscalculations in determining the necessary amount of insurance coverage.

Computer applications in medicine range over the entire span of health care, from purely business and administrative functions to the direct implementation, management, and recording of patient care.[8] The physical harm that may result from software error is said to mandate strict liability in tort standards, although some distinction between the computer's functions as a library resource to store and retrieve information, as a tool in diagnosis and treatment of disease, and as a monitor of a patient's physical health should be made.[9] It is argued that the application of strict liability "may drive vital products from the market and cause severe harm to the health and welfare of the public. . . . Strict liability is an inappropriate standard to apply to medical software because the public interest in the availability of the product outweighs any enhanced accountability of the developer."[10]

NOTES

1. See generally Lawrence, "Strict Liability, Computer Software and Medicine: Public Policy at the Crossroads," 33 Tort & Ins. L. J. (Fall 1987) at 1–18.

2. Note 13 Computer Law & Tax Rep. 4 (October 1986).

3. Supra note 1.

4. See Reece, "Defective Expert Systems Raise Personal Injury Liability Issues," N.L.J. (October 12, 1987) at 24.

5. See Gemignani, "Product Liability and Software," 8 Rutgers Comp. & Tech. L. J. 173 (1981), and Reece, "Litigation over Faulty Software: Complex and Full of Difficulties," 9 N.L.J. (April 20, 1987) at 22.

6. For example, note Chatlos Systems, Inc. v. National Cash Register Corp., 479 F. Supp. 738 (N.J., 1979), and W.R. Weaver Co. v. Burroughs Corp., 580 S.W.2d 76 (Tex. App., 1979).

7. 359 F. Supp. 1095 (ND Ill., 1973).

8. Supra note 1 at 2.

9. It should be evident that computers are composed of "hardware" (the machine itself) and "software" (the set of instructions that tells the computer what it is supposed to do and how it is to do it). Without "software" the computer cannot operate!

10. Supra note 1 at 17–18.

10.2 Acid Rain

Acid rain is defined as "the wet or dry decomposition from the atmosphere of acid chemical compounds"; and although the man-made pollution affects all inhabitants, it also attacks the worker in the workplace with new and additional as well as aggravated threats of occupational injury, disease, and death.[1] A 1982 survey by the U.S. Congressional Office of Technology Assessment reported that half of the 9,400 lakes in twenty-three states had been adversely affected by acid rain, and that of the 117,000 miles of streams, 23,000 miles were "acid-altered."[2] The increased content of sulfur dioxide in the atmosphere is a hazard to human health as well as to crops and buildings.[3]

To combat acid rain it has been suggested that not only should polluters pay, but also that an excise tax be paid by producers of chemical compounds, specifically SO2 and NOx. A federal governmental fund to provide financial assistance for cleanup of acid rain damage and for compensation to victims is also advocated.[4]

NOTES

1. See Acid Precipitation Act of 1980, 42 U.S.C. 8901 et seq at Section 8901(c).
2. See Freedman, Hazardous Waste Liability (Michie, 1987) at Section 1.8.
3. Note McCartney, "Acid-Rain Control Difficult Under Existing Law," Trial Magazine (November 1987) at 77 et seq.
4. Id. at 78.

10.3 Future Injury

Should damages for future injuries or for being put at a greater risk of future damages be compensable? At common law it would appear that no award could be made for an injury that has not occurred, on the theory that such future injury is merely speculative or that a windfall might otherwise be awarded to a claimant.[1] But with respect to occupational disease, as opposed to occupational injury or death, which is not only latent, but also unique, the courts have in recent years begun to consider concepts that are close to compensating for "enhanced risk," for example. In Jackson v. Johns-Manville Sales Corp.[2] the Fifth U.S. Court of Appeals permitted suit for probability of getting cancer and for cancerphobia. But in Bennett v. Mallinkrodt Chemical Co.[3] the claim for "enhanced risk" was not allowed, since the claim was for future injury that simply could not be maintained on the basis of mathematical probability that injury will occur. "Enhanced risk" enabled plaintiffs to sue now in Bradford v. Susquehanna Corp.,[4] a radiation exposure case, in which the future injury was a mere possibility; in Davis v. Graviss,[5] in which the likelihood of future injury incurring was deemed not probable, but possible; and in Haggerty v. L & L Marine Services,[6] in which the seaman was doused with chemicals and was permitted to sue for cancerphobia plus compensation for medical monitoring and detection. The contrary view is evident in the language of the New Jersey Supreme Court in Ayers v. Township of Jackson[7]:

A holding that recognizes a cause of action for unquantified enhanced risk claims exposes the tort system, and the public it serves, to the task of litigating vast numbers of claims for compensation based on threats of injuries that may never occur. It imposes on judges and juries the burden of assessing damages for the risk of potential disease, without clear guidelines to determine what level of compensation may be appropriate. It would undoubtedly increase already escalating insurance rates. It is clear that the recognition of an "enhanced risk" cause of action, particularly when the risk is unquantified, would generate substantial litigation that would be difficult to manage and resolve.

The Pennsylvania Supreme Court, in Martin v. Johns-Manville Corp.,[8] also ruled that evidence of increased risk was properly excluded by the trial court, and "a jury may not award damages on the basis of speculation or conjecture. Instead, the plaintiff must present competent evidence from which a jury can reasonably determine the degree to which future consequences of a present injury are probable, and, accordingly, what the amount of any damages award should be." Of course, the plaintiff can wait, and when the future injury occurs, bring suit, provided that the statute of limitations has not run![9] In this Florida case the court opined that allowing recovery for the risk of cancer from asbestos inhalation in the workplace would disserve rather than promote the goals of finality and judicial economy. Yet, "because asbestosis, unlike cancer, may be mild, non-life threatening, and relatively inexpensive to treat, many asbestosis victims would not sue were not recovery allowed for the risk of cancer."

When the employer's conduct increased the risk of a particular injury that the plaintiff ultimately suffered, the plaintiff-employee must plead for compensation, not for the injury itself, but for the increased risk of that injury.[10]

Medical surveillance damages[11] have become more common as an element in the recognition of recovery for future damages. As the New Jersey Supreme Court expressed it in Schroeder v. Perkel,[12] the injured party is entitled to recover a "reasonable value of past and future medical services necessitated by defendant's tortious conduct." It is well established that a tort victim is entitled to recover those medical expenses reasonably certain to occur in the future.[13] In Friends for All Children, Inc. v. Lockwood Aircraft Corp.[14] the federal appellate court indicated that medical surveillance damages should be recognized in the absence of a manifested physical injury because "it is difficult to dispute that an individual has an interest in avoiding expensive diagnostic examinations just as he or she has an interest in avoiding physical injury. When a defendant negligently invades this interest, the injury to which is neither speculative nor resistant to proof, it is elementary that the defendant should make the plaintiff whole by paying for the examinations."

NOTES

1. See Laswell v. Brown, 524 F. Supp. 847 (WD Mo., 1981), in which the court, in granting defendant's motion to dismiss for failure to state a claim on which relief could be granted, opined: "A lawsuit for personal injuries cannot be based upon the possibility of some future harm. . . . The complaint is conspicuously void of any allegations that children (of the father who had been exposed to nuclear radiation) have sustained any damage other than exposure to a higher risk of disease and cellular damage."

2. 750 F.2d 1314 (5th Cir., 1985).

3. 698 S.W.2d 854 (Mo., 1984).

4. 586 F. Supp. 14 (Colo., 1984).

5. 672 S.W.2d 928 (Ky., 1984).

6. 788 F.2d 256 (5th Cir., 1986).

7. 525 A.2d 287 (N.J., 1987).

8. 494 A.2d 1088 (Pa., 1985).

9. See Eagle Picher Industries, Inc. v. Cox, 481 So.2d 517 (Fla. App., 1985).

10. See Gradel v. Inouye, 381 A.2d 975 (Pa., 1977), and Hamil v. Bashline, 364 A.2d 1366 (Pa. 1976).

11. See Freedman, Hazardous Waste Liability (Michie, 1987) at Section 9.8.

12. 432 A.2d 834 (N.J., 1981).

13. See generally Slagel, "Medical Surveillance Damages: A Solution to the Inadequate Compensation of Toxic Tort Victims," Trial Magazine (October 1988) at 44 et seq.

14. 746 F.2d 816 (D.C. Cir. 1989); also note earlier cases at 725 F.2d 1392, and 717 F.2d 602. District court opinions are at 644 F. Supp. 1289, 593 F. Supp. 388, 587 F. Supp. 180, 567 F. Supp. 790, 563 F. Supp. 552, 533 F. Supp. 895, and 497 F. Supp. 313.

10.4 Comparative Fault in the Workplace

Plaintiff operated for his employer a planing machine with blades protected by a metal guard designed to close after the board being planed had cleared the cutter head. A board slipped out of his hand and he reached down to catch it; because the guard plate had not closed completely, the cutting blades sliced off two of his fingers and lacerated other fingers. In Lippard v. Houdaille Industries, Inc.[1] the injured employee sued, alleging that the planing machine was defective and unreasonably dangerous; his employer replied that the injury resulted solely from his carelessness in placing his hand near the cutting head. The trial court instructed the jury to assess a percentage of fault against the plaintiff-employee if it found that his negligence had contributed to his injury. The jury found his damages were $75,000 and that he was 50 percent at fault, and entered judgment for plaintiff in the sum of $37,500. The Missouri Supreme Court reversed, ordering the lower court to enter judgment for the full amount of $75,000, thus not recognizing the comparative fault ruling of the trial court. Under strict liability in tort, the defense of comparative fault or comparative negligence was simply not cognizable![2] And the court concluded:

We conclude that there should be no change in the Missouri common law rule, as established in the *Keener* opinion, that the plaintiff's contributory negligence is not an issue in a products liability case. It should neither defeat nor diminish recovery. The defendant may sometimes make use of the plaintiff's alleged carelessness in support of arguments that the product is not unreasonably dangerous, or that the alleged defects in a product did not cause the injury, but these are traversing claims not appropriate for instruction. If the defective product is a legal cause of injury, then even a negligent plaintiff should be able to recover. . . . We adhere to the view that distributors of "defective products unreasonably dangerous" should pay damages for injuries caused by the products, without reduction because a plaintiff may have been guilty of carelessness.

It should be noted that California and Hawaii apply comparative fault in all strict liability cases with no limitation on the level of plaintiff's culpability.[3] Some states have refused to apply comparative fault principles to strict liability.[4]

NOTES

1. 715 S.W.2d 491 (Mo., 1986).

2. It should be noted that three years earlier the same court had, in Gustafson v. Benda, 661 S.W.2d 11 (Mo., 1983), abolished the all-or-nothing rule of contributory negligence as an absolute bar in negligence cases in Missouri.

3. See Daly v. General Motors Corp., 575 P.2d 1162 (Cal., 1978), and Kaneko v. Hilo Coast Processing Co., 654 P.2d 343 (Hawaii, 1982).

4. See Melia v. Ford Motor Co., 534 F.2d 795 (8th Cir., 1976), and Young's Machine Co. v. Long, 692 P.2d 24 (Nev., 1984).

10.5 Assumption of Risk

The doctrine of assumption of risk acts to bar or reduce an employee's recovery for any harms caused him because of a risk he knowingly takes. In Maddox v. City of New York[1] a professional baseball player with the New York Yankees slipped and fell at Shea Stadium in the ninth inning of a June 1975 night game. Apparently, while running to his left for a fly ball, his shoe hit a wet spot, and he slid and got stuck in a mud puddle, causing the buckling of his knee. The injury required surgical procedures that forced his premature retirement from professional baseball. He sued the city of New York (owner of Shea Stadium), the lessee (the New York Mets professional baseball team), the general contractor, the architect, and the consulting engineer; other defendants were brought in by way of third-party suits and cross claims. Basically, his claim rested on the drainage system, which he contended was negligently designed, constructed, and maintained. During his deposition he testified that he was aware of the wet and muddy condition of the playing field and of the particular puddle into which he fell. The defendants moved for summary judgment on the basis of assumption of risk. Plaintiff-employee of the New York Yankees countered that he had assumed only the risks of the game, not the risks of the playing field, which was admittedly in an unreasonably dangerous condition. But the New York Court of Appeals affirmed the dismissal of his claim, and pointed out that plaintiff was a professional athlete "more highly trained and in a better bargaining position than persons injured by consumer products." The court also rejected his contention that he assumed the risks of the game, but not the condition of the playing field because the assumption of risk doctrine applies "to any facet of the activity inherent in it and to any open and obvious condition of the place where it is carried on."

It is said that electrocution accidents are the fifth leading known cause of workplace deaths, with more than 50 percent of the total occurring in the construction industry.[2] Assumption of the risk is obviously a factor in defending against claims based on such accidents. Prominent among defendants are mechanical equipment manufacturers of cranes, derricks, aerial hoists, pole-diggers, and concrete pump trucks, along with construction entities and electrical utility companies.[3]

NOTES

1. 66 N.Y.2d 270, 487 N.E.2d 553 (1985).
2. See Mongeluzzi, "Electrocution Accidents on the Job," Trial Magazine (March 1989) at 69 et seq.
3. Id.

10.6 The Bhopal, India, Industrial Catastrophe

It was on December 3, 1984, that more than 3,000 Indian worker-citizens died and more than 200,000 others sustained serious and disabling injuries when the Union Carbide plant in Bhopal, India, emitted the poisonous gas methyl isocyanate over a twenty-five square-mile area.[1] As of 1989, efforts at securing adequate compensation for the thousands of Indian worker-citizens injured, diseased, or dead as the result of inhalation of the poisonous gas have been frustrated. The defendant is not willing to even consider the government of India's demand of $3 billion in damages; the defendant is content to rest on its old offer of several hundred million dollars.[2] On May 12, 1986, the federal district court for the Southern District of New York[3] dismissed the lawsuit on forum non conveniens grounds and transferred the action to the courts of India. On January 14, 1987, the Second U.S. Court of Appeals affirmed the transfer of the case to the courts of India.[4]

On November 1, 1988, the India Supreme Court, in a public pronouncement, asked both parties to settle their protracted legal dispute over liability and compensation. The highest Indian court commenced hearings on the substantive arguments,[5] and the settlement in February 1989 of $470 million would appear to be totally inadequate, judging by the public reaction in India and in other countries around the globe. What the American multinational corporation saved in compensation may well result in a greater loss owing to ill will and contempt for the "ugly American."

NOTES

1. Note Wall Street Journal (December 4, 1984) at 3. The chemical attacks the mucous membranes, eyes, nose, and throat, and injuries include blindness, sterility, emphysema, liver and kidney damage, mental retardation, inter alia.
2. See Warren Freedman, International Products Liability (Kluwer, 1987) at Section 17.19.

3. In Re Union Carbide Corporation Gas Plant Disaster at Bhopal, India, in December 1984, 634 F. Supp. 842 (SD N.Y., 1984), aff., 809 F.2d 195 (2nd Cir., 1987), cert. den. 108 S. Ct. 199 (1987).

4. 809 F.2d 195 (2nd Cir., 1987).

5. See New York Times (November 2, 1988) at 12: "On July 25, 1988, in *Garg v. Union Carbide Corp.*, Judge Jacobson of the Connecticut Superior Court at Bridgeport, ruled that the individual plaintiffs (without the Government of India as a party) could bring suit for injuries and deaths sustained in the Bhopal tragedy because the Government of India was not an indispensable party. In the 17-page opinion, the court authorized the plaintiffs and the defendant to 'enter into settlement negotiations under the direction of this court.' Unfortunately, the opinion contains statements such as 'This court does not have to recognize the Bhopal Act if it chooses not to do so. Therefore, any decisions rendered by an Indian court which purport to preclude settlement in Connecticut courts are not binding.' Judge Jacobson's opinion also contains little discussion of the paramount jurisdictional issue, nor does it note the role of Union Carbide India Limited.''

10.7 Exposures to Chemicals and Toxins in the Workplace

A recent survey[1] reported that U.S. employers have, for the most part, generally neglected basic safety measures, particularly in the chemical industry, such as installing overflow tanks for runaway chemical reactions or leaks, locating plants in sparsely populated areas with buffer zones, building dikes for storage tanks, or reducing the volume of dangerous chemicals in storage. Cited was the episode in 1970 when a vapor cloud from a broken propane pipeline filled a ten-acre valley near Port Hudson, Missouri, and then exploded with the force of fifty tons of dynamite, damaging buildings five miles away; four farm families fled in terror from the leak. The Environmental Protection Agency has disclosed that in the five-year period from 1981 to 1986 almost 7,000 accidents with acutely toxic chemicals occurred, killing 135 persons and injuring more than 1,500 persons.[2]

Chemicals embrace more than 6 million substances, of which perhaps 80 percent have been synthesized during the past fifty years or more. New chemicals are being created at the same rate, which means that each month about 10,000 more chemicals will be in existence; fortunately most of the known chemicals have no practical use and many are scientific or technological curiosities. But the 60,000 chemicals in daily use today are significant enough to create millions of different products and millions of different health problems.[3] Chemicals can cause damage to the human reproductive system, can originate malformation of the foetus, and can cause cancer and countless other maladies. It is often difficult to detect these hazards, and even more difficult to demonstrate that a certain chemical has no long-term harmful effect. It is more important to know whether a given chemical is acutely toxic today, but scientific and medical experience has not been fully informative.[4]

Burning plastics is another chemical pollutant, but it is unlike acid rain, which epitomizes the futility of seeking damages for its harmful effects. Burning plastics has been the subject matter of successful suits in the United States by individual plaintiffs damaged by the plastics' smoke.[5] Such chemical forms as polyvinyl chloride,[6] styrenes, synthetic rubbers, resins, and foam, which are oil-based, do burn and do give off thick, black, and frequently poisonous smoke that causes fire deaths. Recovery for damages from these burning plastics will be frequent in the years ahead, both nationally and internationally.

Polychlorinated biphenyls (PCBs) was the subject of a prolonged lawsuit in State of New York v. Consolidated Edison Co.[7] Here the state sought the authority to enforce a six-year-old law designed to protect workers from exposure to toxic substances. At dispute was the enforcement of Section 882 of the New York Right to Know Law, enacted in 1980 to require notice to employees regarding exposure to toxic substances.[8] The particular carcinogen, PCBs, was found in chemical residue in boilers after burning. The court, in upholding the state of New York, observed that it could not "leave in limbo the very employees the legislature clearly intended to be informed and trained concerning toxic substances in the workplace."

Still another workplace hazard is radiation that comes in the manufacturing of consumer products, ranging from ovens and burglar alarms to industrial and military hardware such as power lines and radar. It is simply not understood by bench and bar, as radiation is probably, at best, an example of the latent injury, disease, or damage.[9] There is in the first place a lack of hard evidence about the danger of microwaves, for example, or the harm caused by exposure to what scientists call "non-ionizing" radiation, which excludes x-rays. Workers in high-risk industries have filed numerous workers' compensation claims and third-party lawsuits; the spread of computer terminology in offices has also raised concern over illnesses from cataracts to cancer that could have been caused by exposure to such radiation emitted by video display terminals. About the only court judgment that found that microwaves caused "an occupational microwave radiation disease" was Yannon v. New York Telephone,[10] which affirmed an award of a New York State Workers' Compensation Board to the plaintiff–telephone repairman who had adjusted microwave transmission towers on the eighty-seventh floor of the Empire State Building for more than thirteen years.[11] Of course, there have undoubtedly been many quiet settlements over the years, but without scientific and medical evidence; proof of the injuries, diseases, and damages caused by radiation is most difficult to substantiate.

Defenses of employers and product manufacturers over the years in occupational injury, disease, or death cases have successfully invoked the "sophisticated user" argument.[12] In Littlehale v. duPont[13] two civilian Navy employees were severely injured when a blasting cap exploded prematurely, some thirteen years after the Navy purchased the blasting cap. The court granted summary judgment for the defendant explosive manufacturer in an action based on failure to warn. In essence, the product manufacturer had no duty to warn a "sophisticated user" or an employer of that "sophisticated user." Sixteen years later, in Goodbar v. Whitehead Brothers, Inc.,[14] plaintiffs were 132 foundry workers who suffered silicosis because of exposure in the workplace to silica dust; the federal district court ruled that the employer knew so much about the hazards of silicosis that sand suppliers would be relieved from any duty to warn employees about these hazards.[15] The Fourth U.S. Court of Appeals affirmed the holding, and observed that the sand suppliers could not possibly have provided direct warnings about silicosis to the 132 foundry workers![16]

On the other hand, it would appear that the universal and better rule is that a supplier has the ultimate duty to warn, unless the injuries were totally unforeseeable.[17] In Neal v. Carey Canadian Mines, Ltd.[18] the court held that under Pennsylvania law, the manufacturer's duty to supply a safe product to the ultimate user was not delegable; there is a duty to warn of foreseeable dangers, regardless of the presence of an intermediary, to wit: the employer.[19] And in Whitehead v. St. Joe Lead Co.[20] the Third U.S. Court of Appeals observed that the fact that a supplier relied on a sophisticated intermediary to correct a product defect did not diminish the supplier's duty to warn the ultimate user.

In 1983 the Occupational Safety and Health Administration (OSHA) introduced the Hazard Communication Regulations,[21] which required manufacturers to provide detailed information on all chemicals shipped after May 1986, thereby replacing state and local laws that required workplace warnings.[22] Employers in interstate commerce are required to supply employees with training and toxicity data on workplace chemicals, and the chemical manufacturer must supply employers with detailed information about each chemical shipped.[23]

Proof sufficient to award compensation for injuries allegedly caused by exposure to chemicals and toxins in the workplace may not be present, as illustrated most recently in Briggs v. Pymm Thermometer Corp.,[24] in which the New York court concluded that the employees exposed to mercury fumes at unsafe levels simply did not prove an "intentional tort" on the part of the employer so as to surmount the exclusivity of workers' compensation. A Brooklyn, New York, jury, in 1987, had convicted the owners of a factory of assault for injuries suffered by an employee, exposed to the mercury, who suffered brain damage; but the court overturned that verdict on the grounds that state prosecution was preempted by the federal OSHA. In the instant claim the employees contended that the employer's defense of lack of intentional tort should be expanded to include situations in which an employer intentionally misrepresented or concealed facts to keep employees working in an unsafe environment.

NOTES

1. See New York Times (May 11, 1986) at 26.
2. Id.
3. See World Health Magazine, supra 38, at 28.

4. IRPTC had, before 1985, prepared a legal file on 450 chemical substances based on national and international recommendations as well as mechanisms related to the control of substances in air, water, wastes, soil, sediments, animal and plant tissues, food and beverages, consumer goods, and agriculture.

5. See generally Nat'l L. J. (October 22, 1984) at 32 et seq. After a nightclub fire the manufacturers of polyvinyl chloride plumbing settled for $4 million, In Re Beverly Hills Fire Litigation, Dkt. 77-79 (ED Ky., 1979).

6. Polyvinyl chloride, for example, can yield hydrogen chloride, a precursor of hydrochloric acid, when heated. Polyurethane foam can produce cyanide when burned; other plastics, such as ABS in drain pipes, can act like fuses to spread fires.

7. Unreported ___ N.Y.S.2d ___ (August 12, 1986).

8. See Section 10.8 hereinafter.

9. See N.Y.L.J. (January 28, 1985) at 21–22.

10. WCB #0714-2308 and WCB #0752-3602 (New York, 1980).

11. 450 N.Y.S.2d 893 (1982).

12. See generally Middleton and Shaffer, "The Intermediary Defense in Toxic Torts: Handicapping the Sophisticated User," Trial Magazine (November 1988) at 66 et seq.

13. 286 F. Supp. 791 (SD N.Y., 1966), aff., 380 F.2d 274 (2nd Cir., 1967).

14. 591 F. Supp. 552 (WD Va., 1983).

15. Supra note 12 at 67.

16. 769 F.2d 213 (4th Cir., 1983).

17. Note Section 388(a) of Restatement (Second) of Torts.

18. 548 F. Supp. 367 (ED Pa., 1982), aff. sub. nom., Van Buskirk v. Carey Canadian Mines, Ltd., 760 F.2d 481 (3rd Cir., 1985).

19. Id. at 368 and 482.

20. 729 F.2d 238 (3rd Cir., 1984).

21. 48 Fed. Reg. 53,280 (November 25, 1983).

22. See 48 Fed. Reg. 53,346 (1983).

23. Note 48 Fed. Reg. 53,340 and 343 (1983). The policy behind the rule is stated as follows: "Chemical manufacturers are in the best position to develop and disseminate this [hazard-related] information not only because they have greater scientific expertise with respect to the chemicals they produce, but also because they may be the only ones who know the identity of the chemicals in the first place. . . . .

"Because of the inadequacy of chemical information, the employer cannot or does not take into account the potential impact his or her decision concerning the use of the chemical product may have on others. Employees pay for the inadvertent or advertent errors in judgment by an employer through impaired health, injury, or death. Other members of the society pay through a reduction in production and community welfare" (48 Fed. Reg. 53, 322 and 323).

24. ___ N.Y.S.2d ___ (App. Div., 2nd Dept., February 10, 1989).

10.8 The New York Right to Know Law

The right to know laws are designed to inform, train, and otherwise make the workplace a safe place in which to work.[1] In the New York case of State of New York v. Consolidated Edison Co.[2] the Right to Know Law was instrumental in enabling the state to protect workers from exposure to toxic substances. The defendant-employer argued that the case should be dismissed because the New York Department of Labor and Health had failed to promulgate regulations as required by statute. Three employees, four years previous, had complained that plaintiff-employer failed to give them information concerning their possible exposure to polychlorinated biphenyls, the carcinogen found in chemical residue in boilers after burning. The court observed:

The Right to Know Law was passed in 1980, in recognition "that there exists a danger to the health of employees and their families throughout the state because [of] hazardous exposure to toxic substances encountered during the course and scope of employment" (Declaration of Purpose, §1, L. or 1980 c.551). The New York legislation is among the most stringent state standards ("Responses to Occupational Disease, etc." Geo. L.J. 1231 [1984]). It requires notice to employees, provision of information regarding effects of exposure, symptoms, emergency treatment and proper conditions for safe use of toxic substances. The statute mandates creation of training programs for employees and for maintenance of medical records for a forty-year period for employees who handle such substances. . . .

The Right to Know Law provides for the promulgation of regulations by both the Department of Labor and the Department of Health. While "The industrial commissioner *may* promulgate such regulations as he shall consider necessary and proper to effectuate the purposes and provisions of this article" (§881, emphasis added), the duty upon the Commissioner of Health is mandatory: he "shall promulgate rules and regulations and take all other actions necessary for the effective implementation of this article" [Public Health L. §4802(3)]. However, the only regulations promulgated to date are the Department of Health regulations on disclosure of information on trade secrets (10 NYCRR Part 72 [1982]). Annual reports of the Department of Labor, and an affidavit from an official of the Department of Health, indicate that although some departmental discussion of policy formulation has taken place, no overall regulations are imminent.

At issue is how the Right to Know Law is to be enforced. The statute provides a detailed administrative agency investigative and determination procedure to enforce the section 880 guarantee of employees rights, in the face of employer discrimination. However, the Right to Know Law contains no overall agency enforcement scheme. Nor have regulations been issued to fill that gap.

The statute does provide for enforcement by the Attorney General. Section 882(1) provides:

"1. Civil penalty. Any employer who fails to comply with the provisions of this article shall be liable for a civil penalty not to exceed ten thousand dollars in addition to other damages for which an employer may be liable pursuant to any other provision of law. *The attorney general may bring an action in the supreme court against any person or persons alleged to have violated the provisions of this article.* In any such action the supreme court shall have jurisdiction to restrain violations of this article and to levy appropriate penalties" (emphasis added).

The court then concluded:

The wording of the statute is plain. More elaborate implications, not contained in the factual language, should not be read into the statute. "Where the statutory language is clear and unambiguous, the court should construe it so as to give effect to the plain meaning of the words used" (PBA v. NYC, 41 N.Y.2d 205, 208).

When the legislature intended to detail an investigative procedure for the Commissioner of Labor, it did so quite plainly. In the absence of such elaboration, §882(1) grants the attorney general authority to sue without restraint. Where the Legislature creates specific enforcement provisions, "we will not lightly assume an unexpressed intention to create additional ones" (Fox v. Reich & Tang, 692 F.2d 250, 255 [2d Cir., 1982]).

When statutory language is clear, other contradictory evidence of legislative intent is inappropriate (Civil Service Employees Association v. Oneida, 78 A.D.2d 1004 [1980]). Con Ed proffers affidavits by legislators and their aides, stating that §882 was premised on Department of Labor investigation. Such pronouncements cannot modify a plain statutory mandate. "Post enactment statements or testimony by an individual legislator, even a sponsor, is irrelevant" (Id. at 1005). . . .

However, where as here, the relevant administrative agency has failed to perform and some very concrete definitions, including that of "toxic substance," have been provided by the Right to Know Law itself (Section 875[2]), then the Court itself should act, as it is empowered to do so here; notwithstanding that administrative guidelines might be preferable.

NOTES

1. See A.B.A.J. (October 1, 1987) at 31.
2. Unreported _____ N.Y.S.2d _____ (New York County, August 12, 1986).

10.9 Latent Disease and Latent Injury

It is well to observe that in many instances, the injury or disease is latent and may not arise for decades, or even at the time of the lawsuit. The argument is that what one may suffer in the future does not "create a present cause of action," and consequently such future injury, disease, or damage often goes uncompensated. However, it is submitted that the medical fact that early detection of the injury or disease will facilitate treatment that will cure the impact of the injury or disease (and diminish social and business costs) should push both courts and legislatures to grant currently some form of relief or compensation. Latent injuries were not readily recognized in Reserve Mining Co. v. Environmental Protection Agency,[1] in which the Eighth U.S. Court of Appeals held that the federal district court had abused its discretion in ordering the closing of the taconite-processing plant that had emitted asbestos-like particles into the air because "it cannot be said that the probability of harm is more likely than not. Moreover, the level of probability does not readily convert into a prediction of consequences. On this record, it cannot be forecast that the rates of cancer will increase from drinking Lake Superior water or breathing Silver

Bay air. The best that can be said is that the existence of this asbestos contaminant in the air and water gives rise to a reasonable medical concern for public health.'' Indeed, the fact of injury or disease is complex, and the causal relation of the contaminant to the injury is even more unascertainable. Interestingly, courts have ruled that the cost of monitoring a current injury to detect possible manifestation of future injury is compensable.

As stated by the New Jersey Supreme Court in Ayers v. Township of Jackson,[2] it would be

inequitable for an individual wrongfully exposed to dangerous toxic chemicals but unable to prove that disease is likely to have to pay his own expenses when medical intervention is clearly reasonable and necessary. . . . Accordingly, we hold that the cost of medical surveillance is a compensable item of damages where the proofs demonstrate, through reliable expert testimony predicated upon the significance and extent of exposure to chemicals, the toxicity of the chemicals, the seriousness of the diseases for which individuals are at risk, the relative increase in the chance of onset of disease in those exposed, and the value of early diagnosis, that such surveillance to monitor the effect of exposure to toxic chemicals is reasonable and necessary.

And in Hagerty v. L & L Marine Services, Inc.,[3] in which the plaintiff tankerman on a barge was doused with dripolene, a chemical containing benzene, toluene, and xyolene, and he suffered dizziness, leg cramps, and a stinging sensation in his extremities, the court concluded that he may recover the reasonable costs of periodic medical checkups ''to the extent that, in the past, they were medically advisable and, in the future, will probably remain so.''

NOTES

1. See Rheingold v. E.R. Squibb & Sons, Inc., unreported ____ F. Supp. ____ (SD N.Y., 1975).
2. 525 A.2d 287 (N.J., 1987).
3. 788 F.2d 315 (5th Cir., 1986), modif., 797 F.2d 256 (5th Cir., 1986).

10.10 The Private Cause of Action Under Statute

Generally there is no private right of action or private right of enforcement under a statute unless the statute expressly so states.[1] However, there are exceptions thereto, for it can be shown that some statutes implicitly create that private right of action.[2] In Texas & Pacific Railway v. Rigsby[3] the U.S. Supreme Court, in examining the Federal Safety Appliances Act of 1893, set forth two tests: Is the injured party a member of a group for whose special benefit the particular statute was enacted? Would the primary purpose of the statute be served by inferring that a private cause of action is implicit in the statute? Eighty-two years later, in Cort v. Ash,[4] the highest court added two more tests:

Is there evidence of legislative intent to create a private cause of action? Is the private cause of action one that is traditionally an area of state rather than federal concern? The fifth test was enunciated in 1981 in Middlesex County Sewerage Authority v. National Sea Clammers Association[5]: What is the intent of the legislature? Civil rights statutes like 42 U.S.C. 1983 appear to be readily enforcible by private citizens.[6]

On the other hand, some courts have rejected the implication of private rights under federal statutes.[7] In Milwaukee v. Illinois and Michigan[8] a kind of "inverse Cort" test was articulated in which the existence of a comprehensive federal regulatory scheme was held by implication to revoke previously existent common law remedies. But Section 20 of the Toxic Substances Control Act of 1976 (TOSCA)[9] explicitly authorizes private actions against any people alleged to be violating the Act or any rule issued under the Act, and against the Environmental Protection Agency (EPA) to compel it to perform any nondiscretionary duty under the Act. This section is modeled after the "citizen suit" provision of the Clean Air Act,[10] which was the Congress' first attempt at including an explicit private right of action in an environmental statute. Like the Clean Air Act's citizen suit provision, the one in TOSCA also requires sixty days' prior notice to the EPA and to any potential defendant; prohibits a suit from being filed if the EPA or the attorney general are "diligently prosecuting" an action concerning the same alleged violation, and permits awards of costs and attorney's fees. Despite this broad grant of power to sue, a county has been held to lack capacity to bring a private suit under TOSCA as parens patriae of its residents.[11] So far, perhaps because of the relative newness and complexity of TOSCA, there have been practically no reported cases under the "citizens' civil actions" provision. Probably, although the language is not completely unambiguous, damages are not recoverable under this section. Also, despite ambiguous statutory language, the Supreme Court has held that attorney's fees may be awarded under this section only to parties who succeed on the merits.[12]

NOTES

1. See Freedman, Hazardous Waste Liability (Michie, 1987) at Chapter 5 thereof.
2. Id. at Section 5.4 thereof.
3. 241 U.S. 33 (1916).
4. 422 U.S. 66 (1975).
5. 453 U.S. 1 (1981).
6. See Maine v. Thiboutot, 448 U.S. 1 (1980).
7. Note Universities Research Association, Inc. v. Contu, 101 S. Ct. 1451 (1981).
8. 451 U.S. 304 (1981).
9. 15 U.S.C. 2601–2629.
10. 42 U.S.C. 7604.
11. See Warren County v. North Carolina, 528 F. Supp. 276 (ED N.C., 1981).
12. Note Ruckelhaus v. Sierra Club, 463 U.S. 680 (1983).

10.11 The Asbestos in School Problem

In 1980 Congress recognized that asbestos was also a problem in schools, and enacted the Asbestos School Hazard Detection and Control Act,[1] which recognized that

exposure to asbestos fibers has been identified over a long period of time and by reputable medical and scientific evidence as significantly increasing the incidence of cancer and other severe or fatal diseases [and that], because there is no Federal health standard regulating the concentration of asbestos fibers in noncommercial workplace environments such as schools, school employees and students may be exposed to hazardous concentrations of asbestos fibers in the school buildings which they use each day.

Under the Act the secretary of education is required "to establish a task force to assist States and local educational agencies to ascertain the extent of the danger to the health of school children and employees from asbestos materials in schools."[2] Scientific, technical, and financial assistance is to be provided to local education agencies to mitigate asbestos hazards in schools. There is also a "whistle-blowers" protection provision to assure that "no employee of any local educational agency suffers any disciplinary action as a result of calling attention to potential asbestos hazards which may exist in schools."[3]

The legislation makes clear that nothing in the Act shall "affect the right of any party to seek legal redress in connection with the purchase or installation of asbestos materials in schools or any claim of disability or death related to exposure to asbestos in a school setting."[4]

NOTES

1. See Warren Freedman, Hazardous Waste Liability (Michie, 1987) at Section 3.4. See 20 U.S.C. 3601–3611.
2. 20 U.S.C. 3601(b)(1).
3. 20 U.S.C. 3601(b)(5) and 3608.
4. 20 U.S.C. 3609(1).

10.12 Noise Control Act of 1972

Noise pollution in the workplace and elsewhere is addressed by the Noise Control Act of 1972,[1] as amended by the Quiet Communities Act of 1978.[2] The Act follows the pattern of other pollution statutes in establishing an Office of Noise Abatement and Control within the Environmental Protection Agency (EPA).[3]

Under the Act the EPA is required to establish noise emission standards for products identified as major noise sources, which fall into the categories of construction equipment, transportation equipment, motors or engines, and electrical or electronic equipment.[4] Noise emission standards and regulations for trucks, buses, railroad trains, and other surface motor carriers engaged in interstate commerce are enforceable by the U.S. Department of Transportation.[5] The EPA is required to submit aircraft noise and sonic boom standards and regulations to the Federal Aviation Administration (FAA), and the FAA can accept, modify, or reject EPA-proposed regulations.[6]

The Noise Control Act is enforced by civil and criminal penalties, and also provides for citizen suits similar to those authorized under the Clean Air Act.[7] Many states and localities also have noise control ordinances, but they are not effective in eliminating noise pollution, because they either aim at highly specific nuisances or are so broad as to be poorly enforced. The city of Chicago, in 1970, was the first major U.S. city to adopt a modern comprehensive noise control ordinance;[8] New York City has also adopted an innovative Noise Code[9] that, in addition to the traditional prohibitions against such unnecessary noise as automobile horns, also establishes specific noise emission levels for certain noise sources, uses ambient noise quality zones, and creates an Environmental Control Board to enforce the Noise Code for citizen protests and complaints.[10]

NOTES

1. See Freedman, Hazardous Waste Liability (Michie, 1987) at Section 9.18 thereof. See also 42 U.S.C. 4901–4918.
2. 42 U.S.C. 4901–4918 (Pub. L. 95-609 (1978).
3. 42 U.S.C. 1858.
4. 42 U.S.C. 4905.
5. 42 U.S.C. 4916, 4917.
6. See Illinois v. Coleman, 15 E.R.C. 1798 (D.C., 1981).
7. 42 U.S.C. 4911.
8. Chicago Code Section 17-4 (April 6, 1971).
9. New York City Administrative Code Sections 1403.3-1 to 1403.8.25.
10. See 4 Fordham Urban L.J. 467, 478 (1976).

10.13 The Mass Tort and the Class Action

When catastrophe strikes industry there are likely to be hundreds or thousands or millions of workers sustaining occupational injury, disease, or death. In the past many workers died of radium exposure from mercury on brushes used to paint watches[1]; more than 35,000 persons were injured in 1988 by exposure to yellow phosphorus as a result of a tank car derailment.[2] To prevent such mass disasters, it has been suggested that the product manufacturers should know in advance that the doctrine of strict liability in tort would be applied civilly and that criminal penalties would also be invoked.[3] Mass disasters in the causation. of cancer and birth defects have also occurred, and the problem of logistics for plaintiffs takes the modern form of a class action under Rule 23 of the Federal Rules of Civil Procedure.[4]

Rule 23 requires that the class be so numerous that joinder of all members is impractical; that there are questions of law or that there are facts common to members of the class; that the claims or defenses of the representative parties are typical of the claims or defenses of the class; and that the representative parties will fairly and adequately protect the class. The exact number of individuals in a class need not be shown to have the class certified[5]; there is no need for all questions to be common or that common questions predominate[6]; but there should be "common interests" within the class.[7] The prerequisite of adequacy of class is satisfied if the counsel are experienced and qualified to represent the class.[8] Subparagraph (b) of Rule 23 permits a class action when a class is necessary to avoid possible adverse effects on the opponents of the class or on absent class members; or when the party opposing the class has acted or refused to act on grounds generally applicable to the class. Under Rule 23(b)(3) the questions of common law or fact must predominate over any questions that affect only individual members of the class, and there must be a holding that the class action is superior to other available methods for the fair and efficient administration of the claim. It suffices to state that the prerequisites under subparagraph (b) of Rule 23 make for difficulty. Indeed, the Advisory Committee[9] had opined that a class action is ordinarily inapplicable in the case of a mass accident injuring many people.[10] Most courts have apparently held that the requirement that common questions predominate under Rule 23(b)(3) over noncommon questions is not met in the mass tort actions because of the individual factual and legal issues relating to exposure, damages, specific causation, and affirmative defenses.[11]

NOTES

1. Note Zimmerman, "Minimizing Mass Torts and Mass Disasters," Case & Comment (September–October 1986) at 16 et seq.

2. See Reynolds v. CSX Transportation Co., _____ N.E.2d _____ (Ohio, 1988), delineated in Rudlin and Shebelskie, "Selecting Test Plaintiffs: The Advantages and Pitfalls of Trying a Mass Toxic Tort Case," Trial Magazine (October 1988) at 37 et seq.

3. Supra note 1.

4. See Freedman, Hazardous Waste Liability (Michie, 1987) at Sections 11.2, 10.2, and 5.6.

5. See Fitzgerald v. Schweicker, 538 F. Supp. 992 (Md., 1982).

6. See Payton v. Northrup, 86 F.R.D. 20 (WD Mo., 1979).

7. See Mikani v. Miller Brewing Co., 93 F.R.D. 506 (ED Mich., 1982).

8. Note Fisher v. Plessey Co., Ltd., 103 F.R.D. 150 (SD N.Y., 1984).

9. See Amendments to Rules of Civil Procedure, Advisory Committee Notes, 39 F.R.D. 69 (1966) at 103.

10. See Shields, "Joinder Alternatives: Finding the Best Mechanism to Litigate Mass Toxic Tort Cases," Trial Magazine (October 1988) at 54 et seq. Also see Freedman and Greer, The Law of Toxic Torts (Prentice-Hall, 1989).

11. See Blake v. Chemlawn Services Corp., _____ F. Supp. _____ (ED Pa., January 26, 1988).

10.14 Bad Faith Handling of Claim

The exclusivity of workers' compensation has been overcome by proof of intentional conduct on the part of the employer,[1] by the dual capacity role of the employer,[2] and by the insurer's bad faith handling of the claim.[3] Perhaps sixteen jurisdictions recognize a tort action arising from an insurer's bad faith handling of the claim in first-party situations.[4] But the extension of bad faith claims into workers' compensation has met strong resistance.[5] The Wisconsin Supreme Court, in Coleman v. American Universal Insurance Co.,[6] however, dwelled on the plaintiff-insured's plea that the carrier had on three occasions arbitrarily discontinued his compensation payments, even though the carrier had in its files uncontradicted medical data that he was disabled. Subsequently the Wisconsin legislature enacted a bad faith action with a statutory penalty.[7] The Colorado Supreme Court, in Travelers Insurance Co. v. Savio,[8] recognized the cause of action for bad faith handling of the compensation insurance claim; the insured must offer proof that the insurance carrier acted unreasonably in denying workers' compensation benefits and had knowledge or acted in reckless disregard of the fact that it had no reasonable basis for denying the claim.[9]

NOTES

1. See Section 7.7 hereinbefore.
2. See Section 8.8 hereinbefore.
3. See Schechter, "Bad Faith Handling of Workers' Compensation Claims," Trial Magazine (December 1988) at 66 et seq.
4. See Travelers Insurance Co. v Savio, 706 P.2d 1258 (Colo., 1985).
5. Supra note 3 at 72, citing Aranda v. Insurance Company of North America, 748 S.W.2d 210 (Tex., 1988).
6. 273 N.W.2d 220 (Wis., 1979).
7. See Chapter 9, in Freedman, Richards on Insurance (6th ed., 1989).
8. Supra note 4.
9. Supra note 3 at 66–67.

Table of Cases

Index

About the Author

WARREN FREEDMAN was formerly Liability Counsel and Assistant Secretary for Bristol-Myers Co. Among his previous books are *Foreign Plaintiffs in Products Liability Actions, Frivolous Lawsuits and Frivolous Defenses, Federal Statutes on Environmental Protection, The Right of Privacy in the Computer Age, The Tort of Discovery Abuse,* and *The Constitutional Right to a Speedy and Fair Criminal Trial,* all published by Quorum Books.